D1345779

Ramblings of
an Actress

SHEILA HANCOCK

Ramblings of an Actress

HUTCHINSON

LONDON   MELBOURNE   AUCKLAND   JOHANNESBURG

This edition first published in 1987 by Hutchinson, an imprint of
Century Hutchinson Ltd
Brookmount House, 62–65 Chandos Place, London WC2N 4NW

Century Hutchinson Australia Pty Ltd
PO Box 496, 16–22 Church Street, Hawthorn, Victoria 3122, Australia

Century Hutchinson New Zealand Limited
PO Box 40-086, Glenfield, Auckland 10, New Zealand

Century Hutchinson South Africa (Pty) Ltd
PO Box 337, Berglvei, 2012 South Africa

British Library Cataloguing in Publication Data
Hancock, Sheila
    Ramblings of an actress.
    1. Hancock, Sheila   2. Actors – Great
    Britain – Biography
    I. Title
    792'.028'0924   PN2598.H2/
    ISBN 0-09-168230-4

Set in 10½/12 pt Linotron Ehrhardt by
Rowland Phototypesetting Ltd
Bury St Edmunds, Suffolk

Printed and bound in Great Britain by
Mackays of Chatham Ltd
Chatham, Kent

Contents

Preface

I seem to have spent the last four years incarcerated in my garret, up to my neck in crumpled sheets of A4, or alternatively feeling guilty that I wasn't. Why did I do it? I suppose it was because I was asked. Then chivvied.

My original brief was to write a book about the theatre (*ME.f.Of,or,L.f.Gk theatron f.theaomai – behold*). If you have spent thirty-seven years in a profession, you are bound to have *beheld* a few things about the way it operates. The book was to be based on the tour I was about to undertake for the Royal Shakespeare Company. When I procrastinated, this was extended to embrace as well the year I then spent at the National Theatre after the RSC. The trouble was that as I travelled the country, and then outside it, I could not help *beholding* a few things about the places I visited and the inhabitants and the contrasts. On top of that, these travels coincided with my reaching the watershed of my fiftieth birthday which caused me to *behold* a few things about myself and my past, and living and dying, and what has happened to women. And, lo and *behold* – I did not know where to begin. Or how to continue. And would have stopped. Were it not for Richard Cohen, Kate Mosse and Paulette Land – to whom I am *beholden*.

Actors' life-stories often seem an enviable report of continual theatrical success. If the biographical aspect of this book has any value it is to show that the average actor's life is not like that at all. The theatre is the means by which I earn my living. I like my job very much but it is not my sole preoccupation – which is why, as the book progresses, my original theme cannot *be held* to as my interests are drawn elsewhere.

The main track, then, is the years between 1981 and 1986. During that period I have wandered with the National from London to Aberdeen, from Paris to Chicago, and with the RSC travelled round the backwaters of England and Northern Ireland. I have provided a map to help with my ramblings round Britain and old-fashioned chapter headings to help with the ramblings of my mind. I am afraid this journal does frequently

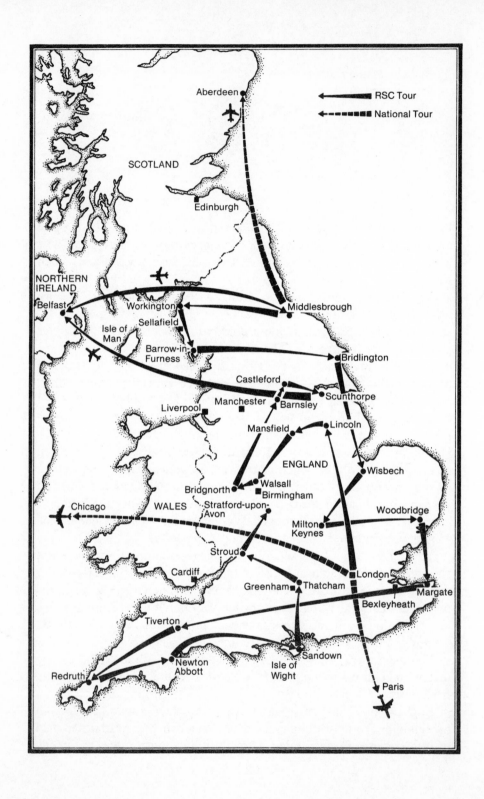

go off down sidetracks and sometimes loses its way entirely. But then this has ended up as a book about my life and it is plain to *theaomai* that I have too.

Photographic Acknowledgments

The publishers would like to thank the following for providing material. Whilst every effort has been made to trace copyright, this has not always been possible with some of the earlier photographs. The publishers would like to apologise for any inconvenience this might cause:

© F. J. Fewster; © Keystone; © Alec Murray; © BBC Enterprises Ltd; © Zoë Dominic; © Manchester Evening News; © Douglas H. Jeffrey; © Christopher Davies, 'Report'; © Sport and General; © Donald Cooper; © Jack Curtis; © Tom Wargacki; © *Daily Mirror*.

PART ONE

PREPARATIONS

1 : Swinging About

On my forty-ninth birthday I was still eagerly waiting for my life to begin.
For nigh on half a century I seemed to have been in frantic preparation
for something that had not yet happened – or, if it had, I had missed it.

Swinging London, for instance. It must have happened: it was in all
the papers. My hairdresser knew all about it. He seemed to be right
there in the thick of it, enjoying it hugely. Come to think of it, hairdressers
are always in the thick of things, enjoying them hugely. But not me. Or
Kenneth Williams.

In 1961 we were starring together in the West End in *One Over the
Eight*, a new-wave revue written by those avant-garde writers, Harold
Pinter, Peter Cook, N. F. Simpson, John Mortimer and other *nieges* of
antan. We were lauded in magazines of the moment such as *Encore* and
photographed in curious poses by curious young men for *Vogue* and
Queen Magazine. One earnest journalist by the name of Tom Stoppard
described me ambiguously as a 'tired chrysanthemum who could put on
a cool blue look that could freeze a humming bird to an oven door', but
by most people we were considered to be the 'in thing'.

Kenneth remained doggedly conservative, on the surface at least, but
I sported Mary Quant dresses that barely covered my crotch, a Vidal
Sassoon fringe that should have come with a guide dog and white
Courreges boots that were a bugger to clean. I was a devotee of the
Maharishi before the Beatles and on one memorable occasion meditated
alongside Elizabeth Jane Howard, Kingsley Amis and two Burmese cats.

All this on the face of it sounds pretty swinging; but it did not feel it at the time. That has been half my trouble; I have never felt much at the time – only in retrospect.

Throughout the run of *One Over the Eight* all I seemed to feel was exhausted. The show – at the Duke of York's theatre – was not as good as Kenneth Williams's previous revue *Pieces of Eight* and it needed a lot of 'selling' – which meant working hard to cover any weaknesses in the material, or as our Dance Captain, Irving Davies, used to put it rather more succinctly: 'Eyes, teeth and tits, darlings – and sparkle, sparkle, sparkle.'

This necessity would sometimes push Kenneth into wild and wonderful excesses. The end of the first half was a sketch by Peter Cook of a man moaning to his wife about how the war had 'held him back'. It was timed to run about four minutes but our improvisations could extend it to twenty.

For instance, Kenneth had one simple line – 'The war clouds were looming' – which would become extended into a surreal tone poem:

KEN: The war clouds were leooooming. Blooming great war clouds. Leooooming on the horizon.
ME: What were they doing?
KEN: They were leooooming, leoooooooming.
TOGETHER: Leooooooooooming.
ME: Looming, were they?
KEN: Yes, they were.
ME: And were they big?
KEN: Yes, they were bleooooming big war clouds.
ME: Bleoooooooming big, dirty great war clouds.
TOGETHER: Bleoooooooooming big, dirty great war clouds. Bleoooooooming, leoooooooooming great war clouds.

And so on, *ad infinitum*. Sometimes the audience loved it. Other nights they were bemused and even alarmed as we got more and more manic. Their confusion would incite us to further madness which only the band enjoyed – although on one occasion it got too much even for them and Don, the drummer, raised a white handkerchief tied to his drumstick, only to elicit an outraged 'Cheek!' from Kenneth, followed by a Williams diatribe about musicians, which took a further ten minutes.

The unpredictable nature of Kenneth's genius was stimulating but demanding. He suffers fools by gladly making them suffer. Despising weakness he attacks it viciously. Strong men, or rather women mainly, have wept on the radio quiz game *Just a Minute*, on which we are both regular contestants in speaking on a given subject for one minute without hesitating, deviating or repeating ourselves. I have often quailed when he has launched into a frenzied attack on my incompetence, starting with, 'I 'aven't come all this way from King's Cross to listen to this rubbish', and usually ending with, 'They shouldn't 'ave women in this show anyway'. He would remind us at frequent intervals, 'I'm a cult, you know – I'm the biggest cult you'll ever work with.'

When we were on tour with *One Over the Eight*, he took agin me for some reason I have forgotten and the atmosphere between us was pretty cold. I remember, during a bleak week in out-of-season Blackpool, descending in a hotel lift in frigid silence with Kenneth and a waiter. As we got out, in an effort to communicate, I commented that the waiter was rather good-looking. From that day to this Kenneth has spread an elaborate story of my torrid romance with a gigolo that scandalised the Golden Mile. Could it be Kenneth who started the whole myth of 'Swinging London'? He would have been capable of it.

After a night of coping with this maverick, it was a relief at the end of *One Over the Eight* to wipe off the 'slap' (the somewhat sadistic name theatre people give to their make-up) and chug home on my Lambretta to my husband in Swinging Hammersmith, dropping off Kenneth on the way at his bachelor flat near Marble Arch. One night, after reading a glowing description of London's supposed cultural and spiritual renaissance in *Time* magazine, I circled Eros on my motor scooter, as one could in those days, with Kenneth on my pillion brandishing a furled umbrella and shouting, 'Where is it, then? Where's it all happening? Where are all the orgies? Why haven't we been asked?'

A few ragged pigeons and a handful of drug addicts were looking pretty left out too. But then people in Piccadilly Circus at night have been left out. Far from the glamorous place that tourists expect, it has always been a dumping ground for the wreckage our society throws out from its various forays into *La Dolce Vita*. The English are not very good at it, if Kenneth and I and the inhabitants of Piccadilly Circus are anything to go by. From the syphilitic, noseless news vendor of the 1950s to the glue sniffers and rack lads, flaunting themselves on the railings in the 1980s, it is an ugly place, this rotting centre of our city, as anyone who has played the Criterion Theatre will tell you. There, the mice eat your greasepaint, then run up to join the rats frolicking in the decaying empty floors above, a monument to a past sweet life which is presumably deliberately being left to decay by a property developer until it has to be replaced by some cost-efficient monstrosity. Down in those stifling dressing rooms, in the bowels of the smelly earth, when I worked there in 1969 in *So What About Love?*, I had to use an oxygen inhaler to get through the long matinee days and would apply my make-up with my feet in the air, to avoid the lurking cockroaches. The front of house is pretty, though. Like life, sometimes.

Admittedly, if I had been asked to join the swingers I doubt if I would have gone. I would have been too tired, too scared or too suspicious – three sure inhibitors of abandoned living. Mind you, every now and then after a show a few other greasy-faced thespians and I would go mad and indulge in roast beef and jacket potatoes with cream and chive dressing at the old Seven Stars Restaurant in Lyons Corner House, Coventry Street. It was hardly a rave-up, but there would be much libellous discussion as to which seven noshers merited the eponymous role of the restaurant that particular week. The choice presented by the clientele that frequented those rooms, now occupied by the slightly seedier world of an amusement arcade, was as wide as the present-day equivalent who go to Joe Allen's. At the moment. They will probably move on soon, leaving Joe Allen's full of men in dark suits with their secretaries, looking for celebrities. Such is the nemesis of all fashionable restaurants.

The plush Caprice behind the Ritz Hotel has now shed its red velvet and gilt along with most of its theatrical crowd, but in the 1950s one could listen to Noel Coward and his entourage exchanging hilarious insults with Frankie Howerd and his (of which I was a junior member) whilst a tremulous Judy Garland held court in another corner. They were all elegantly dressed and bejewelled, whereas the Seven Stars lot, with the exception of the always immaculate John Gielgud, were relatively unprepossessing, as befitted the emerging working-class actors and actresses of the 1960s.

By the time I frequented Lyons Corner House the glitzy days were over. In fact, I can mark the actual day that, for me, they ended: it was when my father was refused entry to the Caprice for not wearing a tie. Public school men, successful businessmen smelling of aftershave – they can cope with these silly rules made to keep men like my father out of their world. They would happily borrow a waiter's tie or give a big tip and sit in a corner making a joke of it all. If they made the mistake at all they would 'carry it off', as my father would say. But not him. His humiliation was appalling. His flushed, frightened face and mumbled apologies for 'letting me down' are lodged painfully in my memory. It was partly in an endeavour to exorcise this image and to take revenge for society's suppression of a good and original man that I returned early in the 1980s defiantly wearing old jeans and a T-shirt – only to discover that everyone else was wearing the same. They probably turn people away for wearing ties now.

When your shaking fist is greeted by an indifferent shrug it can be dispiriting, especially when you have seldom come out of your corner. Which, as I approached fifty, I proposed to do more often. Not necessarily to shake my fist; more to shake up myself. After a lifetime of trying to please, in middle-age I realised I wanted my change of life to be radical. I wished to experience hot flushes of excitement and embark on a giddy last lap; to find out what I *really* thought and wanted. To hell with the opinions of parents, elders and betters, directors, audiences, the *Guardian*, husbands, children and critics, I told myself. I realised I was a mite old to be thinking like this. My mind should have been turning to hammocks and shady hats, to grandchildren and wisdom; but then I have always been late for everything.

I had my first child at thirty-two; my second at forty-two. I became aware of the Women's Movement at thirty-seven; I stopped wearing a bra at forty. I started studying for a degree when I was forty-nine and I am now making my first attempt at writing at fifty-four. I have always seemed to be running after the disappearing bus, sometimes missing it, sometimes leaping on the platform at the last moment and hanging on for dear life. Back in 1982, on the road to fifty, I wanted to settle in and enjoy the rest of the trip with my eyes and ears wide open.

Most people have managed to get some order into their life long before that. Indeed, I knew several young people of twelve, contemporaries of my youngest daughter, who know exactly where they are going. But I spent my first thirty years preoccupied with getting somewhere in the theatre. Where, exactly, I never seriously considered. I had made spasmodic efforts to sort myself out, but dogged determination has never been my strong point.

For instance, I stuck analysis for two years but ended up thinking Freud was a blithering idiot and a misogynist to boot. There is nothing more irritating than a self-satisfied shrink explaining everything you say in terms of imagined envy of his or your father's penis. Logically and emotionally, I disagreed with his every interpretation and finally left him when, during one of my sessions, after a phone call had interrupted us, he pondered: 'It made you jealous that I spoke to someone else, didn't it?' His ludicrously wrong analysis made me announce that I was going and never coming back because I could not bear to lie on his couch and stare at his ugly lampshade a moment longer. The trouble is that analysts make you feel wrong whatever you do. I considered it an act of courage to leave this man who was doing his utmost to make me need him, whereas he smilingly whispered: 'Walking away again, Sheila?', craftily piling on the guilt. I like to think his *sang froid* melted as the door slammed, and that he was left punching the walls of that nasty little room as I ran down the stairs into the fresh air. Most probably he was just as relieved as I.

A more enjoyable undertaking to try to sort out my mind was a degree course I started with the Open University. Having left school at fifteen, I had for many years bewailed my lack of education, and with the OU I found an antidote to my ignorance. But it is damned hard work, and slow too. You can always tell OU students by the bags under their eyes and their inclination to read text-books in the tube or walking along the street – anytime, anywhere they can cram in a huge amount of knowledge whilst simultaneously running a home or job or both. I got into the habit of rising at 5.00 am which has stood me in good stead in trying to write this book. When I did my initial written assignment for the OU it was the first time I had put a thoughtful pen to paper since I left school thirty-four years before, and it took me four days to write two pages. I am only marginally quicker five years later. The degree is broken into six courses which can be taken when you like, with breaks of several years if you choose, or alternatively cramming two into one year if you are in a hurry. As you pass each course you are awarded a whole or half point. Having only managed to get one and a half points by 1987, at my present rate I shall be lucky if I am capable of tottering up to receive my degree, if and when I obtain it.

At forty-nine I had no points. And time, in mid-life, was at a premium. Despite the fact I felt physically and mentally exactly the same as when I was twenty – that is, permanently vaguely ill and muddled – I was nevertheless achingly aware that the chances were I had a much less active life ahead of me than behind me. The sense of panic that this thought engendered was in danger of sending me scuttering up yet more blind alleys, so I deliberately restricted my resolve to a vague intention of taking a good look at what was in front of me in the light of a searching relook at my past experience. That anyway was my unfocused determination, when out of the blue came an offer which was to prove the catalyst I needed.

On 19 July 1982 I was 'Trevved'. This was a word in common usage among members of the Royal Shakespeare Company to describe one of the magic skills of the then Artistic Director, Trevor Nunn. If an actor or actress was being bolshy, or was simply unwilling to do something, it was not long before an arm was fondly laid round his or her shoulders and she or he was led by Mr Nunn into a discreet corner, hideously aware of the mocking stares of the rest of the company. There was much urgent whispering from Mr Nunn, a few chuckles and usually a final smacking kiss – regardless of one's sex – after which the victim would be firmly convinced it was a marvellous idea that her best scene should be cut, or that he should not play the lead in *Richard III* because the first servant was a far superior role. Mind you, his eloquence did not bewitch everyone. During a tedious dress rehearsal of *Macbeth*, Trevor's protracted ponderings on how the murderers should effectively kill off one of Macduff's children prompted Nicol Williamson to suggest: 'Why don't they take him into the wings and you can bore him to death?'

The only other person I know with such manipulative skill as Trevor is now using it to good effect in Hollywood. I remember once sitting intrigued in this particular man's office whilst he tried to cast a rather boring part in a film. He had telephoned an esteemed actor, and was wooing him with urgent sincerity, all the while sipping champagne and pulling faces at me. 'Darling, you are the only man in the world for this part. I won't do it if I can't have you – that's that! The author wrote it for you, my pet. Think of the fun you will have, my darling heart.'

When the 'darling heart' refused, the phone was slammed down with a sharp 'Bastard!' A quick re-dial and the same routine was gone through with a second victim: 'You're the only one for the part! He wrote it for you, my sweetheart. I shall retire if you say no.' This time the fly was ensnared and the phone went down with a brisk: 'Got him, the silly old fart.'

To be fair, the actor was probably simultaneously muttering 'Bullshitter'. It is a game we play in the theatre. I am well aware that a list of several actresses has usually been gone through before an offer reaches me; what is more, they are friends of mine, and we compare notes. Yet these little charades have to be enacted to preserve our fragile egos.

I was once deeply flattered when Arnold Wesker, author of many plays including *Roots* and *The Kitchen*, and founder of the Round House Theatre, phoned to ask me to do a play for him and was very complimentary about my unique suitability for the role. When I told him I was unavailable he asked for any suggestions I might have for the part. I went through a list of about twenty different women, to each of which he commented, 'Not available', or 'Tried her'.

Arnold is charmingly lacking in subterfuge: most actors are better equipped. As we spend most of our working lives pretending, one might

–

as well use the skill to good purpose off-stage as well as on. You cannot confidently march on to a stage and confront an audience knowing there are twenty other people who could do your part better; so you pretend there are not. Self-confidence is an essential part of an actor's equipment and must be preserved at all costs. Which I suppose is why I was happy to allow myself to be 'Trevved'.

Not only that, but Trevor Nunn is a most beguiling man. Having taken over the directorship of the RSC in 1968 as a relatively inexperienced twenty-nine-year-old, he has progressed from a shaky start into being one of the best directors in the world. It was mainly the international acclaim of his production of *Nicholas Nickleby* which opened all manner of interesting doors to him, from musicals about pussycats and roller-skating trains to opera and films.

This coronary-inducing workload was apt to make him somewhat elusive at the RSC but, in my two years acting with the company, I had managed to buttonhole him to suggest he allow me to direct. This could be deemed bold considering I had never acted any Shakespeare before my season with the RSC in 1981. That invitation to act with the company had come about mainly as a result of my taking part in a workshop led by director Ronald Eyre, in which I had to perform a speech from a part in which I would never be cast. I had offered what I hoped was an innocent if somewhat mature Juliet. This had somehow inspired Ron to cast me as the pushy Paulina in *The Winter's Tale* and suggest me to the director John Barton for the wicked Tamara in *Titus Andronicus*. It was a surprising jump from a teenager expressing pure undying love to a mother inciting her sons to rape and subsequently eating them in a pie, but I was delighted with the offer.

In true democratic company style I was also required to play the two-line part of an outlaw in *The Two Gentlemen of Verona*. One of these lines was addressed to a young man called Valentine:

'And partly, seeing you are beautified with goodly shape, and by your own report

A linguist, and a man of such perfection as we do in our quality much want . . .'

The other was:

'Know then that some of us are gentlemen.'

A heavy emphasis on the word 'some' in the latter line, and a breathless, leering delivery of the former, plus the acquisition of a large blunderbuss from the props department, turned the part into a sort of sex-starved *Annie Get Your Gun*, frantically lusting after the young hero. This made for a lot of laughs from the audience (and indeed, I regret to say, frequently the cast) but some confusion in the plot, which displeased our venerable critics more than a little.

Not, however, as much as did my Tamara in *Titus*.

It was obvious to me that the lady was decidedly foreign, not at all like those boring old noble Romans, so I decided to distinguish her from them with an accent. I opted for something vaguely German for Mrs Gaul, which admittedly ended up as a cross between Marlene Dietrich and that little fat Nazi in *Rowan & Martin's Laugh-In* programme on television, but in my naivety it seemed sensible to me. However, I soon learned you do not do things like that in Shakespeare. They sneered at my efforts from a great height. In fact, the double bill – as this very long evening of *Titus* and *Two Gents* was called – was a critical and box-office disaster. Yet, still I was consumed with a burning passion for the Bard. Coming to Shakespeare so late in my career meant that I did not take him for granted. I marvelled at his relevance to the present and revelled in having such a wondrous scriptwriter. But although *The Winter's Tale* was more of a success, after *Titus* I had little hope of the company requiring my services much longer as an actress, let alone as a director.

Besides, the RSC was an impenetrable male stronghold with seemingly no policy for firing old or hiring new directors, so the chances of them taking on a woman seemed slim. I was dumbfounded, therefore, when in July 1982 I received a 'Trevving' letter from Mr Nunn containing the following paragraph:

> I would dearly like you to be the Artistic Director of the Royal Shakespeare Company Small Scale Tour of 1983. Run it however you like. I believe in you, your judgement, your taste and your skills. Direct one of the productions. Act a big part in one of the shows. Choose the company. The itinerary. Decide whether to go to a festival (like Edinburgh) or not. Make it headline news wherever you go. Wagons roll.

My pride and excitement were overwhelming, but I could not help wondering how the letter had come about. I knew there had been a big planning meeting held at Windsor a few weeks before. It was probably in an hotel, but in my mind's eye I felt sure it must have been the castle itself, with Trevor presiding on a large throne, Terry Hands on a slightly smaller one and 'the boys' (as I came to call the other directors) seated like knights below them.

In 1987 Trevor has moved aside, leaving Terry Hands in overall control, but in 1982 they were joint Artistic Directors of the company and the rivalry between them – usually friendly – was acute. Their court of young associates would usually side with one or the other, so that there were Terry men and Trevor men. (Being no man's woman could be lonely, as will emerge later.) Occasionally the two leaders would be thrown together in an endeavour to tame 'the young Turks', as Terry christened the associates, yet despite all this the planning meetings were amicable, rough-and-tumble exchanges with much mutual support, despite the odd bit of bitching.

At the time my letter arrived I had never been present at such inner sanctum occasions, so I visualised this dignified assembly in Windsor Castle discussing my virtues at some length then solemnly casting the unanimous vote that would entrust me with this supreme honour. I now know a far more likely scenario.

They would all have been slouched in a smoke-filled room for hours, drinking tea from plastic cups, desperately trying to plough through an horrendously overlong agenda. The workload at the RSC is every year more onerous. Then there were only two theatres in Stratford: now, in 1987, the new Swan Theatre makes it three. They still have a Newcastle season and two theatres at the Barbican plus, from 1987, the Mermaid Theatre. All these demand numerous productions – as well as various European tours, visits to the USA, videos, and commercial productions like *Les Misérables* (or *The Glums*, as it is known by the company) to boost the revenue. When the topic of the tour cropped up there was probably a horrified realisation that, despite their obligation to the Arts Council to tour in 1983, not one of them had a spare moment in which to organise one. The dialogue probably ran like this:

TREVOR:	(*looking at his watch*) Look, I've just had an idea that I think would work brilliantly. Sheila Hancock wants to direct. Let's give it to her.
BILL ALEXANDER:	(*who headed the last tour and was still looking exhausted two years later*) That will serve her right.
GENISTRA MCINTOSH:	(*harassed planning director who frequently resorts to irony in her losing battle with the intransigent males*) Good heavens! Surely you're not going to let a woman in?
TERRY HANDS:	(*smoothly, smilingly reasonable*) Now don't be absurd, Genny. We have nothing against women. We want people who are *good*.
GENISTRA MCINTOSH:	Oh, silly me! I had forgotten there hadn't been any good women for the past ten years.

TERRY HANDS:	I think it's sexist to have a woman.
	(quizzical looks all round)
TREVOR:	*(still looking at his watch)* Look, it's getting late and I've got another six meetings tonight. What do you think?
THE BOYS:	Great idea. Thank God for that. Can't think of anybody else. What time is this bloody meeting supposed to end?
TREVOR:	Right, that's settled. Next item?

Momentous choices and decisions at the RSC can be made in just such a casual manner. The miracle is that more often than not they prove successful. True, I had worked a lot in the regions and had some directorial experience, but on the other hand I had little in administration – and, on top of that, minimal education compared to this charmed academic circle.

Whatever their motives, here suddenly was the adventure I was seeking. I would be visiting in and around areas I had been to before in my thirty-odd years in the profession, so that I could relive and reassess my past experience. At the same time I would see for myself, instead of through the eyes of the media, something of Britain in the 1980s. It would provide just the reappraisal of myself and life in general that I was seeking. I would have the opportunity to set up and run a company along the lines I believed right, working in a way that I deemed valuable. My aspirations were immediately pretty high-flown, not to say pretentious. I was deeply proud of being a member of the RSC and, having been thrilled by many of the company's productions, I passionately wanted more people to share that experience.

Only a small percentage of the population really knows what good live theatre can be like. I myself grew up in a background where the most one usually saw was a panto at Christmas time, which was frequently confusing and often awful. I have a vivid memory of seeing, as a child, a very fat genie of the lamp in sagging green tights, who burst for some reason into a spirited rendering of 'Because You're Mine' when he first appeared before Aladdin. In the general sexual ambiguity of male mothers and female sons my young mind was not particularly disturbed by his seemingly overcharged affection for Aladdin, merely bored by his holding up the story. That sort of show was not conducive to devotion to 'the Drama', and had that panto been the first show I had seen I doubt that I would ever have wanted to go to the theatre again. But in fact my first visit to the theatre was to the Holborn Empire to see *Where the Rainbow Ends* performed by the Italia Conti School with my sister, Billie, playing Will-o'-the-Wisp. I was at the time a patient in Great Ormond Street

Hospital for Children but they allowed me a night out. The vision of my bossy sister transformed into a dainty sprite with gossamer wings gave me a lasting belief in the magic of the theatre – and a violent nose-bleed.

I was also fortunate enough to have a dear aunt who occasionally took me to shows. Once we went to see Alicia Markova dance *Giselle* at the Woolwich Empire. Arms and hands and feet had been purely functional parts of the body to me till then. I truly thought Markova was some magic creature – I could not believe she was real. It was only much later when I had friends in the Royal Ballet Company that I observed the all too real blood, sweat and tears that went into that sort of perfection.

The main attraction of my outings with Auntie Ruby were, I confess, the sausages, beans and chips and knickerbocker glories in Lyons Tea Shop afterwards; but I did get one or two glimpses of live theatre, which was more than most of my friends. Sadly the same is true today. Most people never stir beyond the television set for their entertainment, and there is a feeling that theatre – particularly classical theatre – is not for them. Now, here I was presented with an opportunity to reach out to new audiences.

After the initial elation, however, I began to get cold feet. The job would mean killing hours, separation from my family and another year earning must less money than I could by other means. (In fact, I was simultaneously offered a musical with a four-figure salary per week.) The hierarchy of the RSC is highly cultured, dedicated and gifted, and I was unsure that I could find the confidence to assume authority among them. As an actress I had survived by being outrageous and cunning. These qualities would not do for a Royal Shakespeare Company director, however. Come to think of it, they were not ideal for a Royal Shakespeare Company actress. During the rehearsals for Edward Albee's *All Over* back in 1967, with Dame Peggy Ashcroft and a generally illustrious cast, I was putting on my usual larky act when Peter Hall, the director, tetchily told me I was like a small child splashing about in a pool whilst everyone else was trying to learn to swim. (Doubtless he had not observed during the preview the night before Angela Lansbury slowly crossing and uncrossing her eyes while sitting with her back to the audience, supposedly engrossed in a long monologue I was delivering.)

The fact is, the more erudite my fellow artists and directors, or anybody, the more 'common' I become, and I have frequently blushed inside hearing my cheery cockney insults at times when they are quite out of place. At least I am not alone in this behaviour. I was once at a premiere with a young hairdresser called Barry Krost. His background was similar to mine, having been brought up in a working-class area of London. We found ourselves in a reverent line-up to greet Princess Alexandra. Even I was mildly shaken when he chirruped: ''Allo Princess. Where's yer crown, then?' She only paused momentarily before entering politely into a discussion with us about the problem of royalty striking the balance between informality and their subjects' delight in pomp and ceremony.

Barry is now a multi-millionaire film producer in Hollywood where he has launched his own bank.

I did warn in the preface that my trains of thought were hard to follow. It gets worse later, but for the moment I am going to Buckingham Palace, which can't be bad. To my surprise, I had been invited to have lunch with the Queen and Prince Philip. These little get-togethers are presumably to keep the Royal Family in touch with their subjects' points of view, which on that occasion, coming as they did from a man from the DHSS, a rabbi and me, were pretty diverse. Over the brandy snaps, we discussed vandalism which Prince Philip strenuously deplored. I found myself protesting boldly: 'Well, it's all right for you, love, living 'ere.'

My carefully RADA-trained voice is apt to lapse into its natural accent – only more so – when I feel inadequate. At the same lunch, I should have learned a lesson in graciousness from the Queen who, when I inadvertently trod on one of her corgis, ignored its yelp and calmed my confusion by saying: 'It's her own fault. She shouldn't be the same colour as the carpet.'

Would that I had such dignified *savoir faire* instead of this penchant for quips. I have frequently seen confusion glaze the eyes of the nice intellectuals of the RSC when confronted by my frolics. None of this would do for the Artistic Director of the RSC Regional Tour 1983. But how would I change my approach to fit in with this formidable team?

On the receipt of the momentous letter I had informed 'Them Upstairs' in the administration offices that I would like to discuss the proposition. However, Trevor having departed on a trip to New York, I heard not another thing. During the weeks of silence and anticlimax that followed, all my uncertainty about the proposal churned round in my mind. Eventually, as so often happens, I just found myself doing it. This was partly because, as is the RSC's wont, everybody simply assumed that I had agreed to take on the job. That is, until I resigned; which I did before I was actually engaged.

2 : Big Is Not Beautiful

ADMINISTRATION AT THE RSC – THE ACTORS' UPRISING – JOAN
LITTLEWOOD – CHOOSING THE PLAYS – BROODING ABOUT
MONEY – THE STRANGE WORLD OF PETER PAN – TERRY 'GAU-
LEIGHTER' HANDS – LIFE AND DEATH IN THE BARBICAN – THE
DOUBTFUL PLEASURES OF HIGH TECH – BATTLE FOR THE
RIGHTS OF *KISS ME KATE* – THREE BRICK WALLS – RESIGNATION
– RESIGNATION WITHDRAWN

There is an assumption at the RSC that an offer of a job is tantamount
to an acceptance, and once enlisted you will serve for as long as you are
needed. At the end of each Stratford season there is much hurt disbelief
when some actors depart at the end of their one-year term instead of
automatically continuing on the two-year Company cycle to Newcastle
and subsequently to London. Hence, since I was already under contract
as an actress and had been offered the new job, nobody deemed it
necessary to discuss further how or if I would undertake the frightening
task of organising a nationwide tour.

Having previously only directed in small companies with little resources, I reassured myself that working for one of the 'Centres of
Excellence' would be a piece of cake. I vaguely knew that on the seventh
floor of the Barbican was something called 'Administration', which I
visualised as a well-oiled machine that would undertake all the boring
jobs, leaving the Artistic Director free to swan around being artistic. One
day in September 1982, in search of this miracle, I ascended from the
murky depths of the actors' regions of the Barbican to this floor that was
rumoured to have windows, and embarked on the obstacle race that
would lead to my resignation six months later in February 1983, when
my post had *still* not been confirmed.

On the seventh floor there are, in fact, a few skylights under which
slaves a small band of women who service the male hierarchy. Without
these women the organisation would grind to a halt. They work ridiculous
hours, put up with the vacillations of the male directors with stoic

patience, and sort out all the muddles. In fact, they play the usual role that women do in most organisations and families and get similarly little thanks for it. If they ever stamp their feet they are deemed difficult, nagging and hysterical – epithets that, applied to men, translate as strong, meticulous and passionate.

The possibility of a woman joining the ranks of those to be serviced was, I suspect, greeted with slightly mixed feelings by this harassed group. In a male-dominated world women develop strategies to get things done: one is to flatter and cajole the men into line, but this works less well with a member of your own sex. I had experienced a similar dilemma when I had had a bumpy ride for the first two weeks of rehearsals of *Dandy Dick*, which I directed for the Cambridge Theatre Company in 1981, with an actress who later admitted she was disconcerted at being directed by a woman, as she realised there had always been a sexual frisson, usually unspoken, between herself and her male directors which had actually helped her work. The desire to please, to be admired, to be 'mastered' – base-products of most female conditioning – is still lurking in many of our psyches. I too have simpered myself into a frenzy with certain men who understand no other female language. Unfortunately it is a vicious circle – the more we behave in this way, the more men get used to it. At the RSC, where jobs for actresses are so few and the female staff have to get through a well-nigh insuperable workload, the male/female games continue. They merely widened the gap.

I had become aware during my two years with the company of a similar rift between the management and the actors, so I resolved to bring about a more healthy attitude in my approach. Moreover, the choice of an actress to lead the tour seemed to indicate that the hierarchy themselves saw the need for some bridges to be built.

For many years the movement towards actors and actresses having more say in the whole presentation of theatre has been stirring within the profession. Simon Callow's book *Being An Actor* brought the matter into public debate, but Ian McKellen's Actors Company, started in 1972, was a previous demonstration of the excellence that this participation can produce, and the group that he and Edward Petherbridge formed at the National Theatre in 1985-6 (of which I was a part) was a development of this trend. But more of that later.

This uprising by the actors is partly a reaction to some of the puppet-masters that have, in recent years, suppressed our creativity so as to manipulate us into directorial and design concepts which dazzle the critics, and occasionally the public, but have little real content. The eternal joke in the ranks is how often 'great' productions have been a fluke. Several eminent directors, with the critics' seal of approval, are actually nothing more than good casters – usually working with brilliant designers, lighting men and composers. Time and again a director is hailed as a genius when he has done little more than be a bloody nuisance. Great productions are frequently the result of panicky actors getting a rush of adrenalin from terminal fear on a first night and pulling off some sort of miracle. Unfortunately, this has no more foundation than an instinct for self-preservation, so that later performances fall apart – which is perhaps why the public is so often disappointed by a show that has been acclaimed by the critics. Lovely original concepts are all very well, but what really thrills are good performances. It is that living link between artist and audience that is the unique quality of theatre, which no other medium possesses; yet it is quite usual for highly praised productions to contain performances which we in the profession, including the actors giving them, know to be appalling.

It is a modern phenomenon – directors' theatre. Actors always used to run things themselves – Shakespeare, Garrick, Wolfit, Atkins, Quayle, Olivier, to name but a few. And, with all of them, the excitement of their productions lay in the performances.

Just before this new fashion for directors, Theatre Workshop was in its heyday. The success of this company, run by Joan Littlewood – also an actress – lay in her ability to squeeze every ounce of talent out of people. Any people. She created an atmosphere in which actors felt cherished and their opinions valued: the shows were created by the whole team, with her at the helm shaping and inspiring. In the programme of *Oh What A Lovely War!* the authorship of the piece is attributed to 'Charles Chiltern and members of the cast'. If you did not contribute fully you suffered. After seeing this show, I asked Victor Spinetti why his part, so strong in the first half, petered out in the second. He replied: 'I had flu – so she forgot about me.'

It was Joan Littlewood who gave me the most liberating experience of my career. I had been sentenced to eight years of weekly repertory, doing one play whilst rehearsing another virtually fifty-two weeks a year. The published moves in the French's edition, the first characterisation that came into one's head and a vague approximation of the words were the best we could manage, sometimes with more lively results than those born of ten weeks' agonising, but nevertheless on the whole being pretty stereotyped. After my audition with 'La Littlewood', she laughed uproariously at my rendering of *St Joan*, led me into an improvisation and, pushing her woolly cap back on her head, declared: 'You're a lovely clown, my darling. Why are you wasting your time doing all that rubbish?' She considered most shows other than her own 'rubbish'.

She had a genius for discovering what was inside you and moulding it into something valuable. Her shows were bursting with life, with artists stretched to their limits, taking risks. Olivier is said to aspire to amaze himself with his own daring, and this was her demand too. She eschewed anything grand. The highest compliment was to be deemed a 'nutcase', the greatest reward a night out in a sleazy club where her favourite 'villains', the Krays, would ply you with presents you dared not refuse.

Having performed herself, she was supremely sensitive to an actor's feelings. Rehearsals were sacred. Everyone present took part, including cleaners from the auditorium and even, on one occasion I remember, a startled visiting plumber. There were tears and much laughter, but most of us utterly trusted her with our talents and inmost emotions – which must have been a huge responsibility for her. Indeed, it was not until we witnessed her collapse at the death of her beloved manager and lover, Gerry Raffles, that we realised how much she had needed his support to take on that responsibility. Without him she could not continue to find the strength to persuade our dull minds of the glory of her proposed modern Vauxhall Gardens – her 'fun palace', with its walls of light and spaces for love, games and life – the ultimate participation, in which the audience were to be the performers. After Gerry's death the people who loved her watched helplessly as she drifted around. Sadly, nothing has ever persuaded her to return to the theatrical scene, but she has remained the guiding light for many of us who are still in the thick of it.

The ascendancy over Joan of the male academic mafia was a process of theatrical evolution. The theatre, like life, goes through cycles that are products of one another. After all the raw emotion and bursting energy that had been developing, possibly into indulgent vulgarity, it was inevitable that a more ordered, intellectual approach should take precedence. 'Text' and 'research' became current jargon. The person in charge of the artistic presentation was now known as the 'director' instead of the 'producer'; the title of producer was relegated to cover the person who juggled the books. Significant, that – 'direct' as opposed to 'produce'.

They were great times, though, the 1960s. The new academics were certainly 'swinging' the theatre in new directions. Peter Hall, John Barton and friends changed the look and sound of the classics. It could not be more exciting than Olivier and Quayle's era in the 1950s at Stratford, but it was certainly fresh and alive. Meantime Jonathan Miller, Alan Bennett and Peter Cook were driving nails into the coffin of old-time revue, the texts of which had, till then, been of secondary importance to the artists. It mattered little what Gingold, Max Adrian, Dora Bryan, Bea Lillie and others were saying; it was how they said it. Brilliant performers that they were, the originality of the material of the Fringe boys was of prime importance. Sacred cows grazing in much larger fields were shot at, as opposed to the mini-targets of the old, trivial school. Jonathan Miller has said that 1961's *Beyond the Fringe* came out of frustration and wanting an 'evening of contempt and venom in order to lance boils': not, I think, the motivation of the likes of dear old Alan Melville.

Actors and actresses have grown up as a result of these rapid changes of approach. I confess to a slight regret that there seems to be no adequate vehicle now for eccentrics like Kenneth Williams and Fenella Fielding. But the new blood of the working-class actors and writers that came in with the Royal Court Theatre and Joan, followed by an influx of university-educated actors (a phenomenon virtually unknown when I first started in the business in 1950) have brought us to the point of Ian's company, Simon Callow's book and Anthony Sher's *The Year of the King*, which clearly demonstrates a modern actor's intellectual approach to his role. There is a hugely successful season mounted every year entirely by the RSC actors themselves defiantly called *Not The RSC*. Actors now want, and are ready to take, more responsibility for the presentation of their work.

It was something I proposed to bear in mind on the tour, and to that end I asked five actors and actresses who had been with me in the company over the previous two years to participate in preliminary discussions.

The obsessive egotism usually attributed to actors and actresses was certainly absent from this group who met in my dressing room at regular intervals and gave unstintingly of their time to discuss the general objectives and plans for the tour. During this period I was doing *The Winter's Tale* at the Barbican, and Paulina fortuitously has a long wait off-stage in the second act. I filled it with chat and reading plays. It was sometimes rather difficult to switch my mind back to the beautiful scene in which Paulina restores Hermione to the reformed Leontes whom she has hidden from his wrath, and one disastrous night I had a complete black-out during one of my speeches, substituting, after a long, groping pause, the word 'twig' for 'bough' in the line:

'I, an old turtle,

Will wing me to some withered bough.'

After the solemn magic of the statue scene, 'twig' seemed somehow ludicrously inappropriate and the whole company dissolved into giggles, shamefully ruining the end of the play for the bewildered audience. It was a classic example of how inappropriate it is to substitute anything for Shakespeare's own words.

Though my performance in *The Winter's Tale* may have suffered, the meetings were very productive. I haunted the London Library and the British Theatre Association and between the five of us we read dozens of possible plays. I seemed always to get lumbered with Restoration pieces, which I find torture to read, and the Russians, which are even worse with their constantly changing, unpronounceable names which necessitate endless flicking back to the cast list. I eventually opted out and resorted to reading collected criticisms by Agate and Tynan. It was nice to put the critics to good use for a change, and interesting to realise that Tynan was a great critic because he gave you a crystal-clear picture of a play or performance that you had never read or seen. Finally we realised that we need not have strained our eyes because, after much agonising, we decided our main productions would be two plays we knew very well: *Romeo and Juliet* and the musical, *Kiss Me Kate*.

Romeo and Juliet has all the elements of a good yarn that will appeal to young and old – fights, dances, colour and excitement – as well as being a play that people think they know, but which I felt could be seen from a new perspective. As a bonus, we had in our group some perfect actors for the leading parts, particularly Juliet Stevenson for a potentially heart-rending Juliet.

Kiss Me Kate was chosen partly because the RSC company from which the tour ensemble was to be mainly chosen was very strong in musical talent. I also considered it could be changed from a spectacular, glossy American musical into being more vividly about the touring Shakespearian company of its subject matter. I wanted to perform it with English accents and did a lot of preparatory work translating the idiom to make it sound right. The music would be played by the cast on stage with new orchestrations using Elizabethan sounds and solo guitars and pianos, making it arise more naturally out of the action than music does from a pit orchestra. We would not try to ape an American production, which the English are not usually very good at anyway; it could be about us, and would have a marvellous immediacy, as well as demonstrating that the RSC not only do Shakespeare but also other classics – including musicals. I hoped that the Shakespearian scene from *The Taming of the Shrew* could be extended and the whole show could be a joyous celebration of the Bard. Another member of the discussion group, Bernard Lloyd, had a beautiful singing voice and was a natural for the leading man. Both plays also provided good parts for Roger Allam and Geoffrey Hutchins, established RSC players, who were also in the group. All this pleased me, as I happen to believe that if you have talent in a company you should choose shows that display it.

We would, I was sure, be criticised for being too popular and not ambitious enough, but having studied the returns for previous tours I had been surprised to discover that a 100 per cent box office was not so easy to achieve. And I wanted to be popular. Subsidised companies should take risks with new writers and rarely performed classics, but we felt that this tour had different criteria. We would be frequently going to places where the RSC had a stuffy image and where the classics frightened people to death – to places, in fact, like the ones I had grown up in – and we were keen to destroy these preconceptions. We formulated plans for workshops, to involve each of the communities we visited. We schemed on ways to bring in new audiences. We resolved to commission a piece of new writing for a play to be performed in the morning, a strategy I was keen on adopting having personally experienced the desolation of the unemployed at that time of the day. And, to attract women trapped in the home with young children, we planned to run an additional workshop for their little ones concurrent with the morning play. For the company to crowd in all this during a three- or four-day turn-around, with all the travelling involved, was potentially overwhelming; but our idealism was not easily crushed.

The previous tour, two years before, had travelled with a 500-seater auditorium that was erected in sports centres, civic halls and the like. The rows of tiered seats could be grouped in any way around the acting area to give a conventional, in-the-round or three-sided auditorium. It meant that one could set up in places usually associated with other community activities that did not have the mystique of theatre buildings and, of course, in towns not blessed with any theatre at all. Once we had decided on the seat lay-out, it would remain constant and save time-consuming rehearsals to adapt to different stages – as well as ensuring perfect visibility from every seat. The local people would be involved in erecting and dismantling it, as we could not afford many stagehands and the actors would be too knackered to perform if they did it. This proved to be a positive advantage in terms of community involvement. Its disadvantage was that there would be factories, village halls and small spaces that could not accommodate it, so we resolved to take our morning play to those. Discovering that the seating we wanted to hire was much in demand for snooker contests, I considered it wise to book well in advance, but here encountered a certain reluctance on the part of the RSC management to talk about money. Not for the first time, moreover.

Thus I began increasingly to brood on the finances. I discovered that the Arts Council was, in principle, prepared to give us some money for the tour but it was to be matched equally with sponsorship. As no budget had yet been prepared it was fairly difficult to assess how much we needed to apply for but, in any case, when I did approach the sponsorship officer, Jane Jacomb-Hood, she was in the process of compiling begging letters for shows that needed their money yesterday; a tour that was scheduled for a few months ahead was the least of her worries. The Tory dream of people rushing to sponsor the Arts, particularly as they give them little financial incentive to do so, puts a heavy burden on the likes of Jane, who was single-handedly trying to persuade business tycoons to part with money for plays they would not cross the street to see. Neither, for that matter, would – or do – Mrs Thatcher and most of her friends, which probably accounts for that lady's overall indifference. In smaller companies it is the hard-pressed artistic directors who are saddled with the task of raising money – to the detriment of the job they should be doing, not to mention their blood pressure. Whilst sympathising with Jane's priorities, I was nevertheless disconcerted to find I was planning a project for which there was as yet no sign of funding. It seemed a good idea to acquaint Trevor with my problems and plans so far.

This was not as easy as one would imagine. By this time it was November 1982, and I was deep into rehearsals for *Peter Pan* directed by Trevor and John Caird. I was simulating the archetypal earth mother, Mrs Darling, whilst my own neglected children were lucky to catch a fleeting glimpse of their preoccupied parent. The first fortnight of rehearsals was spent playing marvellous games, led by Trevor and John, and hilarious improvisations on childhood. The enthusiasm with which we all reverted to infancy gave us a deeper understanding of Barrie and his strange world where growing up is so regretful. We frolicked around, sometimes erupting into childish violence, while Trevor and John usually prowled the sidelines closely observing our antics, except for one occasion when I dragged an embarrassed Trevor in as a teacher to adjudicate on a violent injustice being wrought on me in the playground by an aggressive little Tony O'Donell, who was to play one of the Lost Boys. As always with improvisations, I found the return to the text a huge anticlimax – particularly as I had to grow up and glide around as Mrs Darling, being the perfect lady and uttering ghastly sentimental lines about my children's 'silver voices'. Some of the situations created in the improvisations were so much more robust than the dated antics of Barrie's children that I regretted that our text-purist directors would not incorporate them as Joan Littlewood would have done.

The fact that I spent a good deal of rehearsals being a snotty-nosed kid, combined with the intricate complications of the production, meant that I was never able to corner Trevor long enough to discuss our plans for the tour. Having by this time twigged that nearly all communication at the RSC was done by internal memo, I eventually sent him the following:

> Dear Mr Nunn,
> I am writing officially to crave an audience with you. I offer lunch, dinner, supper, a bottle of champagne or my body in return for half an hour's individual attention.

The rest of my offer was sadly rejected but I did get a meeting at which he approved of our plans thus far and made soothing 'Trevving' noises about the money. However, with the distraction of *Peter Pan* and limping as he was towards a well-deserved year's sabbatical from the company, I suspect he would have approved anything.

During his year away the overall control of the company was to be in the hands of Terry Hands, his joint Artistic Director. I had been experiencing a few problems in enlisting a company to tour because he was simultaneously trying to cast a West End version of his production of Peter Nichols' musical, *Poppy*. The double lure of the West End and good money was proving an unfair match to three-night stands and RSC minimum salaries, not to mention the superior advantage of keeping in with Terry Hands as opposed to Sheila Hancock. So, as Trevor was about to disappear into his monastery, or wherever sabbaticals happen, I surmised it was time to make Mr Hands's acquaintance.

I was somewhat nervous about approaching him, not least because of his nickname, 'Gauleighter' Hands (acquired, I am sure, for no other reason than his predilection for wearing black). In my two years with the company I had only met him twice, the first time when he was devastatingly charming to me after my Shakespearian debut at Stratford as Paulina, and the second after the last performance of the notorious double bill in which I had offered to an unsuspecting public my aforementioned Tamara in *Titus Andronicus* and second outlaw in *The Two Gentlemen of Verona*. I met him and his RSC associate directors, Barry Kyle and Adrian Noble, on the steps of the Arden Hotel where they had doubtless been drowning their disbelief. This time he could summon up no more than a bemused slow shake of his head, performed in perfect unison with the other two speechless young genii. I boldly told them that I had, in fact, been toning down my performance that night as I knew they were out front, at which Terry gulped and disappeared into the shadows. All the more reason, I deduced, that I should get to know him; and he me.

I nervously approached his secretary for an appointment and was invited into his office. Having groped my way to a seat in the subtle lighting, I contemplated this legend as he engaged New York in a high-powered telephone conversation. He was frequently on the phone to New York. There he was, then, on this first occasion, wearing the statutory black, his sensual lips smiling and sardonic eyes mocking, poised panther-like in his chair. I stuttered out my worries and he at once made light of them. I had been 'Trevved'; now I was being 'Handled'. I enjoyed one or two subsequent visits to his lair, listening, fascinated, to his ability to demolish someone with a well-turned phrase, so subtle that it was several moments later before you flinched or laughed, and I relished his powers of derision, usually turned on himself. As I said before, there are RSC Trevor men and Terry men and never the twain would meet; but I found them both equally beguiling. And unavailable.

Being unavailable was a full-time occupation for all the men at the RSC and, as I discovered later, at the National. Indeed, the RSC acting company even requested Jimmy Savile to fix up a meeting with Trevor and Terry on *Jim'll Fix It*. There are so many locations that they could all be at, so many meetings they could be attending, that I would defy MI5 to trace any one of them at any given moment. This unavailability may account for the high percentage of broken personal relationships they have. Whilst I was working with the company two of the directors lost the women they adored; neither could understand why lovers and mothers were not prepared to take second place to the 'greatest company

in the world', and were appalled when I suggested that they should give
up the idea of marriage. Sadly they were also romantics, and romantic
workaholics make rotten husbands.

I was really getting into the accepted method of sending memos, but
few of them seemed to be received or acknowledged. I found this curious
and began to get paranoid. My only previous experience of the running
of a company had been as associate director of the Cambridge Theatre
Company, which the highly organised Jonathan Lynn ran in close
association with his small team in such a way that he could simultaneously
write *Yes, Minister* without neglecting either job. The organisation of the
RSC was teaching me to appreciate the truth of the adage, 'small is
beautiful.'

It had, for example, been a bad experience to move from our season
in Stratford with its small-town friendliness, and a short stay at the
Theatre Royal, Newcastle, with its overcrowded intimacy, to being the
first company into the vast new Barbican centre. Having initially found
the building with great difficulty, we were astounded to discover that
this wonderful new complex was designed in such a way that our rehearsal
rooms were airless tombs in the bowels of the earth, the dressing rooms
were several floors from the stage and the lifts kept sticking. The
air-conditioning was such that one night Stephen Moore, one of the
actors in *A Doll's House*, was actually forced to stop a performance to
apologise to a sweating, expiring audience in the aptly named Pit Theatre.
The whole place had less atmosphere than the average airport and we
became convinced that this theatre, so generously given to the RSC, was
in fact a nuclear shelter for the City of London Fathers. We searched
for a secret tunnel leading to the Mansion House and worked out exactly
which of the strange machine rooms and mysterious iron doors would
be utilised come the holocaust. Most of us desperately hoped that our
shows would not be in the repertoire that night, as being vaporised
seemed vastly preferable to incarceration in the Barbican. After the
intimacy of Stratford and Newcastle we were appalled at how we lost
one another in the Barbican, both physically and emotionally. The band
was buried in some little room it took weeks to find. God knows where
the stage staff were lurking, as I hardly talked to any of them until the
technical rehearsals of *Peter Pan* brought us together like recruits in a
war.

The vastness of these stages, inherited from the 1960s designs, was
pushing shows into more and more spectacle, and the peak was reached
with *Peter Pan*. This pretty little story was to be blown up into a gigantic

epic. Kirby flying-wires were spurned for computer-controlled miracles that went up, down, sideways. The set revolved, came in on trucks, divided, flew and danced – sometimes.

Our first preview was converted into a dress rehearsal where a bemused public sat and watched endless cock-ups, at one point dancing on the stage with the company whilst the staff unhitched a technical knot. The audience staggered home at about midnight, trying to explain to baffled children why Peter Pan flew into the nursery and was then to be seen dangling for some time in mid-air until a strange man in jeans came on and lowered him to the ground; and why, when the children flew out of the nursery window to Never Never Land, Wendy was left behind muttering 'Oh shit'. It must also have been difficult to account for the man in overalls clinging to the chimney pot, desperately disentangling a curtain that hung crookedly from the sky as Mrs Darling's house jerked forward, ending dangerously near the edge of the stage. After this particular drape refused to rise up into the flies (the area above the stage) in subsequent performances, I and the said stagehand invented an interesting sub-plot about Mrs Darling's lover, and he would give me a jaunty wink as he slid down the wall of my house and disappeared into the night. In fact, so many of the stage staff were caught fighting with bits of the machinery when the computer-controlled lights relentlessly revealed them that I believe they considered negotiating appearance fees and joining Equity. I suppose when the children took off out of the window to Never Never Land and soared on rather visible wires to the Barbican roof it was breathtaking; but not when the wires did not function and one, or sometimes two, Darling children were left in the nursery. Or, worse, when the Darling children went but Peter Pan was left, muttering: 'Bugger it, and I've got a friend out front tonight too.' For my part I used to hold my breath and shut my eyes as they bumped against the window frame, getting yet more bruises. At the beginning of the show the full company came on in darkness to recite the start of Barrie's book. I would seize the opportunity of the black-out to ask Miles Anderson, who played Peter Pan, how he was that night. On one occasion he rasped bitterly: 'Well, apart from a dicky ankle, bruised shoulders, a fucking awful sore throat and piles, life's an awfully big adventure.'

At the same time as we were cancelling performances and bringing in the safety curtain mid-scene whilst we sorted out things that had gone wrong, the National were fighting with a rogue water tank in their production of Alan Ayckbourn's *Way Upstream*. On more than one occasion punters were trekking in from afar to see the two great national companies, only to be told that those wonderful new theatres were closed because of technical hitches. Throughout my years of tatty theatre work the show had somehow limped on, but now, with the new technological advances, it constantly groaned to a halt. All this made me look forward with pleasure to touring with no sets or complications – just the audience, the actors and the play.

'Barbicanitis' was pushing the entire company into more bad temper and acrimony than was usual, so it seemed an apposite time to put up the following notice in the dungeon-like Green Room. This was in keeping with my policy of constant communication of plans so that casting should not be the usual hole-in-the-corner process that it was at the RSC. The notice read:

> The Small Scale Tour is probably going to start rehearsing for ten weeks when *All's Well* finishes in August and will be on the road from the beginning of October till the end of January. I would like to know which of you in the existing company are interested in the idea – subject, of course, to parts offered. It is an arduous venture which I think should only be considered by people committed to the idea of taking our work to remote and theatrically deprived areas. I do also think it will be exciting and fun, and for some of you Barrow-in-Furness and Wath-upon-Dearne may be preferable to the Barbican.

It is unusual to approach actors before a director is fixed because a good one is, for most of us, a criterion for the job, brainwashed as we are into believing they are all-important; but this time I dearly wanted people to join because of the nature of the work. And they did.

In response to the notice there were many snatched chats in the wings, even signals on stage during the play, indicating the keen interest people had in a company along the lines I had envisaged. The idea of taking a musical on tour found particular favour, and this made us keener than ever to procure the rights of *Kiss Me Kate*, which our great ally, Colin Chambers, the RSC Literary Manager, set about doing.

This led to the first brick wall.

After a series of delays and muddles it transpired that the National Theatre wanted *Kiss Me Kate* too. I had urgent meetings with various representatives of Bella Spewack, one of the writers, who was old but very much alive and kicking furiously to protect her property. To them I explained my ideas in detail, pointing out that the style of our show and the itinerary of the tour would in no way clash with the National's plans, which I understood to take the form of a big follow-up to their huge success with *Guys and Dolls*, so there seemed no reason why both companies should not do it. At this early stage the Old Vic was also nibbling after the rights, but it ended up as a straight battle between the National and the RSC.

Despite my assurances I was furious when I was told that the National categorically refused to allow us to perform the show on tour if they did it in London. Obviously a big London production was more attractive to the agents than our little cut-price version. I rushed round in a frenzy trying to contact someone to back me up. I wrote to Richard Eyre and Peter Hall at the National, to which there was never a reply – non-communication presumably having spread across the river – and tried to find David Brierley, the General Manager of the RSC, or Trevor Nunn, to lend weight to my pleas. They were, of course, unavailable.

I ended up shouting to all and sundry that if I did not hear from either of them in two hours I was resigning. Miraculously, they were traced before the end of the day and Trevor proceeded to 'Trev' around in all directions. There was a further saga of missed phone calls which culminated in the National winning the rights, and us being barred from performing *Kiss Me Kate*. The rights were presumably locked away in a little drawer for a few years in the South Bank bunker until, in 1987, they were given to the RSC after all, allowing them to mount a lavish production in Stratford and London. It is rather sad really. The people of Workington and Scunthorpe would have enjoyed our version, I think; but I am sure Miss Spewack and the National did not lose any sleep over that.

Rather than the group agonising further over the choice of a play, I felt it fairer all round to enlist instead the opinions of the potential customers. Who were they? Where were all these venues? Nobody seemed to know. Moira Hunter, who had been the administrator of two previous tours but had now left the company, kept being mentioned as a possible source of information. I contacted her and confided that the machinery for setting up the tour was proving more Heath-Robinsonish than I had expected. She gently informed me that she had organised the last one from half-way up a ladder on a shelf in the Warehouse Theatre, which made my nomadic borrowing of any available phones or corners of desks in the relative comfort of the Barbican seem luxurious. Her undiminished enthusiasm for the new tour and the obvious need for someone with experience in the practical side led me to request that she be engaged to join us. After, of course, ascertaining that she was fool enough to want to. This too was greeted with the usual rush of inactivity.

After a bit of fruitless hammering at this second brick wall I gritted my teeth and, in accordance with my policy of allowing the actors to make the decisions, moved on to choose directors with an expanded think-tank. I was profoundly relieved when they agreed to let me direct one of the plays yet to be decided. If they had turned me down it could have been embarrassing, as it was to prove with the selection of a director for *Romeo and Juliet*. It was a glorious reversal of the norm for actors to be assessing the relative merits of people they wished to employ. Having decided an RSC tour should be directed ideally by staff directors or actors, I approached several in descending order of preference, starting with actors presently with the company or who had been in the recent past. I made a trip to Paris to try to lure Peter Brook back to England, thinking the nature of the tour would appeal to him. It did, but not enough. For various reasons our other first choices were unavailable or unwilling, which led to my circulating a list of possible directors, now extended to include some people outside the RSC. It read:

> It would help me greatly in the choosing of a director for the Small Scale Tour Shakespeare production and morning play if you could look at the enclosed list and assess the directors thus:
>   3 ticks for fantastic
>   2 ticks for very good
>   1 tick for all right
>   A cross for over my dead body
> I swear to you that the list will be shown to no one else – not even other members of the group. After I have looked at them I will tear them up and eat them.

I am afraid I broke my promise and the resulting lists and added comments I have locked away in a dungeon to be chortled over in my dotage. The group obviously relished the task as much as Bernard Lloyd who started his reply: 'Dear one, you are camp! It's the sort of game we would have cherished at Christmas . . .'

The unanimous favourites proved to be the artistic director of the Royal Court Theatre, Max Stafford-Clark, and Jane Howell, a much-admired freelance director – several of the remaining in-house directors having been given a definite thumbs-down. Having had no guidelines laid down, apart from Trevor's original letter, giving me, as I saw it, total freedom, I duly asked for their availability to be checked by Joyce Nettles, the casting director.

Thus I collided with my third and final brick wall.

At first my request appeared to be ignored, but when I persisted I was told by Colin Chambers that he understood it would be deemed 'a political move to go outside the resident directors'. Just who had expressed this opinion I could not discover, nor what I was supposed to do, as all our in-house choices had turned us down. Anyway I decided I had had enough of ricocheting off brick walls and was not ambitious enough to try scaling them or better still knocking them down. I had no programme, no administrator, no co-director, no facilities, no money, and nobody seemed to care. So I resigned – even though I still had not been officially contracted.

I wrote a lengthy memo explaining my reasons, culminating with the loaded cry that I simply wasn't 'man' enough for the job, and circulated it to as many people as I could. I then hid. Looking back now, I realise how tedious this whole business must have been for them all. They were used to coping with this understaffed muddle. The Priestley Report on the RSC identified this lack of planning in the organisation and recommended earlier decisions on which plays were to be performed and on casting. No doubt efforts have been made to bring this about, but it is difficult to get everyone together for decisions as the relevant people are rehearsing all the hours God sent either in Stratford or London. I suspect there was also a superstitious fear that their huge success might be damaged if they altered their approach and became too streamlined. Every now and then a crisis blew up as a result of the pressure – both Genistra McIntosh, the superb planning officer, and Joyce Nettles, the dedicated casting lady, have resigned since I left the company in protest at the impossible strain imposed on the staff and actors, although Genistra returned later in another capacity. Usually people just had the odd moan and then got on with their jobs. Now here was this woman causing an irritating minor crisis.

Nevertheless, my flamboyant gesture did reap results. After much 'Trevving' and 'Handling' I was asked to lay down conditions for resuming my job – most of which were accepted by 'the boys'. We were to liaise over casting, with no unseemly or underhand battling for artists, and the final decision was then to be left to them. My company was to be the nucleus of the next year's Stratford season with a guaranteed offer of parts; *Romeo and Juliet* would go into the Stratford repertoire and John Caird was to direct it. In future I was to attend company planning meetings where I could fight my corner; Moira was to be officially engaged; and, principal joy and status symbol, we were to be given an office.

Feeling somewhat ashamed of the upset I had caused, and grateful for the new-found support that had been expressed, I sent out the following statement-of-intent memo:

OBJECTIVES OF THE SMALL SCALE TOUR

i) To take the RSC to members of the British public who support the company with their taxes but have little opportunity to see their work.

ii) By the nature of our venues, our approach to the work and activities involving the local communities, to endeavour to break down the barriers that exist between some people and the theatre – particularly classical theatre. In pursuit of this aim, Moira and I will do our best in preliminary field-work to ensure a broad-based audience.

iii) To enjoy the experience of returning to the basics of actor, text and audience, untrammelled by the complication of large buildings.

iv) To develop a strong ensemble that, having endured together the rigours of the tour, will form an exciting nucleus on which to base the 1984 Stratford season.

v) By adventurous casting to discover or develop potential in artists that may have been underused in the company so far.

As a result of strengthening the links with the organisation as a whole, I hope the tour will enhance the reputation of the company throughout the country, and when they return will feed back an energy and commitment that will nourish the main operation.

With those grandiose but sincere intentions I commenced the real work with renewed enthusiasm.

3 : Under Way

During my skirmishes on the seventh floor I had from time to time
noticed out of the corner of my eye an alien, clean-shaven face lurking
amongst the five-o'clock shadows. On a couple of occasions a sober suit,
graced with a stylish club tie, had very politely and only slightly nervously
flattened itself against the wall as I gushed down the narrow corridor.

When, in May 1983, I was summoned to give evidence to their owner,
I ascertained that the club was ominously something to do with rifles
and the suit adorned the person of Mr Clive Priestley, CBE, emissary
from Mrs Thatcher & Co to investigate the financial affairs of the RSC.
One can only joyously surmise their reaction when his resultant report
proposed a considerable increase in the Government's grant to the
company.

As we all do with reports, I merely read the press accounts of the
conclusions of Mr Priestley's painstaking task for the Government, until
one winter's day in 1984 I came across it in the British Museum and
idly thumbed through the details, only to be stung by the following
passage nestling in the section about the tour:

ADVANCE VISITS/PLANNING

The budget for this is unusual. No normal touring company would plan over
so extensive a period and in such detail. But it is in the nature of the RSC,
and this special kind of tour to unconventional venues, that this order of cost
must be incurred. The RSC believe from their past experience of such tours
that a personal involvement of the Director through the setting-up period

and throughout the performing weeks themselves is as essential as his/her presence during rehearsals. Initial planning for the tour started in the late Autumn of 1982 while Ms Hancock was under contract as an actress. The RSC believe that unless they had offered a contract to Ms Hancock immediately after the end of her performing contract in March 1983 the uninterrupted availability of her services and thus the essential continuity of the planning of the tour would not have been secured. The Arts Council of Great Britain believes this to be an inevitable cost in engaging someone like Ms Hancock whose charisma and energy are vital to an enterprise of this kind. The ACGB believes it to be costly, however, and in future tours they would not contemplate funding such a long pre-tour employment.

The spectre haunts me of future generations of theatre researchers regarding me as a greedy hussy who demanded a 'costly' fee for the privilege of her 'availability': despite the passing compliments, the implication was that I was paid some kind of retainer rather than an honest salary for working harder than I ever had in my life. A few weeks after this shock in the reading room I happened to see David Brierley, General Manager and financial whizz-kid of the RSC, at a function given by the Mayor of Stratford-upon-Avon; during that worthy gentleman's solemn address, I hissed my fury at him for not sweeping away those innuendos, nor questioning the ACGB's criticism of our planning 'in such detail' whilst condemning the lack of organisation in other departments. Fresh from gloating over his increased bounty and at that moment trying to butter up the Stratford councillors, I could appreciate David's indifference to my personal niggle. I console myself that apart from one in the British Museum and doubtless a dusty copy piled up with all the other reports in a cobwebby attic of the Arts Council building in Piccadilly, little will remain for posterity of Mr Priestley's diligent research.

Nevertheless, for the ACGB and government records the following are just a few of the things I was doing during the period when the Arts Council thought my presence unnecessarily 'costly'.

Unlike the National Theatre, the RSC has no 'normal' touring department. Moira Hunter and I were, in fact, it. My resignation tantrums may have secured us an office but we still had to beg, borrow or steal the facilities of various other departments to help us, when they could be extricated from the complexities of the rest of the organisation. To type my business letters I had to kidnap any random secretary who dared to pause for a coffee or fag. Offices would become frenzied hives of activity and women would leap into cupboards at my approach.

Rumours had leaked out about our proposed tour and we were already becoming inundated with invitations from towns all over the British Isles. Any 'normal' touring companies have a network of dates they book on the phone, but we were looking for places with no experience of theatre and consequently no experience of organising such visits; indeed, in one or two cases, no phone.

So it was that at various times in March, April and May 1983, armed with our measurements and requirements for the auditorium (which, despite having not a penny, we had boldly booked lest we should be snookered by other regular users) and a list of necessary facilities for actors, wardrobe, wigs, fire regulations, etc, we journeyed by rail, road and aching feet round England to choose our venues as well as to suss out if the locals had any ideas for the second main play to replace *Kiss Me Kate*.

My criteria for deciding where to go were: (a) if our presence would be useful (b) if it were physically possible.

The definition of 'useful' was wide-ranging. It could mean there was no theatre at all in the area, or alternatively the existing local groups or theatre needed a bit of a PR boost, particularly with ungenerous councillors, which we could give them by including them in our plans. Maybe the English staff in a school or college were having a tough time with a science-orientated head or, in the case of Scunthorpe with its brave Cultural Festival, a depressed town endeavouring to attract tourist income and new businesses with a changed image.

We visited towns and villages I never knew existed the length and breadth of the British Isles. We met local councillors, head teachers, union leaders, children, parents, the unemployed, all desperate to have a visit from the company. Our introduction as representatives of the Royal Shakespeare Company always brought forth amazingly enthusiastic responses even in the most secluded backwaters, such as I seldom found later as a National Theatre player. I suspect the words 'royal' and 'Shakespeare' have a more venerable ring to them than 'national', with its connotations of petrol and skinheads in union jack T-shirts (although the chic use of the initials RSC alone, as used in London, Newcastle and Stratford, engendered nothing but bewilderment that this erstwhile comedienne was now working for a car-towing organisation).

Over the next few weeks Moira tentatively booked town and village halls, gymnasiums, community centres, factory canteens, prison libraries and covered swimming pools. They were all used by the local community and I chatted to many who agreed that if we were there they would 'give it a go', though many had never been to, nor intended to visit, the theatre, least of all to see Shakespeare. The odd sour note was struck by one or two sports teachers who resented the proposed disruption of their schedules, not to mention the danger to their floors. However, the 'charismatic' Ms Hancock went out of her way to charm these dissenters with stories of how, contrary to popular belief, actors were macho young men who would be grovellingly grateful to receive coaching in their spare moments, and I too was not averse to the odd work-out if they would hold my hand. Several of these establishments had alarming pulse-taking machines which purported to show one's state of health, and as all of them in various parts of the country deemed me near death, I indeed resolved to do something about my decaying heart and body. As it turned out, the only occasion during the tour that I subsequently had time to avail myself of the facilities was to sit on an exercise bike whilst ironing one of the costumes in a gymnasium in Mansfield. There was, I confess, one occasion on Doncaster station, during a shivering two-hour wait in a howling March gale after a visit to Dinnington and Wath-upon-Dearne, when I did wonder what the hell I was doing.

On tatty tours in my youth there had been a certain glamour in hours spent on Crewe station greeting the other passing companies, doing the *Sunday Times* crossword and chuckling over Ken Tynan's acerbic reviews in *The Observer* of our famous colleagues whom we occasionally glimpsed on trains in first-class compartments. However, I had always steadfastly believed that this was only a temporary step on the ladder which would lead up to chauffeured Rolls Royces, West End lights and a comfy old age. I might have endured it less cheerfully had I known I would still be at it at fifty.

Most of the towns I revisited seemed even more barren, ugly and desolate than I remembered them – places like Oldham, for example, where I had spent a year in repertory in 1953. Admittedly, then it had had houses with one outside lavatory between four or more families and no bathrooms or heating apart from the black lead stove in the scullery; but surely to God it was more congenial to live in than the replanned urban nightmare it now is. Anyone who vandalises these obscene sights they are forced to look at day in day out has my total support – *pace* Prince Philip.

Whilst reading in gossip columns of socialites cavorting in London, in these towns people were queueing for jobs, youngsters were hanging around on street corners contemplating their barren futures and teachers despaired of giving their charges hope. The usual considerations of pleasing the critics, my peers, ways of demonstrating my cleverness or enhancing my future prospects – all were forgotten in an overwhelming desire to communicate and entertain. It is very easy in my fiercely competitive industry to lose touch with that fundamental driving force, and I was elated by the strength of my feelings. Writing this as I am in retrospect, I am embarrassed in case it sounds sentimental and matronising, but at the time the regard that I, and later my company, felt for our audiences was genuine and total – a feeling that, chauvinist that I am, I cannot in all honesty claim to feel for the Japanese and American tourists who make up a large proportion of West End audiences.

The more I saw of the places we were to visit and the more I talked to our potential audience, the more I began to think of the suitability of *A Midsummer Night's Dream* as our second play. This glorious work – about reaching out in friendship, coping with love, escaping from an austere society with cruel injustices into the beauty of imagination and untrammelled nature, the dark undertones, the triumph of human resilience, the imagery, the comedy, the music, the recognisable characters and the sheer blazing magic of the play – seemed absolutely what I wanted to offer.

After bending the arms and minds of my support group, I informed the hierarchy of my decision to do *A Midsummer Night's Dream* as the companion play to *Romeo and Juliet*. It was not a popular choice, not least because everyone was still nervous of trying to follow the revolutionary triumph of Peter Brook's 1971 production. But I did not have the same pressures on me to find new interpretations that are usually the preoccupation of directors in London and Stratford. My aspiration was to communicate the play to our particular audience, and if the best way should turn out to be to do it in a white box with conjuring tricks I would have no worries about plagiarism. The ends justified the means.

We next chose our morning play. It proved too late to commission new work but Terry Hands suggested the perfect piece in Edward Bond's *Derek*. It is a short play about a young, brilliant working-class lad who sells his brain to a mindless upper-class twit, and is full of Bond's usual anger and compassion for an unjust society. Just the thing to get them going, I thought.

My determination to reach the right audiences necessitated meetings with marketing people in the various areas to devise ways of distributing the tickets, as well as best placing publicity. Peter Harlock, our indefatigable Publicity Controller, was driven mad by my stipulations for the poster and hand-out material. I wanted none of your tasteful grey or sepias but something vulgar and vivid. Each deadline which would ensure we would have the designs ready by July so that the hand-outs could be circulated well before we opened in October kept passing as I rejected draft after draft. We finally settled on a lovely blurred blue, red and brown image of a crowd of vaguely Shakespearian characters cavorting towards the eye and a slogan I awoke with in the middle of the night: *The RSC – Coming to Town*. Ludicrously simple, but the feeling of circus was perfect. Poor Peter had another nasty turn when he received the programme notes we had requested from Edward Bond – a marvellous diatribe on the uselessness of Shakespeare or other writers' attempts to change a capitalist and war-like world. Tremors went through the building when I insisted that it should be used.

The ridiculous lack of rehearsal space at the Barbican landed us with having to book the dreaded Alford House – better known as Awful House – a youth club near Kennington gas works. Undaunted, we chatted up the caretaker and, by dint of a bit of paint, a few posters and pot plants, made it a more congenial home for our ten weeks' stay: not, at the risk of sounding sexist, a strategy that I think a male directorate would have undertaken. Actors have to rehearse and perform in conditions that would cause a mass walk-out in any self-respecting abattoir, as they are not covered by the Factories Act enforcing decent conditions for workers. I just happen to think they work better where there is a clean lavatory and the odd chair to sit on whilst learning their lines.

As we booked transport, digs and cushions for the hard auditorium seats, I began to get very nervous again about our financial situation. Occasionally I would sit on Jane Jacomb-Hood's desk and jokingly ask for news. The jokes began to wane as we got nearer and nearer to the proposed first day of rehearsals on 1 August and were running up bills with not a penny in the kitty. The Arts Council were still adamant that we would get no money from them without matching sponsorship. We kept trying to cut the budget, which was already pared to the bone. It would have been possible to settle for a smaller company than eighteen actors, but there are other groups doing the really small-scale work and I felt our audiences had a right to get from us something more in line with what Stratford, Newcastle and London were offered. As it was, I intended to use actor/musicians instead of taking a band.

In the quest for money I wrote to every rich acquaintance I had, and wined and dined every boring businessman I could get access to. But to no avail. The tour was on the verge of cancellation when, as someone on the list of charitable celebrities, I was asked to attend a party at London Zoo given by CVS (Community Service Volunteers), an organisation which recruits young people to help the community. They were throwing the party for disabled youngsters and on the day, when I saw the pouring rain, I nearly decided to opt out as I felt my spirits were low enough already. Eventually my conscience got the better of me, so I went with my then nine-year-old daughter, Joanna.

As always on such occasions I could hardly speak for grief, while Joanna and all the young volunteers danced merrily with the helpless little bodies hanging on to their shoulders, or whirled them round the floor in wheelchairs and conversed blithely with incoherent children struggling to speak; they seemed thoroughly to enjoy their company, with no time to indulge in fruitless pity. I did my best and at one point was helped to lift a young boy out of his wheelchair by a man in shirtsleeves. After we had given the lad his tea I asked the man what he was doing there. 'Oh, I paid for this gig.' Oblivious to the pound signs in my eyes, he continued: 'I run the Nat West sponsorship department.'

Poor man. Had he known what a predator he faced he would have kept his pride to himself. Next day he was out to lunch with me, the following day he had promised £80,000 for the tour, the largest amount ever given to the company at that time. So, Mr Priestley, Lord Gowrie, et al, at least my 'unnecessarily costly' salary was covered.

Thus began my lasting friendship with this jazz-loving, untypical banker, Geoff Burnett and his opera-loving assistant, Barrie Collins. I had cause to be even more grateful later when they gave us yet another £10,000 when I ran into problems with the Musicians' Union and another £3,000 when we needed to buy some lighting equipment at Stratford. Nowadays, if I phone either of them socially, I have to tell the secretary first that I am not after money before they will speak to me. Over the years I have had dealings with sponsors who had no interest in anything but the amount of publicity they would get. Barrie and Geoff struck a shrewd deal but were always deeply supportive and knowledgeable about the artistic side of the work. Rare animals in the business world.

Having at last got the money, to my profound relief we were all systems go. I rushed round the country again doing publicity, appearing on TV with a Nat West T-shirt clothing my ample bosom as promised in our contract. Press conferences are not my favourite occupation, not least because all the cub reporters' first questions are invariably: 'Forgive me, but who are you?' or: 'What have you done?' And the old hacks still regret the passing of *The Rag Trade*. For most of the media, as I suppose for the great British public at large, if you don't do TV you are dead. The fact that I have been beavering away in various areas of entertainment for thirty-odd years is of little interest compared with the relatively few weeks of that thirty years spent doing sitcoms. It was slightly undignified to have every TV interview I did to promote this classy tour preceded by a startling clip of me in *The Rag Trade*, losing my skirt and squawking with embarrassment over my exposed thighs and frilly knickers. Although I did relish appearing in a mindless quiz game called *Babble*, at the end of which the continuity announcer enunciated solemnly over those closing, leering smiles to camera: 'Miss Hancock is a member of the Royal Shakespeare Company.'

With the money in the bank, we felt safe to contract the company and staff. We had already been joined by Jennie Smith as stage manager, and it was with no thought of discrimination that I booked five more women to join us in August: Illona Sekacz to do the music, Priscilla Truett to design the costumes to match resident designer Bob Crowley's set design, Sarah Pia Anderson to direct *Derek*, Carol Braithwaite as publicity officer and Jean Newlove as choreographer. They were just the best people for the job, as was Malcolm Ransome to direct the fights. Everyone – the actors, stage management and crew – had to be able to cope with the workload and travel, as well as fulfil that enigmatic definition of a 'good company person'. Roger Allam was the only valiant survivor of the original group of actors, and we next set out to ensnare Robert Eddison who was about to leave the London company. I passionately wanted him for Quince; John Caird wanted him for Friar Lawrence; and both of us wanted him for his consummate skill with the language which we knew would be an example to the rest of the company. As he was then seventy-five it seemed unlikely we could tempt him on this uncomfortable expedition – particularly as we outlined our proposal sitting in his exquisite house in Chelsea, sipping a very good whisky. But we misjudged his indomitable spirit. It was a day of rejoicing for us when Robert said yes, particularly when the esteem in which he is held led five other members of the London company immediately to join us as well.

Believing as I do in the prime importance of the actors in a production, recruiting them is apt to be a more meticulous process for me than some directors. I constantly went to see actors and shows in the regions and drama schools with an eye to finding new people, as it is always preferable to see actors work than judge them from cold auditions. Only then can you tell if that potency with an audience is there, a factor I value above interpretative skill. People can be so utterly different on stage – mercifully for me.

When I was about twenty-one I appeared in Terence Rattigan's play, *Separate Tables* at the Bromley New Theatre. It is a double bill in which the leading lady is called upon to play two entirely different roles, thereby demonstrating her stunning versatility. In the first half she is a beautiful, fortyish ex-model and in the second a plain, repressed little spinster. With only a week's rehearsal it seems unlikely that I can have achieved any great depth in my characterisations, but my mum thought I was lovely, until she overheard a woman in the audience, shortly after I made my entrance miraculously transformed into the frump of the second play, mutter to her friend: 'Oh, hasn't she let herself go?'

However confused that good lady was, a very important London agent was sufficiently impressed to summon me to his presence. The make-up, the hair-piece, borrowed elegant black dress, plus a lot of cheek had obviously fooled him in the first play for his fleshy face fell when he saw this stringy young girl with a funny nose and gauche walk enter his grand office. Being mainly involved in films he was not interested in my ability to fool an audience in the theatre. He sat me under a very bright light and suggested plastic surgery and a good hairdresser, and I went home and had a good cry. I have never forgotten this incident when faced with unprepossessing actors whose work I do not know.

We cast several actors we had spotted in shows. James Simmons was booked on the spot when I saw him at the Shaw Theatre not only playing a brilliant Mercutio but valiantly and elegantly leaping to the defence of his leading lady when, in an after-show discussion, a snotty-nosed, singularly plain lout said querulously: 'I thought Juliet was supposed to be pretty.'

We came across Daniel Day Lewis when he took over from Rupert Everett in *Another Country*. The role of a homosexual public schoolboy was a little different from Romeo and, although his devastating beauty was a positive plus, John Caird was worried about his ability to handle the verse. At his interview Dan was visibly wilting under the intellectual discussion that was taking place, so I leapt to my feet and said: 'Let's have a crack at the balcony scene.'

John has never forgotten my rendering of Juliet and said the combination of the two of us gave a whole new dimension to the play. It also clinched Dan's engagement on the assumption that if the young man could manage to articulate those rapt protestations of undying love to a bespectacled apparition old enough to be his mother without cracking up, he had to have talent.

When Juliet Stevenson dropped out (having decided to leave the RSC), we travelled far and wide in search of a new Juliet. On one such foray to the Bush Theatre we ended up with the perfect Titania. It was crucial to my feelings about *The Dream* that my Titania should epitomise a particular kind of femininity, and lo and behold the perfect-looking girl walked into the pub. John Caird, who is bolder than I, accosted her and, on discovering she was an actress, invited her to audition. Thus we engaged Penny Downie. It was typical of the sort of coincidence one is dependent on for work in our profession.

My very first role in the West End, after years in the provinces unsuccessfully trying to get London agents and managers even to grant me an interview or an audition, came about as a result of joining a queue at the stage door of the Duke of York's Theatre, which I just happened to pass one day when doing a fruitless round of the agents. When I got to the head of the queue I discovered they were looking for an actress to take over a role from Joan Sims in *Breath of Spring*. I read for it and got the part. By a series of similar chances, hard auditions and Joyce Nettles, the casting director, and us keeping our ears and eyes open, we assembled an extraordinary group for the RSC Regional Tour. The last actor's contract was confirmed three days before we started rehearsal. Our small team was already practically on its knees from getting the planning wheels in motion, and at the same time I had been trying to prepare my production of *The Dream*. To get myself back on my feet I treated myself to a weekend at a health farm (for which I may one day send the Arts Council the bill), after which I was ready for the job of integrating all the various parts of our preparation into a productive whole.

I threw a party on our first day of rehearsal in our newly refurbished Awful House on 1 August, and I remember looking in awe at the potent physical combination we had mustered; a pleasure that never palled for me. The male directorate beadily noted that it was a long time since the RSC had engaged so many attractive men, but I was equally certain that they had not seen so many fascinating women before – the tendency having been for rather wet, pretty creatures. John and I had not made a conscious decision to pick dishy people. They were not all conventionally good-looking and came in all shapes and sizes; but every one of them had that quality which I believe all exciting artists have – a sexuality that is challenging and compulsive as well as somewhat ambiguous. I knew as I looked at them that it spelled trouble, challenge and a rough ride, but by God it was exciting.

For some time I had felt the approach to our work at the RSC erred on the side of being too cerebral, so the first few days of rehearsal were spent in loosening up our bodies. I say 'us' as I was playing in the Bond and, therefore, also an actress doing class. The odd fellow occasionally baulked at the bean-bag games I imposed on them, but gradually these disparate elements merged into an integrated group. In very few jobs are people thrown together and immediately forced to reveal their inmost emotions and cast aside all inhibitions. Working on a film, when time is at a premium, one can shake hands with a stranger and minutes later be writhing on a bed in a passionate love scene. But it is easier if actors have time to relax with one another first.

During rehearsal we had the usual text analysis sessions, including the now mandatory consideration of Jan Kott's writings on *The Dream*, which Robert found highly offensive and the women deeply sexist. It would be a book in itself to go through the whole rehearsal process. Suffice it to say I am a great believer in 'getting on your feet' rather than too much chat.

To use one example: Roger Allam, Penny Downie and I had spent ages discussing the scene of Titania and Oberon's first encounter in the woods in which Penny had the famous, ravishing 'Forgeries of jealousy' speech. All set pieces in Shakespeare are intimidating as some in the audience mouth the words along with you while others wait for an original reading. We all three felt overawed by the poetry of the scene, and it was not until we rehearsed it with both of them alternately trying to leave the room/forest and the other using every device to prevent them – seduction, persuasion, force, humour – that we discovered the many colours and changes that drove the scene along and prevented it being just a beautiful recitation.

I regard my director's role as referee rather than as teacher, with everyone having a right to a say, which can lead to battles and occasional violent temperament. I will not pretend that I had no strong opinions about the interpretation of the play, but I was open to changing them and on many occasions did. It takes time, tolerance on everybody's part, plus the right chemistry to create an atmosphere in which anyone can say exactly what they like about other people as well as themselves, and some groups never achieve it; we did.

The event that finally linked us as a company was a day out in some woods near Croydon, undertaken as an exercise to help us with *The*

Dream. We played games to develop our sense of touch, hearing, smell and awareness of one another and the natural world. Robert got lost, all of us were bitten by insects and scratched by brambles and, after the last hectic game of hide-and-seek, we ended in a heap on the edge of the woods, entwined, exhausted and exhilarated.

This new unity, which was subsequently to be a strength and a trial to the RSC, was tested two days later when we discovered our visit to Workington in Cumbria was being further sponsored in the area by British Nuclear Fuels Ltd.

When I first started in the business it was unheard of for actors and actresses to express political views or, indeed, enter into controversies of any kind. There were, of course, exceptions to the rule like battling Sybil Thorndike, but on the whole we were advised to remain impartial and lovable. There is no doubt that immediately you express an opinion you alienate a lot of people. Now that most actors have opted to behave like the common or garden members of society we are, we have to accept that our likes and dislikes will affect people's attitude towards us, just as I have never been able to strike up a meaningful relationship with anyone who likes Gilbert and Sullivan. Since Bob Hope behaved like a pompous ass and spoke his anti-feminist mind when a few women (one of whom was my husband's first wife, Sally Alexander) threw a bag of flour at the stage in a protest against the Miss World competition, I confess, irrational and prejudiced though I know it to be, I have never felt moved to laugh at him again.

Similarly, I have to accept that people will respond in like manner to my outspokenness. My popularity with the general public – those that know me at all – was more widespread during my *Rag Trade* days, when they could believe I was just as innocuous as the daffy character I played in that series, than when I have stood up to be publicly counted on one or two issues more recently. Whenever I appear on *Any Questions* I receive much mail along the lines that actresses do not know anything and should keep their traps shut. Now that could very well be true of me personally, but in general people in the theatre are rather more in touch with society's problems than many of the other, more insular professionals that I have encountered, coming as we do from all classes and backgrounds, as well as researching and getting inside the skin of a whole range of characters in our work. The media representation of a lot of lotus-eating idiots could not be more unlike the working actors I know. Nowadays there is a high level of political and social consciousness within the entertainment business which manifests itself in various colours. Moreover, unlike some people who live and die in one area of life, surrounded by neighbours and like-minded workmates who seldom challenge their viewpoints, actors are constantly – and sometimes viciously – questioned within our union, Equity, in the press and amongst ourselves. This was potently demonstrated to me in our dilemma over Workington.

When the Sellafield question arose the company were torn between two principles. If the money from Nuclear Fuels subsidising the price of the seats was not accepted, many of the inhabitants of Workington with their rampant unemployment would not be able to afford our prices, but if we took it we knew that Nuclear Fuels would use us to enhance their image as benefactors of the area. During rehearsals for *Macbeth* in 1986, when Jonathan Pryce read on a poster that the play was sponsored by Barclays Bank, he felt unable to continue because of their connections with South Africa. The main organisation of the RSC was able to cut back elsewhere in their programming to replace the money that they were forced to ask Barclays to withdraw. I, with my limited budget, had no such room to negotiate.

As the theatre is forced to seek money from all and sundry it becomes increasingly offensive for actors to find themselves sometimes endorsing products and businesses they abhor. There is a group of actors led by Warren Mitchell and Paul Eddington who refuse to work in cigarette-sponsored shows. Judging by Daley Thompson's objections to his Guinness T-shirt at the European Games, sports people have the same dilemma. A similar question of conscience applies to the lucrative field of advertising, although here at least the decision is the person's individual responsibility. Many actors keep body and soul together between proper jobs by persuading the public that one soap powder is better than another, or that such and such glutinous junk will not actually poison you straightaway. I myself can be heard rejoicing in the virtues of a certain lavatory cleaner, and it has earned me more money than several months of work with the National or RSC. But I cannot pretend it feels honest.

Sellafield, as they had renamed it hoping we would forget its murky Windscale past (unaware that it had an equally murky Sellafield future), was a dirty word or two with all anti-nuclear campaigners even before the public at large became nervous after the Chernobyl disaster. It was only fair in a democratic company to discuss the issues. Several of us were active anti-nuclear protesters, and to be seen to endorse something that we had previously opposed would appear hypocritical as well as being personally distasteful. At the time there was much talk in the press about the above average incidence of leukaemia in the area. Others felt equally strongly that we should do the job we were paid for whosoever funded us, as the Arts could not afford to examine every sponsor in terms of what each individual actor believed was right or wrong, e.g. what were Nat West's interests throughout the world? A couple still believed that actors should always be non-political and unbiased, just performing when asked, and objected to the others forcing them to take sides or discuss their private beliefs. One member was positively pro-nuclear from an economic standpoint and wanted to endorse the technological achievement of the plant.

Emotions ran high. Offers were made, led by Robert, somehow to provide the money ourselves, but that would have led to endless complications with other towns and I considered the actors were already subsidising the tour sufficiently with their cut-back salaries. Eventually we came up with what we thought was the perfect solution: first, we reserved the right to say what we liked to the press or public about our donors, and second, we wished to perform *Derek* at the plant itself.

Of course, Nuclear Fuels were delighted with this outcome, having no idea of the content of the play which was against everything this company stood for (or the fact that we would be having an open discussion after the performance), so they readily accepted our terms.

As the Artistic Director I was pleased that the engagement would be honoured, but as an actress I was extremely nervous about what lay ahead – there still being a large part of me conditioned not to offend an audience. The youngsters, however, were cock-a-hoop and returned to rehearsal with a new zest and commitment. However, this was given a sharp check by a visit from Edward Bond to watch a run-through of *Derek*. It is always a nerve-racking experience for actors to perform a play for the first time to the writer. After a dress rehearsal of a production of *When We Were Married*, watched by J. B. Priestley who did not crack his face throughout, Fred Emney said loudly after the final line as Priestley made his way silently out of the auditorium: 'Well, if he didn't like it, he shouldn't have bloody well wrote it!'

Mr Bond did, in fact, laugh but at all the wrong moments and derisively instead of encouragingly. When we were half-way through he stopped us with the pained enquiry: 'I don't know why you are doing this play.'

I have never admired Sarah Pia Anderson more than on that occasion when, with infinite tact and patience, she tried to prise out of Bond what he wanted us to do. Most playwrights are bad at explaining their plays and I am not alone in thinking Edward Bond is worse than most. We ended up shaken and bewildered, but Sarah gently guided us back on the rails. We never saw Bond again, which was a pity because I think, had he come to see the effect we had on some of those audiences, he would have found it more revealing than the preaching-to-the-converted that his works generally achieve at the likes of the Royal Court.

The two other plays were progressing well. It was complicated rehearsing all three shows at once and there were days when exhaustion exploded into anger or giggles and hysteria. There was never time for it to be dull, however, a blessing not felt by many people in their job, something of which Peter Jones who was my partner in a television series called *Mr Digby Darling* used frequently to remind me when I complained, retorting that: 'It's better than working in a glue factory.' He had once visited one and swore that it was the most unpleasant existence anyone could imagine. It is true that I have at times been very frightened, humiliated and unhappy in my job, but seldom bored. My diary of this rehearsal period shows I was often anxious and insecure, but consistently stimulated and amused.

At the end of September 1983, we moved to the Round House for our technical period so that we could practise erecting the auditorium and work in the actual space rather than using tape marks on the floor. Thelma Holt, the brilliant entrepreneur who had run the place, bringing companies from all over the world and the provinces into its theatre-in-the-round and making the restaurant a meeting place for anyone interested in the non-conformist areas of theatre, was sadly packing up after losing a battle to keep it open, but there was a good atmosphere of past glories to inspire us.

Seeing a company for the first time in wigs, costume and lighting can be exciting or disastrous. Actors have a way of drooping inside a costume they do not like that demands frantic changes by the overworked wardrobe staff, but they can equally suddenly take off in a part when the costume gives a new dimension – a pair of shoes or boots can define a walk, a hat or wig can shape a character's expression. Oberon and Titania's airy cloaks seemed to make them fly, and the boys' leather costumes in *Romeo and Juliet* turned them into dashing guttersnipes – they also indelibly dyed their flesh red and black on contact with sweat.

The final dress rehearsals were the usual nightmares, but I was gratified to notice that two security men appeared from the shadows and ended up sitting munching their sandwiches whilst they watched the show. The next day, 10 October 1983, after months of preparation and anticipation, we would finally be embarking on our four-month, twenty-one-town expedition. Would the good citizens of Yarborough near Lincoln be as engrossed as our security friends.

PART TWO

THE RSC

4 : Of First Nights and Fear
Lincoln near Yarborough

SWEENEY TODD – REMEDIES FOR STAGE FRIGHT – SILENT RAPE
– CENSORSHIP – *HERE IS THE NOSE* – LINCOLN – UNION
BATTLES – REGULATIONS – *ROMEO AND JULIET*'S FIRST NIGHT
– *A MIDSUMMER NIGHT'S DREAM* BEGINS – AFTER FIRST NIGHTS
– A DAYLIGHT MATINEE – CHURCHES AND CATHEDRALS

On a bleak October day in 1983 I drove my car off a country lane outside
Lincoln and sat quietly in a field, trying to hang on to reality. Winding
down the car window I smelled the earth, let the tingling rain beat on
my skin and listened to it pounding onto the flat fields, reminding myself
that the two solid chestnut trees by the gate had been there for a few
hundred years and would probably be there for a good many more
without caring in the least if the denizens of Yarborough enjoyed the
performance of *Romeo and Juliet* that night. Furthermore, though I found
it hard to believe, quite a few of them were totally unaware that it was
even taking place.

On first nights I find it difficult to remember that there is a world
elsewhere, but since the opening of Stephen Sondheim's *Sweeney Todd*
at Drury Lane on 2 July 1980 I have been alive to the dangers of this
loss of sense of proportion. The show had been hyped in such a way
that raised expectations beyond reach of realisation – the *South Bank
Show* on TV, erudite articles judging it closer to opera than musical
comedy, a legendary Broadway production with awards and plaudits for
Angela Lansbury in my role, and predictions of a similar triumph in
England that the critics were honour bound to contradict in order to
justify their existence. On top of all that, I had been working for months
to increase my vocal range to encompass the fiendish score, jogging and
swimming to improve my stamina to cope with the physical demands of
the role and, latterly, working long hours with Hal Prince, the American
director, to get this mammoth show on. My regard for Sondheim grew

on acquaintance and was a more compulsive reason for my wanting the show to succeed than the much publicised amount of money riding on our backs, making it the most expensive musical ever mounted at that date.

The combination of these pressures pushed me into a state which I realised on the first night was something more than the usual nerves. These usually manifest themselves as a complete dissolving of the bowels and, lest anything should remain in my limp body, particularly unattractive paroxysms of vomiting as well. The resultant vacuum is a feeling of such shaking awfulness that certainly I would have retired long since were it not for the curious fact that the whole sordid business is over the minute I make my first entrance. Mind you, with this lack of calm preparation and the traumatic shock my body sustains, I have never been exactly at my best on a first night. Quite the reverse. The first time I have ever given a respectable first night performance was *The Cherry Orchard* at the National Theatre in 1986 when I sought the help of a hypnotist, as I will describe later. Would that I had known him six years previously.

Seeing my white face and trembling hands the morning of the first night of *Sweeney Todd* (by which time I was convinced I had lost my voice and certainly did not know the words), my husband suggested a walk in Richmond Park. During the previous sleepless night I had frantically read Stanislavsky's advice on stage fright in which he suggests concentration on the other actors' eyes and the feel, smell and colour of objects around you. In the park I realised I was sick when I startled the deer by clinging to the rough bark of a tree, staring dementedly at my husband, simply unable to move away, the rest of the park and world being much too frightening. Had any of the customers looking forward to their chic premiere chanced to have passed through the park at that moment they might have been more than mystified by the leading lady's behaviour.

I was aware of little else during that first performance, except the texture of the dough in my complicated opening number about making pies, and a vague awareness that some woman was going through my role rather indifferently who I hoped would do it for the rest of the run so that I could go to bed and sleep for a very long time. My return to my right mind was a long and tortuous process during which I somehow never missed a performance, even though there were occasions when it took every ounce of my fragile will not to run from the stage. Mrs Lovett's songs are fast and complicated and one missed word can leave you floundering while the orchestra whirls relentlessly on without you. Dare to think ahead and you are lost. Sweat would drip off my nose as I tried to bring my mind back from the panic of remembering the coming line to the business of delivering the present one. Despite the received opinion that *Sweeney Todd* was a flop, perfect strangers still stop me in the street to say how they adored it, but I was unable to share their relish.

Throughout my career I have approached first nights with a varying battery of weapons. Pills and potions had little effect. Neither have meditation, Bach remedies (essence of flowers), beta blockers, uppers, downers nor, on the first night of *One Over the Eight*, a disastrous overdose of amphetamines that resulted in my mouth literally frothing in the opening number and becoming utterly devoid of saliva by the finale of the first half.

During *The Rag Trade* Miriam Karlin and I would juggle the order of a bath, a glass of champagne and one of those lovely purple heart-shaped pills a nice doctor gave us and from which it subsequently took me months to shake off my addiction. If the show went badly one week we would convince ourselves it was because we took the pill before the bath, or vice versa. I finally decided that, for me, taking two pills washed down by three glasses of champagne lying in the bath was probably not the perfect formula to make the audience laugh, but at least it rendered me indifferent if they cried. I hasten to add that since those frantic days neither Miriam nor I drink before a show, although for both of us the fear has remained.

It is difficult to define exactly why I and some of my fellow thespians are so terribly frightened. Most of us have little real regard for the critics, although it is painfully difficult to swallow bad reviews. When Harold Hobson of the *Sunday Times* decided I was 'Unbearable to the eye and unendurable to the ear' in *So What About Love?* and declared of my husband, John Thaw, that he 'dreaded his every reappearance on the stage', it was quite difficult for us to prance on and be funny the next night. It was even more embarrassing when a few weeks later he recanted his bad review, acclaiming the unpretentious author, Leonard Webb, as 'a new Anouilh' and attributed to me a quality of 'abattage', which I took as another insult until I looked it up, for to be Hobson's choice in those days was to invite derision from one's fellow actors. However, experience reduces the duration of pain after a bad review and self-consciousness after a good one. Audiences are unlikely to turn into lynch mobs. Indeed, when I sit amongst them to watch shows – particularly in the West End – I am surprised at how anxious they are to enjoy anything that is happening, probably to justify the mortgage they have had to take out to buy their tickets. So what is the reason for this fear that could not be worse if one were facing execution?

In my case I have a sufficient catalogue of disasters programmed into my subconscious to make anyone wary, verging on the cataleptic. I am all too aware of the pitfalls waiting to trap me on stage. In my very first job after leaving RADA the producer, as they were then called (he was also the leading actor) did not believe in allowing prompts – a little quirk that re-occurred at the National Theatre with Philip Prowse. Now, no actor likes to take a prompt, but it is reassuring to know that there is someone on your side in the wings – particularly if you have learned a three-act play in five days whilst performing another one in the evenings, as we did in weekly repertory. Maybe he was afraid a prompter would be aware that he had only learned a vague approximation of the author's lines, so that in lieu of a cue we were obliged to detect by the look in his eyes when it was our turn to speak. Unlike him, I found it difficult to ramble on with any old rubbish when I dried and would usually make some excuse to leave the stage and have a quick look at my strategically-placed script. Thus, in the middle of some intimate scene, I was apt suddenly to hear a doorbell or, more inventively, to go and dead-head a rose outside the french windows. We would all have difficult sentences or elusive words stuck in phones, on mantlepieces and scribbled on parts of our bodies. I would have my nose stuck in my script until the instant I made my entrance, when I would drop it by the door ready for later emergencies; except on one occasion in Oldham, when I was depicting sultry Sadie Thompson in Somerset Maugham's *Rain* and missed my cue as I feverishly bent over an elusive speech in the wings, forcing the desperate actor left speechless on stage to come off and drag me on, still grasping my script and with a duffle coat inconsequentially draped over my slinky tart's outfit.

My skill at inventing exit lines stood me in good stead in *The Moon is Blue* at the old Bromley New Theatre. I was not only playing the lead but also assistant stage-managing. In those days there was a tradition that it was unlucky to say the last speech of a play until the first performance, so it did not occur to us until the lover and I went into the final clinch in front of the audience that fulfilling my job as the operator of the manual house-curtain would be difficult. The author would not, I think, have been displeased with the laugh I got as I extricated myself from his arms and said: 'Excuse me, I must go and clean my teeth,' and the even bigger one for the lover's startled reaction. It was a pity that I could not be rewarded for my ingenuity with a curtain-call as I had to pull it up and down.

On another occasion, in West Kirby, I learned deaf and dumb language in one week in order to play the lead in *Johnny Belinda*, but the prompter refused to do the same. Heaven only knows what the deaf people in the audience must have made of some of my frantic hand signals, but one night in this play drying was not my major problem. Sets were, and sometimes still are, made up of a series of pieces called flats which are fixed together by ropes round hooks by a process called cleating. In *Johnny Belinda* there is a rape scene which in those days of censorship was discreetly done behind a pile of hay. In the previous scene I had become aware that one of the flats was not properly cleated and was in danger of falling inwards, which I endeavoured to prevent by leaning on it. Thus it was that my potential rapist was confronted on his entrance with his victim unable, being dumb, to invent a line of explanation and resolutely refusing to be thrown behind the hay stack. The resulting scene would have been risky even by today's standards, but in those days could have closed the theatre and had us all thrown in jail.

It is difficult to credit the inhibiting powers the watch committees and censorship offices had in those days. Guns were blacked out with tape on front-of-house pictures by the Oldham watch committee and the most inoffensive lines were cut. Some more anxiety was programmed into me by the Lord Chamberlain when I was several times reprimanded during the run of *Make Me An Offer* for my improvisations. He was particularly cross on the night of Princess Margaret's wedding when his spies reported that I sang:

'It's sort of romantic like Darby and Joan
Sort of romantic like Margaret and Tone.'

Although, as I said, audiences are very polite these days, when I was younger the bird (as booing and jeering from an audience is called) was not unknown. My friend Dilys Laye chilled me with stories of a dreadful first night in a musical called *The Crystal Heart* at the Saville Theatre on 19 February 1957 during which the audience started calling out quite early in the evening. It became an absolute riot and Dilys stopped the show for several minutes with her unfortunate line to Gladys Cooper in the second half, 'The bird has taken madam.'

I have never been treated quite so cruelly by audiences, but I have had the odd brush with cranks. I had to be escorted by the police from the stage door for a while in *Rattle* when I received a spate of letters from a religious maniac who wanted to kill my character. *Rattle* – a play about a nightclub hostess and a football fan which seems unbelievably coy now – was considered *risqué* in 1962. Strangely the thing that most seemed to shock was that I removed my make-up on stage. Several papers commented on my daring, and one night at that point a lady shouted from the gods: 'This is a filthy play. Where's the Lord Chamberlain?' having presumably managed to enjoy the two-and-a-half hours of mild titillation up till then. The trouble is that everyone's definition of pornography is different. I once had an irate letter from a TV viewer berating me for wearing wellington boots which had obviously triggered off some worrying fantasy for him, whereas other people will look at appalling horrors without turning a hair.

The angriest reaction from an audience I ever had was in 1960 during the first night of a little epic called *Here is the News*, presented by William Donaldson, well-known con-man of Henry Root fame, and directed by John Bird, fresh from university. The audience had good cause, mind you.

We should have expected trouble bringing a way-out revue with material by Ionesco, Pinter and N. F. Simpson to a bank holiday audience in Coventry – particularly when the bills in the town renamed the show *Here Is The Nose* – but we had infinite faith in the apocalyptic theme of the evening. True, it was a motley cast of people, including Cleo Laine, Lance Percival, Richard Goolden (better known as Mr Mole), Valentine Dyall (radio's deathly 'man in black'), a jazz band on stage and a stripper called Kathryn Keeton (who now owns the Penthouse empire with her husband, Guggione) who was brought in at a rather late stage of rehearsal by her sinister then boyfriend.

The said boyfriend had injected some much-needed cash into the production, but this was not sufficient to cover the cost of completing Sean Kenny's innovative set. Had one been able to afford the engine, I am sure the effect of sets gliding effortlessly on and off would have been breathtaking, but as we actors were forced ignominiously to push our sets on before playing a scene, breathless was a more apt description. On top of this the costumes did not arrive. I shall always treasure the memory of the exotic Cleo Laine exposing the safety pins that secured the red velvet curtain she was wearing when she heaved on her set to pant out a sophisticated little ditty called 'Diamonds for the Queen'.

Sean also introduced a new system of back-projection which arrived just in time for the first show. Unfortunately there was something wrong with it which caused the beautiful plates to crack about twenty seconds after they were projected. Undaunted, the operator relentlessly persisted, getting some of the biggest rounds of the evening as each sketch was punctuated with the tell-tale shattered image. Or was that the first night of *One To Another* in Margate? These nightmares are apt to merge.

The lighting in *Here Is The Nose* also left a lot to be desired, but the local spot-operator did his best. In the jolly opening sketch, which has a huge nuclear explosion followed by a black-out in which our faces were picked out in turn by a pin-spot as we spoke, it was not his fault that he always managed to find us just *after* we had said our line. He had no more preparation than the flying technician who managed to get Robin Ray inextricably wound into a border cloth in the first number so that he had to deliver all his lines in subsequent sketches during the first half dangling in mid-air. The sound of seats tipping up during the show and the desperate search afterwards for a pub near the theatre where people were not angrily brandishing their programme, plus many other torments over the years, are etched into my memory, waiting to spring up and frighten me. It took the aforementioned brilliant hypnotherapist of 1986 to change the programme in my mind so I could consider the possibility that things might actually go right.

Back in Yarborough in 1983, as usual, I expected the worst. Hence my sitting in a field near Lincoln wondering why I did it. A director is able to effect the technical smooth running on a first night, but once the audience is in, he or she has to sit back and hope that the magic will happen for the actors. A performance can be prepared meticulously, but in my experience there is no way that one can guarantee that it will work on any given night. I have gone into the theatre dreading the show and the instant I have walked on stage some link has been forged with the audience, lifting the evening into something extraordinary. Equally, I have bounded on, full of myself, and gone slap-bang into a wall of indifference that shatters the evening into pieces. It is not whether an audience is quiet or laughing, although that helps; it is more an almost mystical experience.

There is much that goes on in a theatre which is difficult to explain. Doctors should study the weird ability we have to shake off chronic illness the minute we step on the green (as the stage is called). There must be some secret ingredient that pumps into the system along with adrenalin that, were it possible to isolate and bottle it, would cure all known ills. Fortunately the elixir began to pump into my system as I caught my first glimpse of Lincoln. After driving through miles of utterly flat landscape, it is quite a shock to see the cathedral and castle piled so high on a hill that to reach it you walk with your stomach practically on the perpendicular pavement. We were breaking in the company gently by opening in Yarborough, near the elegant city of Lincoln, replete with good restaurants and antique shops. Very few ugly modern buildings have been allowed to scar this ancient place and, where they do, bits of monumental Roman wall are apt to surface alongside, demonstrating their superior durability.

Our first leisure centre venue of the tour was pretty grand too, rather more thought having gone into its design than the sprawling school alongside it. Not that I could see much on that day as a cloudburst broke over the car park as I alighted from my car. As he greeted me, the manager scarcely noticed the pool of water running off me on to his nice floor, so stunned was he by the rest of the havoc we were wreaking on his usually immaculate building. The aroma alone remained the same. Even with the smell of the greasepaint and the crowd, we were never able to eliminate anywhere in the British Isles that pungent sports-complex perfume of rubber, disinfectant, chlorine and sweat.

The huge main gymnasium was entirely filled with our towering steel scaffold auditorium. I gaped in amazement when I saw the arena with its lighting towers and rising semi-circle of blue and red seats that had grown miraculously in this previously echoing space. People were dashing purposefully in all directions, bursts of music and sound effects suddenly cutting across the shouts and clatter. In the midst of it all John Caird, white and unshaven but black eyes sparkling, was calmly adjusting the lighting for *Romeo and Juliet*.

Rehearsing the two plays together meant that John and I had to work very closely with one another. We were a perfect combination, as I am horribly pessimistic and dreary when I get worried whereas John gets positively frivolous as the disasters pile up. It was with a merry laugh that he told me on my arrival that we probably could not open that night as a representative of the Musicians' Union had arrived to tell us we were breaking yet another regulation.

Throughout the rehearsal period we had encountered endless objections over our use of actors who were also musicians. The rules about this and payment for on- and off-stage music, recorded sound and even the definition of what is music as opposed to a sound effect had caused me sleepless nights, and the need for the aforementioned £10,000 increase in our funds from Nat West. Throughout these complications I had been patient and respectful as I am grateful for the improvement in our conditions that the entertainment unions have brought about, the MU being one of the most powerful. No one has been more exploited than I was in my youth, working all hours of the day and night for a pittance that I could not possibly have lived on were it not for loving parents. On one occasion, whilst appearing at the Tudor Cinema in West Kirby, I was even diagnosed as suffering from malnutrition. Oh yes, I have been trampled under the heel of oppressive bosses with the best of them – and yet, and yet . . .

When I take part in the pious little meetings that have to be held amongst actors these days if a director wants to work another five minutes to finish a dress rehearsal without breaking the budget with massive overtime payments, my subversive mind takes me back to the fun I had at those two-o'clock-in-the-morning sessions in the old days, moaning and giggling and knocking back the vino and sausage sandwiches fried over the little portable hotplates that we all had for such emergencies.

In an overcrowded profession like ours, the unions have worked valiantly to protect us from unscrupulous rogues, and nowadays we are seldom stranded in some God-forsaken dump with a closed-down show and no money for our fare home. However, I am saddened when some actors seem more intent on screwing every last penny out of the boss rather than getting the show on, and it upset me a lot when I discovered it was two of my actors who had summoned this little grey official now confronting me with his rule book, demanding more bonus payments.

The MU has managed to secure some rates and conditions that sometimes interfere with artistic freedom and can result in doing their members out of work altogether. If they had had their way the actor/ musicians in the company would have been receiving a sum far in excess of that of the Equity members, and out of all proportion to the amount of extra work they were doing. I could not up everyone's salaries to match, so my only choice was to drop some of the music. As the budget had always been available for the company to see and the two objectors knew this, I was hurt that they still chose to throw the book at me. I know from personal experience that it is easy to get carried away with demanding one's rights – particularly from a big organisation. When I reminded them that the tour was not part of the main RSC budget and I was powerless to meet their demands (not least it would have been grossly unfair had I done so), they were rather sheepish. It was less easy to convince the MU representative.

I have never been very good with rules. I once threw a large volume of by-laws at a district surveyor in Cirencester who wanted me to cut the beautiful beams in my cottage, that had hung six feet three inches above the floor and which all but giants had managed to avoid for three hundred years, for no other reason than it was the rule. The deathless phrase, 'I'm only doing my job,' passed his lips. 'So did the concentration camp commandants,' passed mine, and the book only just missed his ear.

Similarly, it is no thanks to my handling of the MU man that we were allowed to open. Various phone calls with more tactful negotiators back at Stratford eventually resolved the problem and he left physically unharmed, having graciously permitted us to go on.

Would he too have been awestruck by Illona Sekacz's requiem sung by the actors in the solemn procession that preceded *Romeo and Juliet* as I perceived that first audience to be? If any of them shared my worry about the load-bearing capability of this mini-Epidaurus dumped on their indoor tennis courts before the show began, they showed no signs of thinking about anything but the tale we were telling once it started. The detailed work of rehearsal often makes us forget the overriding importance of the plot to an audience and, as frequently happens, the actors discovered a whole new energy from simply relating the story to eager listeners – many of whom did not know it. A loud 'Oh no, he's not dead!' from a woman on Mercutio's death; an anguished muttering from a little girl, 'She's alive, you fool', in the tomb scene, introduced us to the spontaneous reaction we were to become accustomed to from unjaded audiences.

The superhuman effort the company had all put into the first night of *Romeo and Juliet* and the relief that it worked so triumphantly, plus the drinks consumed in celebration afterwards, were not conducive to facing yet another dress rehearsal and another first performance the following day, this time of *A Midsummer Night's Dream*. In an effort to galvanise them into life I asked for a speed run of the play, which is a run-through entailing all the sense, emotions and actions, performed several times faster than normal. Usually the subsequent performance, done at the right pace, is tighter and livelier as a result. The company were tired and ratty and the general sloppiness led to an accident in which Philip Jackson as Bottom got his lip cut and I had to rush him to hospital. It was not surprising that the first performance was somewhat lacking in lustre, but to me it was profoundly disappointing. At the reception with local dignitaries after our second first night I grinned and scintillated, but I secretly nursed inside the familiar tell-tale ache of anticlimax, until I returned to my grotty digs room and howled my eyes out.

I have never solved the problem of what to do after first nights. Parties are not the answer for me ever since the opening of Joe Orton's *Entertaining Mr Sloane* in New York in 1965. The champagne was flowing in the gross apartment of our Texan millionaire producer until the first review was read out, whereupon it was removed by his friend to the sound of retching coming from the solid gold-tapped bathroom. As the notice said words to the effect of: 'Throw this British cesspool back in the Atlantic', I suppose his reaction was understandable, but I decided there and then that public declamation of my notices was not for me.

Nevertheless, if the show is a hit it is quite nice to mark the occasion in some way. The first time you have a big personal success in your career is an experience you can never repeat and I rather regret that, after what I see in retrospect was a triumph in *Rattle* in 1962, Tony Beckley (a dear friend of mine, now dead), Barry (my later-to-be millionaire hairdresser) and I ended up rather unglamorously trying to jump-start my ailing Morris 1000 outside the deserted Garrick Theatre, which had earlier been ringing with cheers. Similarly, I remember staggering out of the Ashcroft Theatre in Croydon in the teeming rain with a heavy suitcase after a very successful performance of Brecht's *Good Woman of Setzuan* and overhearing a woman, who did not recognise the drowned rat standing next to her at the bus stop, saying: 'Well I thought it was lovely, but you couldn't recommend it, could you?'

I suppose I know what she meant. But the ambiguity of her overheard remark compared unfavourably with the adulation and champagne I saw poured on and down Judy Garland in the Caprice after her appearance at the Palladium – I think they were better at celebration in the old days. I find it particularly difficult to know what to do after first nights when I am on tour – especially when I am depressed.

A plus side of being in the theatre is that your life can change from disaster to triumph in a second. You can be out of work for six months, the phone rings and your agent offers you a serial on television. Michael Billington in the *Guardian* says you are rubbish; you pick up *The Times* and Irving Wardle thinks you are the best thing since sliced bread. You are convinced you will never get inside the skin of a character, then you see a woman going down the street with the perfect walk, try it and everything falls into place. Similarly, I cried myself to sleep on the Wednesday in Lincoln; on Thursday I was unable to sleep at all for excitement.

On the Thursday afternoon we had a matinee of *A Midsummer Night's Dream* for schoolchildren: we were unable to create a black-out because of the windows in the hall; so the show had to be done in daylight without the lighting effects with which Basher Harris had managed, by dint of dappled mysterious colours, to transform our bare space into kaleidoscopic changes, full of atmosphere. Without these and in front of the notoriously critical, if not to say hostile, gaze of the young people of the town, I was not at all confident that the laboured production I had seen the night before would survive. The young people stampeded into their seats, roaring and stamping. Like early Christians, the actors entered the fray and startled them into silence when the Mechanicals galloped on to say hello and played their honky-tonk overture on washboard, drum and kettle.

The derisive quips of the potential troublemakers froze on their lips as it dawned on them that their friends were not as monumentally bored as they expected and were irritated rather than entertained by their interruptions. In fact, they were laughing. And listening. To Shakespeare! At every attempt at a witty sally from one of these jokers, the company turned a basilisk-glance on them and gradually drew them into Shakespeare's world. All the actors had was the language to create the sunlight and shade – a wood, a court – just as in Shakespeare's day at the Globe. They rose like rockets to the challenge and a thrilling display of acting fireworks galvanised the audience. They really did piece out our imperfections with their thoughts. I hardly recognised the company. Figuratively speaking, a performance can be flat-footed, plodding through mud; but they were twirling and prancing on tippy-toes. At the performance's end it was like going into the stable of sweating, highly-strung horses after a race, and oh, were we pleased with ourselves. There is no pleasure in life to compare with a job well done, as my dad always said. After the show this time I knew where I wanted to go – Lincoln Cathedral.

There are times when I am overwhelmed with my luck in life and I want to express my gratitude. I am now a confirmed atheist, for reasons I will later explain, but my earlier devout belief often propels me into churches on these occasions. Not only that, but I like them.

As a child I had many jolly experiences in church with my father. The simple sincerity of his approach to his God, overriding all the antics and boredom of the various religions, has left me with a nostalgic pleasure at being in these buildings. We would visit a different denomination every week, comparing the merits of the choir and preacher as though they were turns on a variety bill. There is nothing more delightful for a child than to share laughter with a parent, and I sometimes see in my offspring the same joy that consumed me as I collapsed with mirth on the hairy hassocks under dark brown pews as my father giggled his way through the confused leapings up and down of an unintelligible Latin high Catholic service.

Dad would have been in his element in Lincoln where they have churches of every denomination – Unitarian, Methodist, Salvation Army, Jehovah's Witness, Elim Christian Fellowship – you name it, they have got it. The cathedral itself is a very cheerful place. On the several occasions I have visited, there have always been either lay people or clergy keen to chat about its history as they arrange their flowers or sweep their floor. The frisson that goes through me as I wander through the shady loftiness is entirely to do with the spirit of people who can design and carve and cull such transcendent magnificence. I love too the grimacing Lincoln imp, high in the wall, which some irreverent craftsman sneaked into all that solemnity. Subtly concealed high in a pillar, this wicked creature with one foot lifted on to his knees glowers down on to the world, unmoved by the choir of angels surrounding him. There are various explanations for his irreverent presence, but I like to think one of the workmen had something dropped on his toe and wanted to protest about mundane human pain amidst all this grandeur.

I once attended a performance of Verdi's *Requiem* in St Paul's. The combination of that superlative building, the ordinary choristers' faces transformed by their pleasure in the sound they were making and the genius of Verdi transported me into a reverie that I was only momentarily jolted out of when the exquisite face of the conductor, Giulini, turned and glared witheringly at a rogue cougher in the congregation. It was irrelevant to me to consider where all this artistry stemmed from. It was there – glorious and to be rejoiced in – and thank you very much Mr Wren, Mr Verdi, Mr Giulini and ladies and gentlemen of the band and choir.

And thank you very much craftsmen of Lincoln in the years 1072 to 1280 and residents of Yarborough in the year 1983 for launching our intrepid little troupe on their way.

5 : Touring and Detouring
Mansfield, Walsall, Bridgnorth, Barnsley and Castleford

MOTORWAYS – MY CHILDREN – BOTTOMS DOWN UNDER –
CONFERENCES – MANSFIELD FUNCTIONS – OBE – THE SHOW
MUST GO ON – THE MINERS' STRIKE – BOSSES – THE MORNING
PROGRAMME – GAZEBO – WORKSHOPS – PRETTY BRIDGNORTH
– NOT SO PRETTY BARNSLEY – MINERS' WIVES – SHAKESPEARE
GROUPIES – CASTLEFORD'S SIGHTS AND SMELLS – HENRY
MOORE – STANDING OVATIONS

And thank you family.

Every time I hear of road-works on the poor old, clapped out M1 I feel a tinge of guilt about the many times I abused it during the tour in order to travel home to London. In fact, I have been using it since the day after it opened in 1959 when motorways were an unknown quantity; I was a nervous passenger as Cleo Laine drove tentatively for the first time along this new monster with her husband, Johnny Dankworth, edgily instructing her about lane discipline. In those days your windscreen wipers fought a losing battle against the remains of massacred winged insects. They seem to have subsequently learned the rules better than us and now live happily in the verges which have become wildlife sanctuaries. Every time a new motorway gouges out more beautiful countryside I lament, but I fear that I have been only too glad to use them to snatch a few extra moments with my long-suffering husband and children.

They, along with my electric blanket and teasmade, are the absolute essentials of my life without which I could not exist. Yet I neglect them shamefully: the kettle of my teasmade is all furry, my electric blanket is lethal for want of a service, Marks & Spencer's are kept in profit by my husband's purchase of their ready-cooked dinners, and my children think a stable background is a home for horses. Yet I love them all to the edge of idolatry.

Having always found little boys very alarming with their tongue-tied shyness and their soppy turns, I was very relieved to give birth to two girls and acquire yet a third, Abigail, as a stepdaughter. My oldest daughter, Melanie, and I have ricocheted through endless dramas. Her adolescence was for me – a person with a conservative upbringing – a traumatic coming-to-terms with all that is threatening in modern society. There is a chasm between my pre-pill, pre-drugs, pre-TV generation and hers. The goodnight kiss on the doorstep, shared Woodbine in an air-raid shelter and apples scrumped from a neighbour's garden of my childhood are as far removed from today's entertainments as the Enid Blyton books and Sunny Story magazines I read. For years, Melanie and I screamed and collided and I broke the record for the number of invitations from the headmistress to come to 'have a little talk about your daughter'.

The youngest, Joanna, is suspiciously angelic – no doubt only to make the contrast more devastating when she reaches the evil teens. It is a pleasure to buy a pair of shoes with Joanna. In contrast, I still shudder with shame at the memory of disowning my oldest daughter in Selfridges when she lay on the floor and screamed because she could not have a pair of satin pumps with diamanté clips to wear with her school uniform. No child has ever been able to scream louder or longer than Ellie-Jane – as I call her, amended with good reason by Frankie Howerd when she was a baby to Smelly Drain. She chewed the Selfridges carpet for a full fifteen minutes after I walked away and left her, peering back occasionally to see if she had subsided. When a woman muttered to me, 'What a dreadful child', Peter-like I agreed and slunk off again. As a rule, though, I enjoy my daughters' company. They have always been with me at work whenever possible. In fact, two weeks after Ellie-Jane was born in 1965, I was acting in the film *Carry On Cleo* and would rush off the set every three hours to feed her in the dressing room where she was waiting impatiently with my mother. On the frequent embarrassing occasions that film is repeated on television, should Ellie-Jane dare to criticise my definitive rendering of Senna Pod, wife of Hengist Pod, inventor of the square wheel in early Britain, I remind her that it was her greed that prevented me etching in the finer details of my role.

This desire to have them with me has introduced them to dressing rooms, wings of theatres, usherettes and dressers and hardened them to sleeping in lumpy beds, or on floors or chairs in digs and hotels all over the world.

Fortunately, Joanna is addicted to hotels. The more plastic they are the more she likes them. Her 'absolute favourite in the world' is the Holiday Inn in Birmingham (never mind that it is virtually impossible to get off the adjacent motorway to enter it). Once there, she is ecstatic about every new synthetic discovery, rifling the drawers and bathroom for free goodies: soap, shampoos, bath foams, plastic bath mats, plastic-encased milk, tea, coffee and chocolate send her into transports of delight. She was only momentarily confused once by a small plastic carpet beater which I decided was something strange for tired business-men. Joanna was convinced it was a fly swatter, undaunted by the protest that no fly could possibly enter this hermetically sealed world. John concurred with her, surmising that it had been delivered in error and a lot of people in a Holiday Inn in Cairo were probably equally confused by their consignment of plastic rain hats.

Abigail and Melanie have had their moments in hotels too. My husband and I were rather confused by the size of our bills at the end of each week in a hotel in Melbourne when we were appearing there, only to discover that while we were at the theatre and their grandad believed them to be asleep in the next room, they were in fact ordering massive meals from room service. They told me ten years later that they also amused themselves by stopping the lift at their floor and flashing their bottoms at the startled people inside.

The small hotel in Mansfield in which Joanna joined me for her half-term holiday did not rate highly. It had no plastic shower caps. (From bottoms Down Under to plastic shower caps in Mansfield – my rambling has really reached incoherence. So I will tenuously link back from this detour by informing you that we have now taken the *Midsummer Night's Dream* Bottom to Mansfield in Nottinghamshire, our second venue.)

The shower-capless hotel in Mansfield was full of Pakistanis on some trade conference. Hotels are always full of people conferring. Throughout the tour I became increasingly bewildered about the number of non-subjects people could find to confer about. I finally divined the object of the exercise was nothing to do with exchanging information but merely a way of using excess profits as some kind of tax dodge, in the same way business organisations are now taking over Henley, Wimbledon and Glyndebourne. Not only does it provide an opportunity for bosses to patronise the proles, it also allows the rank and file to drink themselves into a coma and sexually harass anything in a skirt. Only the odd secretary is allowed to join the men on these alcoholic junkets, very definitely no wives – apart sometimes from the managing director's lady being gracious – so any other woman in the hotel is seen as fair game, especially actresses because we all know what ravers they are. The other pernicious sex maniacs are commercial travellers or, as they now call themselves, representatives.

We started by politely fending off these motley Lotharios when we sat down, wanting a quiet drink and a chat after the show, conceding that they were probably lonely and misunderstood and it was difficult for them to grasp that women on their own in a bar were not necessarily prostitutes or desperate for male company. But we ended up never going without the men, or alternatively nipping our inebriated suitors' approaches in the bud with a ripe obscenity that frightened them to death. After all, back home they were ordinary little men with ordinary little wives who would not say boo to a goose. Confronted by a group of spitting, surrogate ganders they ran a mile. The desperate searching of a drunken man for the answer to life is truly pathetic – those wild-eyed creatures in silly bobble hats and scarves after a big match, rolling around Soho, distraught that their erotic dream has turned out to be a tacky rip-off. We met identical men in Burton suits, eyes swivelling with drink and despair, in every corner of the British Isles.

Like Joanna they seemed to relish these plastic, faceless emporiums. Frequently we had no choice but to use them, as theatrical digs are now a thing of the past and the average small guest house will not accommodate our strange eating and sleeping times. Apart from the accents of the staff, these hotels manage totally to ignore the identity of the surrounding area and remain relentlessly characterless. But what diversity of landscape, architecture and people is to be found in Britain!

The next two weeks alone (the loose core of this chapter), when we covered Mansfield, Walsall, Bridgnorth, Barnsley and Castleford, were to disprove any illusions that anything north of Watford Gap is one amorphous mass.

For instance, Mansfield is a mere thirty-odd miles from our previous venue near Lincoln, but could not be more different. The very lie of the land declares its priorities. Whereas Lincoln soars upwards to the Gothic grandeur of the cathedral, the streets in the centre of Mansfield descend to the pivot of the market place with its workaday wooden trestle stalls. It is a no-nonsense, proper little town that tries to do things correctly. They do not always entirely succeed, however.

Rising from the centre of the stalls in the market place, for instance, is an imposing, if somewhat worn, monument built by public subscription in the nineteenth century to pay tribute to one Lord George Bentinck. But it still awaits the statue of him that it was meant to house, and as I could not find anyone in Mansfield who knew who he was I doubt if they will ever complete it.

The Mansfield sense of occasion was much to the fore in October 1983 at the reception given for the company in the Victorian town hall. We were ushered reverently into the committee room and were aware that it was a privilege to be sipping sherry in this small front parlour, with its reproduction wardrobes and dressers and utility brown table serving as a desk. Flocked wallpaper was covered with local pictures and certificates, plus, needless to say, a picture of the Queen and Prince Philip over the slate and marble fireplace that housed a two-bar electric stove. Our way of dressing contrasted awkwardly with the neat Sunday-best suits and dresses of our hosts, who proudly showed us the chains of office and local regalia. The lady town clerk nervously made an imperfectly memorised speech of welcome and they made me a presentation of a little lead soldier-type Robin Hood mounted on a wooden plinth. The people of Mansfield are inordinately proud of Robin Hood, whom they claim as entirely theirs rather than Nottingham's.

At the many civic functions I attended in Mansfield I almost felt I could have worn my OBE without being ridiculous. I usually keep very quiet about my OBE – partly because I think it was a mistake and they might take it back, and partly because I made such an idiot of myself when I received it. First, I went in my clapped out MG which made an unholy row in the courtyard of Buckingham Palace, and then I yelped in panic, waving my naked hands at the smooth Major Domo when he instructed us to keep our gloves on if the Queen wore hers. Visions of soiling Her Majesty's immaculate kid leather with my sweaty, bare skin appalled me until a sweet housemaid hissed at me from behind a pillar, proffering a pair of immaculate white ones. Designer John Bates would have killed me if he had seen their startling brightness against the subtle greys and beiges of the outfit he had lent me for the occasion, although he did resignedly accept the huge holes that another equerry had to drill into the pigskin jacket to put a pin in to allow the Queen to hang my medal. Once inside the impressive investiture hall I forgot all the instructions, leapt forward too soon and practically caused them to call out the guard to protect the Queen from a suspected assassin.

My Mother – 'You are the most beautiful woman I know'

Family portrait in our Sunday-best. *From top left*: Sister Billie, Dad, Auntie Cis, Grandma Hancock, Me, Mummy

My Mother and Father as I most remember them – laughing

Above left: With my friend Julia at the Latham Road street party on VE Day

Above right: Earning my keep digging ditches in Holland whilst hitch-hiking round Europe

Below: Frothing my way through St Joan at Dartford County Grammar School

Curriculum Vitae: Sheila Hancock. Blonde, 5ft 8½ins, Juvenile – Juvenile character –
Leading lady – Character woman

Above left: The rape scene in *Johnny Belinda* at Oldham Theatre Royal – horizontal as opposed to vertical

Above right: A love scene with Ivor Burgoyne in another repertory production. It could be any one of a hundred plays any time in the 1950s

Below left: Giving my breathless juvenile in *Charley's Aunt* at Tudor Cinema, West Kirby, with a disbelieving Iris Derbyshire. The gloves, hat and parasol didn't help a lot

Below right: *Reefer Girl* at Oldham, 1954. My mother's comment: 'When are you going to play some pretty parts?'

All this talk of medals and hob-nobbing with the royals probably comes strangely from one who is not on the whole fond of the Establishment. Indeed, as I grow older I am becoming anarchic to the point of senility. Nevertheless old habits die hard. Intellectual socialists wag the finger at royalty and ritual, but my roots align me with the people of Mansfield. Happy occasions dancing in vast crowds outside Buck House and going 'Up West' as a child to cheer the Lord Mayor's show nestle cosily in my memory. I shamelessly wept off my false eyelashes whilst watching Charles and Di's wedding on the telly in the canteen at Stratford between entrances, oblivious to the sneers of my more radical fellow actors. Rationally I accept all that 'opium of the people' stuff, but like others of my background I love an excuse for a knees-up and a good cry.

I find it impossible to follow any particular ideology that forces me to suppress my natural instincts. When I was a small child, in pre-war days, my mother was even reluctant to let me join the Brownies, so frightened was she by any kind of factions or movements that smacked of Nazi Germany and Hitler Youth, and I have inherited her fear of blind allegiance to any doctrine. I believe implicitly that it is right to put your friend before your country or your cause. I salve my conscience by thinking I would be an awful nuisance to any cause anyway with my questions and my doubts: I am not a joiner. But when invited, I was delighted to become an Ordinary Officer of the Civil Division of our Most Excellent Order of the British Empire, after checking up that I did not have to swear my allegiance to anything or anyone – except that nice Queen and a non-existent empire.

A title or a decoration was not necessary, however, to impress the people of Mansfield, celebrity of any sort being rather thin on the ground there. Having been seen on the television I was treated with an awe only shared in the town, I was told, by Frank Carson and the Bachelors, even though I could have sworn that one of us at least had been dead for years.

Whenever I go to the provinces I am struck anew by the public's strange perception of actors. Londoners become accustomed to seeing the odd well-known person, but it is unlikely that people in Mansfield or the like will ever meet an actor face to face, so do not realise they are not missing a thing. Time and time again on the tour we would be told, with a mixture of amazement and disappointment, that we were just like ordinary people. It used to be held that one should not spoil the magic by being seen to be ordinary off-stage, in much the same way as one was not supposed to have an opinion, but it is not easy to appear elusive whilst shopping in Waitrose. I actually find it hugely comforting when seemingly beautiful or clever creatures turn out to be ordinary. If anything, I found the exotic girls in the Lido show in Paris (in which my elder sister, Billie, appeared) even more stunning on-stage after I had seen them slouched, gossiping in the dressing room in various states of undress, doing their knitting and *petit point*.

Mansfield certainly saw us stripped of our artifice. On the second night our generator blew all the fuses and the hall was plunged into darkness in the middle of a scene. My heart sank as I went on to explain the problem to the audience and beg their indulgence to our continuing with the minimal circuit that we managed to rig up. I need not have worried, of course, because there is nothing an audience likes better than to take part in a theatrical Dunkirk.

I think it was at Torquay that I was playing in a mystery thriller in which the last act was the obligatory scene in the library with all the suspects being summoned to give their alibis to the detective. The set was the usual ill-painted book flats, single door and a large inglenook fireplace, and as the actors came on it gradually became obvious that the doorhandle was dodgy. There was a steadily increasing rattling and shaking before each character's entrance, accompanied by a steadily increasing chortling from the audience. Everyone managed it after a struggle without being too thrown except for the poor ASM, playing the maid. Mesmerised, we watched as the entire set swayed with her efforts to get through the door. We listened, transfixed, as she hurled herself against it, then endeavoured to carry on with the scene when she at last propelled herself on stage. By this time the audience was beside themselves with joy, and the suspense of wondering what she would do whilst watching her loading up her tray with tea cups, having thoughtlessly shut the door behind her, was infinitely more exciting than anything in the plot. She got an ovation when, after studying the door for a moment and contemplating her loaded tray, she turned on her heel and exited through the fireplace.

I am a great believer in letting the audience in on things going wrong and have no time for the 'the show must go on' tradition. Occasionally one is confronted with an audience that just does not want to know and nothing you can do will involve them. I have never had the courage to stop, but I have every sympathy with Nicol Williamson who, after trying to cope with a particularly noisy group of young Americans at a performance of *Macbeth*, eventually got off his throne, walked calmly to the footlights and, in iambic pentameter, gently said:

'If you don't shut up a colleague of mine
Will pass amongst you with a baseball bat.'

Whereupon he readjusted his crown and continued the play to a stupefied silence.

Similarly, there have been many times when I would have loved to have emulated Monsewer Eddie Grey who, during a particularly rowdy panto performance, while doing a gag routine with Max Wall, both dressed as women, finally said: 'I'm not having this – I'm off mate,' whereupon he stalked off the stage, went to his dressing room, took off his dress and went home to London, never to return. That immortal sentence has become a catch-phrase in our family, although writing it down does not imply the right intonation of drawling indignation that is essential to its potency.

I am not sure which town drove Eddie Grey to such lengths but it could not have been Mansfield.

They obviously loathed *Derek* but our production was simply greeted with polite distaste, and the attempted discussion afterwards was a disaster as the local audience were too kind actually to tell us what they thought. One could understand later during the miners' strike in 1984 how affronted they were by the brash approach of Scargill, and indignant at the denial of what they considered their right to a ballot. Equally, when I returned to Mansfield in 1986 some of the working miners I spoke to were still calmly sticking to their guns, whilst acknowledging that the striking miners probably had a point – difficult to deny with pits closing and unemployment at fifteen per cent, despite the loyalty of most of them to the Coal Board. Yet the town appeared to be thriving in comparison with the next venue.

I missed the comforting neatness of Mansfield when, four days later, I drove towards Walsall, passing burnt-out houses and shops barricaded against rioters. There are streets of beautiful houses as well, but I am haunted only by my first impressions. Our venue, Bloxwich, on the outskirts of the town, was tricky to find and I got lost searching for it in the wilderness of nearby Willenhall and Darlaston. Acres of rotting, rusty industrial estates, the dank, stinking canals, neglected houses, decaying rubbish – a vista of desolation that sears the mind.

Walsall has only recently suffered a rapid decline, having once been one of those areas where a local boy could easily make good. At the comprehensive we visited they had, some time before, had a party for the retirement of an old caretaker and invited back boys from the 1960s. The teacher, also a local, described proudly and without a trace of envy how the playground was full of the Rollers and Porsches of the boys who had left and built their own businesses – probably in the same factories that were in 1986 rotting away up the road.

It must have been easier to relate to a boss who has come from your own school or street, just as it was probably easier to like or hate the local mill or mine owner who lived in the big house in town rather than a vast, faceless multi-national, or to trust a local lad like Arthur as opposed to a stranger with a funny accent and American know-how like Ian MacGregor.

It is customary in the working classes of this country to be wary of bosses. I have worked for some of the nicest managements in the business but I have always felt impelled to treat them with graceless suspicion. I hope my company felt less divided from me as the ultimate stopper-of-the-buck because I also worked alongside them as an actress. It is difficult not to feel close to one another when standing in your knickers in some ladies' lavatory, making-up in a hand mirror.

I had to face the fact that, though our main plays were packed out in the first three towns, the morning session was proving something of a disaster as it had been under-publicised. We performed this short play with no sets, lighting or props at other small venues in and around the towns we visited with the main plays. For the first few venues there was confusion about this arrangement and the people stayed away in droves. We performed in the morning hoping to cater for the unemployed and women at home with small children for whom two of the company ran a simultaneous workshop; sometimes they showed the resultant work to the grown-ups after the discussion which followed the performance of *Derek*, but the idea as a whole was not yet working.

By far the most successful part of the morning's entertainment was that presented by the small children. The boot of my car was filled with dressing-up clothes from home and these, together with the improvisations they did, inspired some pretty potent drama. Polly James was the Peter Brook of the kindergarten, and probably reached her peak later in Tiverton with an epic production of *Snow White and the Many Dwarfs* in which her over-large cast was employed as trees and wind and birds to present a very surreal forest scene. However, I was nowhere near as successful as Polly in my part of the morning entertainment, which was, after I had played my part in *Derek*, to lead the discussion with the audience. I soon realised that just to say: 'Any questions?' was pointless. The extremist political members of Equity had nothing on me at those three first venues as I filled the resulting silence with revolutionary gobbledegook that left the listening teachers, education officers and mystified youngsters thinking I was raving mad.

However, help was at hand. Wherever we went on the tour I tried to make contact with any professional companies in the area, and in Walsall I was lucky enough to meet Graham Sharrock, a member of a 'theatre in education' group called Gazebo who are based at Darlaston. He invited me to watch their work in a mental hospital, which proved a revealing experience.

My only previous glimpses of the inside of a mental hospital had been in the 1960s when I used to visit a young drug addict, Gracie, of whom I became very fond. After being arrested for drug offences, with my persuasion she chose to go into hospital on a 'section' rather than prison. I expected them to help her and was appalled at the lack of care she received. After several weeks she was let out, and a little while later she died of an overdose.

Perhaps that is why I was so moved by the work I saw Gazebo doing in Walsall. The audience with whom I waited were severely subnormal. One man was fiercely punishing his hands with vicious rhythmic clapping; several were obsessively rocking backwards and forwards in their chairs; one was flattened, face on to the wall, as if trying to engrave her shape on it; amongst the anguished howls and grunts one woman's voice rang out sweetly singing the same phrase over and over again. Some of them looked quite normal, until they attempted to speak when their mouths either gaped out of control with tongues lolling, or seemed to be hinged so tightly that they became locked in savage contortions.

I found it difficult to believe that a group of actors, or anybody, could penetrate their world and I was sweating with apprehension for Gazebo when they came into the room singing and dancing. They presented a simple play about running a restaurant, leading to a situation where they needed help and gradually, with superb skill, they drew in almost all of the patients to participate, according to the limits of their ability. The woman's song was listened to, probably for the first time in years. Obsessive actions were translated into cleaning tables, for which gratitude was offered. One woman who could not take the huge step of entering into the scene had a table pushed towards her and she wrestled with eating a boiled egg. After much effort it was demonstrated to be solid and she eventually joined the laughter and applause that greeted her joke. The actors patiently endeavoured to unite them in song and dance, taking as much time as was necessary with the individuals who wandered away. It was a superb example of the kind of teaching drama that groups are taking into schools and hospitals all over the country – a part of theatre work that gets little media coverage.

I picked the Gazebo's brains about the other work they did in schools and asked their advice about how to construct the *Derek* discussions: thanks to them the shape, I hope, was thereafter more stimulating. But it could still be an uphill struggle.

In the areas of high unemployment throughout the country I noticed a resignation and paucity of ambition amongst the young folk. Questions about their future were answered by indifferent shrugs, and girls who looked beyond getting married could see no further than hairdressing as a career. They had a cynical contempt for the firms that were manipulating the then YOP schemes to obtain cheap labour, but the girls particularly did not seem overly angry that wages were being undercut and working conditions deteriorating because of the lack of jobs; particularly curious given that the media and Government has been bombarding them with materialistic propaganda all their lives, but that is how it seemed. The overall impression I got was that a lot of them had no idea what to hope for and there were too few people going the right way about helping them to discover. There were many difficult kids who appeared to be just ignored and left to run wild, and some of them were little bastards, but at the risk of sounding arrogant I never once saw the actors in the workshops unable to handle any of them; on the contrary, I sometimes saw them wreak miracles, impressing even the most disillusioned teachers.

We had already been prepared by the RSC education officer, Tony Hill, and voice teacher, Cicely Berry, but we gradually adapted their methods to suit the young people we worked with. We devised all sorts of ways of shaking them up at the start of the session. Many were there under duress – particularly the boys. Some of the girls were touchingly dolled up to the nines, usually in skin-tight skirts and heels, at the prospect of meeting some actors, so our first task was to get them leaping about to shake off their inhibitions and sulks. By a series of games and ploys and our own enthusiasm, we got monosyllabic youngsters to relish words and their regional accents and play with their language. They made wild guesses at what the more obscure words in the Shakespearian texts meant, including 'adamant' being a pop star! These workshops underlined for the company the absolute necessity for us to do the plays with clarity, and we must have succeeded to a certain degree because a young lad in Walsall did actually thank us for translating *The Dream* into modern English.

We learned to woo or jostle the quiet ones out of their shyness and target the difficult ones into interested involvement and constructive showing off. In the bad schools it was less easy, but we never utterly failed. There were always one or two in whom we lit a tiny flicker of daring or enjoyment. They were once like the little goers in the morning workshops and that energy must still be there somewhere. To my mind, nothing unlocks children more effectively than acting.

Way back in the 1940s I had been fortunate enough to attend Upland Junior School in Bexleyheath, Kent, where, without any thought of being progressive, we seemed to act out every lesson – probably as a desperate means of keeping, by active participation, the attention of a class of over fifty infants. I have a vivid recollection of being Africa in geography; and, in elementary science, feeling the first stirrings of the resentment of a supporting player whilst I revolved in a worldly fashion round my friend, Brenda Barry, who stood superiorly on the desk, radiating as the sun. Not only have I never forgotten the facts I learned so graphically, but I am sure that every child in my class was more confident as a result of this exhibitionism. Anyone who has been a seven-year-old Hannibal astride a seven-year-old elephant, clambering over several seven-year-old Alps, has to develop some sense of his or her own importance.

We all need to be valued; in Walsall the shrewd headmaster had delegated a group of tough boys to organise the car park and they ordered the drivers into line with all the commitment and zeal of little Arthur Scargills. Similarly, a group of boys, decidedly not into the Arts, were assigned to help put up the auditorium which they did in record time. I found them laboriously sketching it the next day, to be signed by me with the timing added as evidence of their achievement, and I was doubly thrilled when they wandered in on the last night to help with the packing up and caught the end of the play, which they were furious to have missed, and insisted on me telling them the story: which is not easy with *A Midsummer Night's Dream*.

The reaction of the people who did see the two main plays in Walsall was wonderful. It had got steadily better in each of the three towns we played. This is probably because our performances were becoming more confident, but also because the audiences did vary in the degree that they expressed their approval. For instance, during our visit to Yarborough I

received a letter from a local apologising for what he considered the
'cool reception' to *Romeo and Juliet*, and describing his fellow citizens of
Lincoln as 'reserved and rather diffident'. I had actually been well
pleased with the reaction, until I compared it with the warmth of
Mansfield and, yet again, with exuberant Walsall. Here the Mayor leapt
to his feet on the first night to admit to the audience that dread of this
particular official duty had been replaced by a determination to get a
ticket straightaway for the next night. The reaction was more restrained
in the next town – Bridgnorth. On the first night a man in the interval
said to me noncommittally: 'Mm, yes, is it a success?'

This cautious need to discover what others thought before committing
himself to an opinion irritated me after the openness of the people of
Walsall.

Bridgnorth is a lovely place, though. Nowhere were the sudden
contrasts of England more vividly demonstrated than in the twelve-mile
drive between Walsall and Bridgnorth. I went through the dereliction of
Darlaston again, grimly humming 'Jerusalem', but the song dried on my
lips as within a few short miles I was undulating through the beautiful
curves of the East Midland countryside.

After Walsall the black and white houses and clear river of Bridgnorth
appeared almost sentimental. Despite the steep cliff dividing the high
and low town, there is a leisurely smoothness in this agricultural centre
which is totally absent from the towns we had previously visited. The
audiences were definitely middle-class. And nothing wrong with that.

Middle-class – a state much envied and respected by my parents –
has become a term of abuse these days, along with do-gooder, liberal,
peace campaigner, and lady as opposed to woman. However, despite my
preoccupation with making the theatre available to all people, I recognise
that at present the bulk of the theatre-going audiences and, therefore,
my bread and butter, comes from the middle-class. There is no doubt,
however, that less sophisticated audiences are more robustly demonstra-
tive. We picked up our most dedicated converts to the Bard in the next
venue of Barnsley.

Unlike Mansfield, Barnsley is Scargill country. No attempt is made
to prettify it – it is a town of straight lines. The old cottages of the mining
villages outside the town, such as Hoyland where we actually performed,
are built of square-cut stone into square-shaped houses as unrelenting
as those on the more recently built council estates. The town hall is a
rectangular building with a square tower and the new shopping precinct
that scars the town centre is all straight blocks of cement. Only 'Arthur's

Castle', as the Victorian Gothic office of the NUM is known, breaks the rule with rebellious arches and towers. Look closely as you walk around the town: the shops are quite stylish, and the windows of the houses are bedecked with beloved ornaments, while the curtains declare each person's individuality. It is uplifting how the drape of a piece of net can show such defiance.

The people of Barnsley are defiant. They were the last to return to work during the miners' strike and the scars of it still run deep. When I revisited in 1986, unlike Mansfield there was no polite acceptance of the other person's point of view: then, it is difficult to be polite when you are still paying off debts for standing up for your very way of life, and if not already one of the twenty-one per cent unemployed in the town, in constant threat of becoming one.

Possibly the only good thing to come out of the strike is the emergence of the women as active participators in the affairs of this macho coal-mining society. Perhaps D. H. Lawrence's women would have been less destructive if they had been given a voice and a similar outlet for their intelligence. On reflection, it was the research I did about women in mining areas and the frustration I felt when playing one on TV in 1985 in Lawrence's play *The Daughter-in-Law* that increased my sympathy with the women in these colliery towns. There is something about the women of Barnsley. I noticed it when we visited even before the strike. None of your respectable Mansfield cardigans for them. I loved the way they flaunted their fat bottoms in tight jeans, undaunted at their town having been nominated the fifth tubbiest in England, as well as top for tooth decay and deaths from smoking. There is a marvellous do-or-die spirit in the people that was epitomised by the group of locals who became Shakespeare groupies. They had never seen any of his work before; in fact, few of them had seen a live show. Thousands of people on the tour wrote lovely letters and told us nice things, but this lot came all over the country to see the shows again and again. I revelled at the sight of them sitting amongst the 'lahdy-arses' at Stratford's Other Place, wearing their funny hats emblazened with 'Bottoms Up', 'I Love Willies (plays)', 'Snout like Shakespeare', 'Up the Bard' and 'Puck-Off'.

Yet another convert from Barnsley wrote:

I had never seen a Shakespeare play acted before this week. My only experience was reading *MacBeth* around the class when I was about twelve. I had a vague idea of the plot of *Romeo and Juliet* (the wrong vague idea as it turned out) and *A Midsummer Night's Dream* meant someone running about in a donkey head. My wife bought the tickets while I was away, I work on an oil rig and I don't suppose I would have gone at all. I sat enthralled for both plays. I don't remember three hours passing as quickly before. After *Romeo* last night I felt exhausted, drained, so God knows how the players must feel.

Thank you Miss Hancock for two experiences I won't forget in a hurry and please say thank you to all your company. It must be very hard work touring but I am glad you do it. Maybe the buggers at the Arts Council will give you a bit more cash next year.

Thank you again.

And thank you Barnsley.

We were still in Scargill country when we moved on to our third colliery town. Mansfield and Barnsley had their fair share, but Castleford wins hands down in the slag-heap stakes. I thought the surrounding countryside had become more hilly until I realised it was a mountain range of tips. However, the really distinctive feature of Castleford is its odour. There is a sewage works as one enters the town, another as one leaves and the fertiliser on the fields is singularly potent – maybe it is fresh from the chemical works which dominate the skyline. Whatever, the combination of this and other industries blends into a pungent mix of yeast, sickly sweets, old-fashioned anaesthetic and tar, and one cannot escape it.

Or, apparently, resist it. It should be sold as perfume. Several of the towns we went to in 1983/4 I have been drawn to revisit, but none more frequently than Castleford. I love it. Strange, with its smells, frothy polluted river and evil, belching, squat chimneys; but it also has rows of comfortable little industrial cottages with inviting windows and back-yards, a warmly welcoming old-fashioned indoor market with guinea pigs, nails, tea-towels, carpets, loose biscuits, sticky buns and mugs of tea, as well as girls and old ladies with pretty hair and men and women with wit and warmth.

On one of my visits in June 1986 I discovered that the week before, uncommented on by the national press, there was an accident in the chemical plant a short distance away from the school we originally performed in back in November 1983. In the staff room I laughed lest I should cry as the teachers told me of the saga of ineptitude that surrounded the incident. At about 9.15 am a cloud of vapour was seen billowing from the works towards the school, trapping latecomers in its coils. (The headmaster wryly mused that it was an efficient lesson in punctuality.) The children were quickly shut up in the school, the windows closed, then everyone sent upstairs, as per the emergency drill. No alarm bell had sounded so the headmaster phoned the works to see if there was an emergency. Yes, he was told, there was, but it was not thought to be lethal so they had not bothered with the alarm. At five o'clock two men with buckets came to the school, informed the staff that it was 'contaminated' and proceeded to wash the windows of the ground floor. They did not bother with the old part of the building, which is empty anyway because of rot.

A couple of weeks later the firm gave notice in the local paper of their intention 'to familiarise people with the sound of the public warning siren required by the Control of Industrial Major Accident Hazard Regulations (CIMAH)', so presumably, for some reason, they assumed a little test was a good idea. No one seemed to question the fact that a whole town was being asked to live constantly under the sort of threat that required an alarm system, against which their only defence was to shut the windows of their houses and go upstairs; nor, for that matter, had any fierce objections been raised to the leak, as a town with mines and factories closing daily cannot afford to be 'difficult'. Anyway, insurance companies were paying up for pitted cars without a quibble, though a blind eye was turned to shrivelled trees and the long-term poor state of children's lungs.

Through the doors of the rotting part had passed the young Henry Moore and I thought it merited a snapshot. A passing youth commented sadly: 'Are you taking our decrepit school?' I am sure that the teachers could not be bettered, but I cannot help thinking that it is a bit unfair that some kids have the playing fields of Eton while others have the chemical stained scrublands of Castleford.

Henry Moore would be proud of the art work, though. There is a brown and black picture of miners underground at the school which he did as a lad, with all his later chunkiness and solidity, as well as a lovingly carved wooden memorial for pupils who died in the war. The work of today's students, proudly displayed in the school entrance hall, has a similar blatant talent. It is strident and individual, and the pictures I saw on my visit in 1986 showed some of the frustration felt by a generation that has watched their parents' year-long bitter struggle in the miners' strike, and more recently suffered personally from the teachers' dispute. The teachers are a wry, self-deprecating lot, but their banter conceals a very real pain from the divisions their strike has caused between each other, and between them and the pupils. The deputy head told me that he was leaving because he had had enough of 'this grotty place', and had always had dreams of working in a lovely town with a beautiful house, beaches and nightclubs: he was taking up a headship in Barnsley.

By the time we reached Castleford, the company was utterly involved in what they were doing and the thrill of the power they perceived they had was pushing them to great heights. On the last night there the entire house stood up and cheered their lungs out, refusing to let the actors leave the building.

Now, in the West End for a musical like *Annie* or *Sweeney Todd* a standing ovation is par for the course when whooping Americans force reluctant, embarrassed English punters to rise to their feet at the drop of a hat. But in Castleford High School gym it is something else. I am the first to admit I am a wimp on these occasions, but my cheeks were not the only ones wet with tears that night. In a conventional theatre one can bring in the curtain and, if necessary, the iron (as we call the safety curtain) to send an audience home, but it is not so easy in a gymnasium where the dressing rooms are the gents' and ladies' toilets adjoining the hall. There is something almost frightening when an audience really wants more, as they did that night, refusing to go home. When I did the little number called 'It's Sort of Romantic' on the first night of *Make Me An Offer* in 1959, I was stunned when the audience clamoured for more. The song was very short as it had been thrown in at the last minute to cover a set change, so when the audience shouted: 'Encore! More!' I was reduced to shouting quite angrily: 'There bloody well isn't any more,' (and got my first reprimand from the Lord Chamberlain).

Shakespeare did not write encores either, but as in Walsall and Barnsley a good few drinks were quaffed with the audience and teachers into the small hours. It was exhilarating for all of us to have such direct reactions, to feel so appreciated. This letter – another of hundreds we received – is typical:

> How I wish I had the ability to get over to you adequately my gratitude and joy after last night's *Romeo*. I feel deeply in the debt of you and the gorgeous Roger Allam, Day Lewis and all.
>
> ... I feel I want to pack up, leave wife and my very dear son and follow you lot, and I am not a star-struck youngster – I am fifty-four!
>
> For the first time in my life I was near the front. I could have reached out and touched the boys and girls acting and for the first time in my life I wept in the theatre. I didn't think I would ever do that.
>
> I rarely wish I was loaded with money, but if I were I would come and pour champagne all over you. And then pay the cleaning costs.
>
> Tomorrow night I will be right at the front. I will be the one laughing loud.

Goodbye my dear, dear Miss H.

Please tell your team what it all means to this one, dull, ageing member of the public.

P.S. Dear God, that Roger Allam! Quel actor.

Poor Roger was dogged by that last phrase for the entire tour – particularly after one of his less good performances – but all this was heady stuff.

We reached a peak of success at Castleford which I feared would be difficult to sustain. Pride cometh before a fall, to quote my mum. And she was right.

6 : Progress
Scunthorpe, Belfast, Middlesbrough, Workington, Barrow-In-Furness

FLIXBOROUGH – SCUNTHORPE'S PROGRESS – DIRECTOR'S NOTES – CORPSING – *THIS IS YOUR LIFE* – STAGE MANAGEMENT – SMALL PERFORMING SPACES – FEAR OF BELFAST – THE DIVIS FLATS – THE FALLS – PERFORMING IN BELFAST – COMPANY DISCONTENT – DRUNKS – IRISH FRIENDS – MIDDLESBOROUGH INSIDE AND OUT – SHOPS – OLDHAM – JOYS OF WORKINGTON – SELLAFIELD – PETITIONS – IDEALISM V NECESSITY

'It's better than a special week at Scunthorpe Baths' has always been a joke phrase in the theatre. A 'special week' is a clause inserted in a contract meaning you have agreed to an incredibly low salary which the management will not henceforth regard as your going rate – so they say – a 'special low' fee being a favourite trick of the BBC. I had hitherto thought that Scunthorpe Baths was a mythical venue made up to sound funny. But I was not laughing a lot as I drove through a thick fog to throw myself into an all-too-real 'special' four days in this low watermark of actors' careers and the signpost to Flixborough swirled out of the mist three miles outside Scunthorpe.

Whenever I hear glib reassurances about the safety of nuclear and other potentially lethal establishments I think of Flixborough. The machines may be perfect but what about the men? Having been brought up as a child to believe that clever people in authority like politicians, doctors, judges and that all-encompassing word 'experts' know best, it is difficult even now for me to grasp what a bungling load of idiots most of them are. Particularly scientists and engineers. Worldwide – from the disastrous cockers-up of the American NASA programme to the Russian variety in Chernobyl, from the neglectful bunglers who killed 144 people, of which 116 were children between the ages of seven and ten, in Aberfan to those who finished off 2,352 in India's Bhopal. A quick read of the

Government report on the Flixborough accident is a crash-course in human fallibility.

In March 1974, when one of the reactors in the Nypro plant in Flixborough cracked, a little group of fools decided to take it out and mend it, and without even bothering first to work out why it had gone wrong, attempted to keep production going by linking together two other reactors with a temporary join to bridge the gap. This they did as badly as I would mend a fuse if I did not have an 'expert' with me, as they did not because of a vacancy in a crucial job – except that I would at least look at the instruction manual. If they had bothered to read theirs they would have found that it told them not to do almost everything that they did. Anyway, by mending my fuse I would not be likely to run the risk of killing twenty-eight people, injuring hundreds of others and damaging 1,821 houses and 167 shops for miles around. And they were lucky. The whole place blew up and caught fire on a Saturday afternoon, 4.53 pm on 1 June 1974 – a lovely day, as everyone poignantly remembers – when there were only a few staff on duty and the surrounding villagers were nearly all some distance away at the steel works gala which providentially was taking place that day.

The report, if it were not so tragic, would make hilarious reading, with its saga of tools locked in sheds and DIY bungling, but perhaps the funniest thing of all is that after the disaster had obliterated the works they rebuilt it at vast expense, only to discover that the product they manufactured, caprolactum, was no longer in demand. So they had to shut it down.

No, all in all it is hard to have much faith in the captains of industry. Or the 'experts' who dodder their way into disasters. What frightens me is the more powerful the things they invent the bigger the risks. However, they will doubtless continue to whirl us madly around on the wheels of progress. It is funny how this much-vaunted progress always seems to hurt the people it is presumably progressing for. I am sure it is making someone happy somewhere, but I have to say it was not the people of Scunthorpe in 1983, the height of the recession there, which had begun with the 'rationalisation' of the steel works. Rationalisation – another word that has acquired ominous overtones. The gloom when we went to Scunthorpe was almost tangible, despite their defiant cultural festival, of which we were the star turn.

Happily when I returned in 1986, unlike Walsall, Castleford and Barnsley where things had deteriorated, Scunthorpe had been much improved by being made an enterprise zone at the end of 1983. They fought against the miners during the strike to keep the coke coming, to save what remained open of the steel works, and one could see their point. Since the money has been poured into glamorising the area, Skippingdale, on the edge of Scunthorpe, a barren place when we performed *Derek* there, has blossomed into a colourful group of hyper-market stores, flags flying and money flowing. A new council estate in the town is one of the best designs I have seen in the country, and just down the road there is a splendid leisure centre opened by Kevin Keegan. Even if the run-down Unemployment Advice Centre, nestling between it and the splendid new Co-Op, reminds one of the have-nots, never mind, the haves are apparently doing all right thank you. Yes, Scunthorpe now is superficially full of swish and bravado. But when we went in November 1983 it was a dismal place, providing a suitable back-drop to a dismal four days.

Scunthorpe Baths could be quite an impressive building were it given a wash, but its grubby exterior is difficult even to find amidst the muddle of the busy Doncaster road. I never really felt confident about the weight of our auditorium pressing down on the floor laid over the pool and worried that, whereas an aquatic version of *A Midsummer Night's Dream* would probably be heralded by London critics as new and exciting, it might prove difficult to justify in the Verona of the Capulets and Montagues and could necessitate writing in a move to Venice. The shows, in fact, were well received but, after the ecstatic reaction in Castleford, the company had become a bit greedy and the feeling of anticlimax, together with echoing accoustics, made for some sloppy work.

As a director I am notorious for my notes. It is a constant bleat of actors that most directors disappear after the first night, but they are just as resentful if the director never leaves them alone. Particularly on the tour when I was constantly around, I niggled and fretted until the actors would scream and run whenever they saw me approaching with my dreaded reporter's notebook. It was necessary, however, as performances shift slightly with repetition, particularly with a play as delicate as *The Dream* where there is a very fine line which, if crossed, turns the play into something gross. This happens especially in comedy where an audience's laughter can trick you into believing you have got it right, but you have to be sure that the laughs are there for the proper reasons or you will be led in quite the wrong direction. For instance, in the first meeting between Bottom and Titania you can get belly-laughs with sexual innuendo and double-takes, but there is a much richer vein of warmth and awe to be mined. It is also very easy with the repetition of performances to become automatic and not think each thought as though for the first time: when speaking Shakespearian verse, this can lead to a hollow 'voice beautiful' delivery.

Another fatal result of a long run is the giggles or 'corpsing' (as it is known in the theatre), which is an apt word as it is not at all funny but rather killing yourself with laughter that is shameful, and agony to control. It is not so bad when something has gone awry, particularly if the audience are in on the joke, but it frequently attacks actors for no reason at all. There are people with whom I just cannot work because a certain twinkle in their eye sets me off. I had a dreadful time in *Absurd Person Singular* at the Criterion Theatre in 1973 when the nasal whine and ingratiating manner which Richard Briers assumed in his role forced me to play every scene I had with him back to back. One dreadful evening he had started the performance trying to conceal a slightly bent stiff neck and when rising from kneeling under the sink managed also both to wallop his head and do something painful to his back. But, instead of getting the sympathy one would expect from a fellow actor, he scarcely got one line of dialogue from me without it petering out into helpless laughter as I looked at his contorted face and body. There is nothing worse for an audience in a comedy than to sense the actors laughing at it themselves and I suffer the tortures of the damned trying to control myself.

So it is strange that, despite my own behaviour, my attitude to an audience is actually deeply puritan. During the run of *Bed Before Yesterday* in 1976, I was told they were going to do a documentary about the author, Ben Travers, on his ninetieth year. I protested vehemently when they said they wanted to film the end of the play from one of the boxes during the show, complaining that it would ruin the theatre audience's pleasure. I moaned to Ben about it when we did an interview and I threw tantrums with the technicians, demanding that their equipment be hidden by curtains. I spent the whole day in a thoroughly nasty temper. All the way through the performance I whinged to my fellow actors about how badly the play was going as a result of the presence of the cameras. It was only when the applause suddenly died during the curtain calls as Eamonn Andrews walked on with the dread red book that I realised the whole thing had been a put-up job to trap me for *This Is Your Life* and that Ben, the company and the entire audience had been in the know. Having believed that I could tell if people were lying to me up to this point, particularly my own family, I have been wary about trusting anyone since. This graceless behaviour during the whole incident was only excusable because it really did stem from a deep concern for the audience's enjoyment, a concern difficult to equate with my predisposition to corpse. This was reflected at the end of the Stratford season where there is a party at which joke awards are given by the company to one another. It is to my eternal shame that, elder statesman as I was in 1982, I received the ironic title of 'Most Professional Actress'.

With my reputation it was understandable, therefore, that my fellow actors found it a little difficult to stomach my harsh notes on their behaviour in Scunthorpe, and they retaliated by revolting *en masse* about the curtain-call. As the rapturous receptions meant these were usually interminable we invited people to come on stage and dance with us. Observing from the audience I had seen the thrill it gave the participants, and the company did it so charmingly that I had not been aware of how profoundly it embarrassed them. Most actors loathe being themselves with an audience, as opposed to acting a character, but since working with Joan Littlewood it had never been a problem to me, so I was not very understanding about their reluctance. They also thought the whole idea was in bad taste. I fear they were later backed up by the London critics, but on the tour I was less concerned with matters of aesthetics than with involving our audience. I am still arrogantly convinced my motives were right, if not my method. (Adrian Noble and Howard Davies improved on this in the following year's tour by making the whole performance a promenade.) Eventually, after heavy persuasion, the company agreed to continue; but they were not happy.

Neither were the stage staff. It was about this time that I got the following memo:

FROM: STAGE MANAGEMENT
SUBJECT: NON EXISTENCE
In a number of press reports so far it is being stated that:
'Sheila Hancock is leading a company of eighteen.'
'Sheila Hancock is leading a company of eighteen actors carrying their auditorium tortoise-like around the country.'
'With her band of eighteen RSC brothers and sisters . . .'
What happened to the other fourteen?!

Their resentment was understandable as on get-in days they were working a fifteen-hour day, and in between a luxurious thirteen-hour day.

I hope I am usually appreciative of stage management, having done it myself, and I rather regret that few actors nowadays have a chance to do the same as there is now a new breed of workers specially trained for the more complicated technical job it has become. When I was young most actors served their apprenticeship combining acting in small parts with ASM-ing (assistant stage-managing). I spent many happy hours pushing a wheelbarrow round various towns in the British Isles, 'propping' – which means begging, borrowing and stealing furniture, ornaments, carpets, etc. to dress the set. I once demolished several graves in Bromley churchyard, ripping off ivy to tart up an ill-painted wall in *The Scarlet Pimpernel*. I too have been on the receiving end of unfair abuse from temperamental actors and directors who needed a scapegoat, and I had liked to think I was more considerate as a result. Therefore I was depressed that I had thoughtlessly caused resentment among our excellent team.

All told, I did not feel over-confident that I was leading the company as well as they deserved. A director's job can be lonely, so I was comforted when Barry Kyle, one of the RSC's associate directors, paid us a visit and tried to restore my confidence by praising the productions, even if he did temper it by pointing out that it is easier to succeed in a small space. Despite smarting somewhat in my then-sensitive state, I do agree with him.

It is a myth that the proximity of the audience makes it difficult for actors. Of course they have to be truthful, but most of them do not find that difficult. What is more difficult is enlarging and projecting that truth to fill a big auditorium. In addition, when you are remote from an audience up on a stage they examine more critically the way you move and speak and it demands more technical skill. The worst moment in any production process is when you move from the rehearsal room to the stage: everything you have worked on seems to fly away from you as soon as it has to be magnified. Small spaces do demand attention to detail, however, as a PS in one of our fan letters proved: 'One small complaint. Please could Tybalt take that piece of blue sticky tape off the sole of his boot because it looks a bit silly when he's dead.'

The comment about the relative simplicity of small spaces was not meant unkindly, and Barry was very supportive. The only other thing that cheered me up in Scunthorpe was the billiard hall opposite the baths. Realising he was on to a good thing as far as his bar revenue was concerned, the owner kept it open for the actors till all hours, and it was a change to have somewhere to go after the show apart from Indian restaurants which, along with the Chinese, are the only places that stay open late in the provinces. We had curry and sweet and sour coming out of our ears.

Despite the late nights potting the reds the company did improve the plays during the four days in Scunthorpe, and I tried to ingratiate myself back into their affections. Instead of a dog in *The Dream*, we used a fox fur on a piece of string which, in the hands of Simon Templeman, became a living, breathing, very funny creature. I put the following note up on the board:

> The show was much improved last night. Thank you. However, I am sorry to say that the dog was OTT [over the top]. In future I will not work with children or fox furs.

They were, however, not in the mood for banter and I cannot say I found Scunthorpe a bundle of laughs either. Even when I returned in 1986, wondering at the town's apparent renaissance, I had a stand-up row with a man in uniform at one of the gates of the steel works. I was taking a photograph when he rushed out of his box and ran aggressively towards me, gabbling frantically into his walkie-talkie. He officiously tried to prevent me taking pictures as it was 'not British Steel policy'. I started trying to reason with him about my civil rights and the law of the land as I knew it (which I was not altogether sure of myself, having already encountered the strange police force that prowled around Sellafield, not to mention the guardians of Greenham Common). In my nervousness I found myself babbling on about 'tax-payers' money' – a phrase I really never thought I would use with such Thatcherite self-righteousness. So I left Scunthorpe in 1986 almost as sickened by myself as I had been in 1983.

Almost, but not quite. In 1983, as well as feeling inadequate at my job, I was ashamed of the fear I felt of going on to Belfast, our next venue. The fear of the unknown for me invariably proves to be much more terrible than the real thing so I hoped this would prove to be the case about what I expected to find in Northern Ireland.

When we set out in November 1983, relationships between England and Ireland were at a pretty low ebb with bombs going off in London and Belfast. It did seem, at the very least, foolhardy for the Royal Shakespeare Company to be marching in with one production in which religious bigotry was highlighted and another in which a group of men donned bowler hats and orange decorations and played pipes and drums: an unwittingly tactless choice which only dawned on us as we flew over the uncompromising H-block of the Maze Prison in a rather rickety little plane.

I am a nervous flyer at the best of times, but this flight was not helped by the presence of a waxen-faced Enoch Powell, looking like Hitler in his latter years, whom I assessed was even more a prime target than us. The security on arrival at the airport, the road blocks on the road into Belfast, the Green Goddesses driving along with rifles sticking out of the back seemed to confirm my worst fears, as did the body search as I went through the entrance of the strongly fortified Forum Hotel where we were to stay. Just as with Sellafield's failed attempt to obliterate the memory of Windscale, the change of name from the Europa did not erase the awareness that it had been, and is, an unpopular place. I was, therefore, already pretty jumpy when Roy Hattersley, who was also staying there, engaged me in a conversation near a front plate-glass window.

I had to come to terms with this panic, so I decided to grasp the nettle on my first day and visit the trouble spots of the city. Fortunately I was restrained from hailing one of the black taxis which the IRA are involved in running as a service for the parts of the Falls Road area that no bus or minicab will enter. They would not happily have transported someone with my accent, but I was fortunate enough to find a person who would, as long as I kept quiet and did what I was told. Neither of which things I find easy, but it was worth it to gain access to places and people that are usually out of bounds to strangers.

There are a few areas, as a result of the tour, that I would truly rather be dead than have to live in but, without any doubt, the Divis flats in the Lower Falls has got to be top of the list. The district of Pound Loney was replaced in 1973 by a gruesome estate emulating the Le Corbusier brutalist style of architecture. Pound Loney was apparently in a poor state but, as in Oldham, no attempt was made to regenerate the existing closed community. Instead it was razed to the ground and the inhabitants encouraged by cloth and laity alike to appreciate this 'adventure of living in high flats' and playing in 'streets in the sky', as the Northern Ireland Housing Institute put it in 1962.

Well, I suppose it is an adventure of sorts to live in a place where an estimated thirty-three people have been killed around your front door when terrorists have battled it out with the police and the army. Some of the kids certainly drum up a bit of excitement by joy-riding cars into the estate and setting fire to them, as well as having the odd sniff of glue. But I doubt if the family of four-year-old Jimmy McGivern who drowned in an open sewer find it very exciting, despite the few hundred pounds given to them by the builders whose neglect caused his grotesque death. Perhaps it was them who scrawled 'Is there life before death?' on one of the concrete walls. Or a relative of one of the many suicides. The Northern Ireland Office may protest that it is 'emotive and ridiculous' and 'grossly exaggerated' to say that the Divis is some of the worst housing in Western Europe, but I suspect only the rats and cockroaches like it very much. Perhaps the British Army find it convenient for their helicopter pad and surveillance post on the highest tower but the foot patrols must have felt the 'adventure' was beginning to pall when one of their number was blown up by a ten-pound bomb not so long ago. How any of the people living there have found the strength to organise themselves into residential groups, drop-in centres and advice and educational groups, God only knows. I would be one of those who retreat into an alcoholic stupor and give up.

It would be presumptuous of me to venture any solution to the Northern Ireland problem. Or even, not being Irish or religious, to attempt to understand it. One thing that did strike me, though, was the seeming relish with which the men played their war games: the swaggering youths outside the Sinn Fein headquarters, the soldiers with guns protecting the police patrols, the orange men on their parades, the rabble-rousing speeches of the various leaders – all have about them a grim pride and cockiness that you see in little boys playing soldiers. I know there are women in active roles on both sides of the Irish divide but on the whole I got the impression of men asserting their maleness while the women cleared up the resultant mess.

And what a mess. Not just the Divis. Burnt-out houses and cars, broken glass and litter all over the Falls area. Police stations and vulnerable buildings completely concealed behind concrete and barbed wire. And the wall. That ugly barricade dividing streets, houses and minds. The graffiti would appear colourful were not the messages so full of hate. Then there is the bleak estate where Bobby Sands grew up to achieve fame by starving his young body to death, and where his mother was told to shut up as her job was over when she begged for some quiet from the crowds outside her house after his death. Or, at least, that is what I was told. It is often difficult to separate fact from fiction.

I talked and looked and tried to understand. People kept stopping me in the streets and, even as armoured cars with guns sticking out cruised by, would say, 'It isn't so bad as they say, is it?' In terms of being

frightened they are right, it is not, but in other ways it is much
worse.

Not for all the residents, mind you. I had little to do with the booking
system in Ireland and, it being a 'cultural festival', our audiences were
certainly not coming in coachloads from the Falls or Shankill areas to
the Queen's University where we were based. The sniffer dogs going
over our seating and dressing rooms were unusual, but the audience that
poured in looked a bit like the one in Bridgnorth.

I was very nervous as the requiem at the beginning of *Romeo and Juliet*
started and the smell of incense filled the hall. The usual laughs in the
first scenes were completely absent. I was in a sweat, thinking the
audience was disapproving of the religious emphasis, but the cast obviously felt vibrations that I was missing and played with a contained
beauty. There was a radiant moment in the balcony scene when Dan
Day Lewis and Amanda Root, as Romeo and Juliet, gazed at one another,
holding a long pause as if unable to communicate their love out loud,
and I swear the world stopped revolving. At the end of the play there
was one of those rare silences in the theatre when an audience cannot
even move to applaud. This was followed by minutes of fervent and hard
clapping. No cheers, but there was an intensity about the reception that
showed that for them, like the company, each line had suddenly taken
on a new depth.

The effect of *Derek* was equally powerful. We performed in a dilapi-
dated club, dressing all together in a room which was in the process
of being knocked down – a process we accelerated when Simon Templeman leant on a wall causing it to collapse. There being no chairs
he was leaning to recover his strength after the shock of poking a
suspicious parcel which responded by playing Happy Birthday.
Presumably a macabre joke, revealing the same sense of humour
that made the audience roar with laughter at lines like, 'He doesn't
like killing people' and, 'Be a man in a man's world,' at which the
women in the audience hooted, leading me to believe they too recognised the quality I had observed in their menfolk. There were
babies crying and children running about but the audience was the
best we had had for the Bond. They loved the send-up of the army
and the Establishment, and the discussion afterwards was fiery and
exciting.

At least *I* found it exciting, but the company was getting fed up at
some of the conditions I was expecting them to work in. The two actors
who were supposed to be running the children's workshop at the club

had found themselves instead nursing fractious babies and objected to being child-minders. In my enthusiasm I had begun to exploit their generosity and they were right to point this out to me. Besides which they were tired.

The hotel was full every night with rampaging Irishmen so one had little rest. The women were no slouches at rampaging either. One night there was a really violent bout of fisticuffs between two women in the bar and most nights the carousing went on until the small hours. Lying in bed, listening, took me unpleasantly back to my childhood bedroom over the public bar in the Carpenter's Arms in King's Cross where I had sometimes trembled for my mother's and father's safety down below amongst identical shouts and murmurs.

All this alcohol proved too much to resist for one member of the company who managed to get himself paralytic before the show. Ever practical, I plonked him in the shower and plied him with coffee. My pub background has not enamoured me of drunks, but there was something appealing about this little fellow standing chubbily naked in the shower, protesting that I had destroyed him with one of my notes. Almost as appealing as the story of Richard Burton and Peter O'Toole falling in the road as a result of Peter's endeavour to carry Burton home. When a sober Alan Bates passed by, script in hand, and told them he might be relinquishing the theatre for a while and joining them in the film world, Burton stretched up a hand from the ground and cried: 'Welcome to the gutter.'

There was a lot of drowning of sorrows by all of us in Belfast. Two company romances foundered. Ian McKellen visited us and was generous and helpful, but managed to upset Dan with some of his advice about Romeo. Problems multiplied, tempers flashed and tears flowed. Mine too, for the stupidity of the inhabitants, our ancestors, various governments and me. For the whole week the company played with dedication and joy, but off-stage they were obviously finding me a pain and the feeling was, frankly, mutual.

I took refuge in the Irish theatre community. Many of them were feeling rather left out of all the international theatre high jinks in the town and were quite surprised when I sought them out. It was my pleasure. I was thrilled by the new writing over there, the stylishness of the ensemble acting and the conversations off-stage. Being in the Belfast theatre circles, I felt the adrenalin roaring as it does in New York. I argued furiously and laughed a lot in clubs, pubs and restaurants as I forced myself to leave the company alone when I was not working with them. As the week progressed, hardly a note did I give or demand did I make.

On my last night in Belfast I went to a concert of work by Prokofiev and Shostakovich given by the USSR State Orchestra. A platform full of scowling Frankie Howerd lookalikes created lightness and grace but looked unmoved by the music they were making or our passionate response to it. I looked forward to meeting them at the party afterwards, but it was not to be. After a long wait we were told that the Russians had been ushered into a coach and whisked back to their hotel outside the town away from all the other performers. It seemed that in Belfast even the artists were to be separated.

So, a fractured jig of a week came to an end and I limped home to London for Sunday lunch – oh, the joy of crispy Yorkshire pudding and home-made gravy – before charging off to our next venue.

Middlesbrough is only about a hundred and fifty years old, springing to life by supplying coal, iron and steel, and sadly at present dying just as quickly as demand for these products wanes. Of all the towns we visited, this had the highest rate of unemployment, a shaming thirty per cent. But even this figure did not paint a true picture of what misery that actually meant, as it was averaged out over all the inhabitants. The truth is that on some estates there was seventy to ninety per cent unemployment amongst the men. Positive efforts are now being made to regenerate Middlesbrough and one can only hope they are as successful as in Scunthorpe, but in 1983 I did not find it a cosy town as I battled my way through a gale across the wasteland surrounding our digs. The walk to the venue was no more uplifting. The cheerless road in front of the town hall is not a good example of town planning. On one side of the Gothic pile is a thirties theatre, the old Empire, now a Mecca social club which looks about as sociable as the Reverend Ian Paisley. The grey of the town hall blends quite nicely with the pink of the Empire, but it cannot take on the brown and black shiny glass monster that towers beside it, nor the grey concrete building over the road.

Inside the buildings it is another story. The town hall, for instance, is a gem, decorated with flair and imagination. The fumed oak panelling could be oppressive were it not for the bold decision to pick out the ornate roof beams and window frames in dazzling white, contrasting with the terracotta walls and enhancing the colourful stained-glass windows. The result is at once dramatic and warm, and I marvelled that they would allow us to desecrate their lovely hall with our muddle.

The inside of the spectacular shopping precinct also belies its drab exterior. Glistening marble floors, shiny silver pillars and dazzling over-head lights make the Cleveland Centre one of the flashiest of the new shopping complexes that are erupting all over the country. At the centre of the arcades, daylight is allowed in to illuminate a huge model of Captain Cook's ship dangling precariously overhead. I am mystified by this obsession with shopping centres. Many towns we visited seem to be spending millions on building these gigantic complexes and nowhere was the irony more apparent than in Middlesbrough. Can it be that, while thirty per cent enviously look on, seventy per cent are indulging in a desperate orgy of spending before they too just have to watch?

Am I alone in not enjoying these vast super- and hypermarkets? As I lacerate people's heels with my nasty wire trolley (because they never run straight), as I rush backwards and forwards trying to find where everything is, desperately searching for a human being who will talk to me rather than stamp things with little guns or give all their attention to sinister computerised tills, I long for the joys of Castleford's old-fashioned market and my childhood Saturdays doing the weekly shop for my mother.

Whoever invented plastic wrappers destroyed the joys of shopping. I suppose we are all too busy to stand and chat while the shopkeeper slices and weighs but I miss the smell and feel of loose products. Fat bottles of whirly barley sugar or paragoric pieces, snapped with pincers and tipped into crisp white bags, whole cheeses miraculously cut with wire, bacon guillotined by an evil machine to just the thickness you want: all so much more appetising than those tightly wrapped parcels in refrigerated cabinets.

My mother worked at one time in what was considered to be a big shop in the 1940s and 1950s: a family firm called Mitchells of Erith. Comfortable ladies and neat gentlemen ran their various departments, taking pride in counter displays of gloves, hankies, discreet undies, artificial flowers and hats, and the neatly stacked rolls of material which they ripped flamboyantly into the length required. I would sit on the high stools provided at the counters so that the customers could pass the time of day and watch, spellbound, as the money was fed into a magic contraption which then flew off on wires to the cash desk. My mother ran a tiny library of mainly romances or thrillers. Then she started up and managed a restaurant in the store, looking so pretty in her smart 'business' dress made on our old-fashioned Singer sewing machine from a Butterwick pattern, cut out on the kitchenette floor. The dignified courtesy the salesmen and women showed the customers contrasted with the larky jokes that went on back stage in their staff cloakrooms and canteen. It was a lovely place and I looked forward to my Saturday visits. The daughter of the owner, Wendy Cope, has become a poet, and I am not surprised.

Yes, shopping in the old days was a friendly, sensuous business. There are not the same smells and textures in the Cleveland Centre in Middlesbrough. And the inhabitants do not chat much. But they do smile. The people of Middlesbrough are surprisingly cheerful. The faces one passes are often gently smiling, as though they know something better about the town that they are keeping to themselves. There are some nice parts tucked away in corners. For instance, there are some beautiful modernised rows of Victorian industrial cottages, with the old cobbled paths between the backyards still intact and some of the streets pedestrianised so the children can play there unharmed. They have been echoed alongside by several streets of modern houses built in 1980 along the same pattern, including the back entrances. Old ladies sit in chairs outside their front doors in summer or at their parlour windows in winter. Maybe I am unduly romantic about this sort of housing because of eighteen months spent in repertory at Oldham in 1951 and 1952. It was the first time I had been up North and to begin with I could not understand a word anyone said. Neither could I stomach at first the staple diet of pint pots of tea, mushy peas and chips and sloppy hot-pot cooked over the kitchen range. The toilet arrangements of washing in a tin bath in front of the same stove or braving the public bath-house (where I first learnt the potency of Mornay Pink Lilac bath cubes for drowning out the smell of carbolic) were a bit of a culture shock too; as was trying to use the outside lavatory while people chatted outside awaiting their turn. It all took a while to get accustomed to.

Eventually Ethel and Bert, my landlady and landlord, got used to the RADA accent and treated me like the daughter they could not have. I relished every moment of my time in Oldham. The Lowry landscape was like a foreign country for me to explore with its mills and hilly, narrow, cobbled roads, crowded with back-to-back houses. I enjoyed life there from the crack of dawn when I heard the knocker-up coming down the street, tapping on the bedroom windows with his pole, followed by the clatter of clogs on the cobbles as people went to the mills, to last thing at night when I would stumble out, long after hours, from the Shakespeare pub opposite the old Theatre Royal. This has now been razed to the ground, and was pretty far decayed when I was there. People would put up their umbrellas in the stalls during the show as the rain spattered through the roof. My first three shows were *Pick-Up Girl*, *Reefer Girl* and *The Respectful Prostitute*. This last slipped in by mistake because the director had no idea it was an arty piece by Jean-Paul Sartre. My anxious mother wrote and asked me when I was going to do 'nice' plays, but I was as happy as a sandboy. The audience took me to their heart and, worried about my skinniness, would bring me little offerings of pies and goodies. I fell hopelessly in love with the leading man and acted all our love scenes in various awful plays with gut-wrenching fervour. His wife was in the company, and anyway I was a very moral eighteen-year-old, so the only expression allowed of our love was on-stage or longing looks in the wings. These were frequently intercepted by his patient spouse who had seen it all before – many times.

Oh, the sweet agony of it all, pouring out my heart to Ethel as she whitened the front stoop with her hair in the metal Dinky curlers she wore all week, except Saturday night when she went to the pub or a dance (after which there was invariably a punch-up with Bert). She and the neighbours and I all compared notes about our sex lives: or at least they did while I listened, pretending a worldliness I did not have. They were ripe, raw, rollicking women and they generously took me to their ample bosoms. Nobody died or gave birth alone or unloved in that road in Oldham, the doors were open to all-comers, the backyards were shared. People worked terribly hard in foul conditions in the mills but they enjoyed their families and their homes, their illegal betting shops, wakes week, religious walks, outings to Blackpool and their pubs and clubs.

I do not know for sure, as I have not lived there, but that corner of Middlesbrough looks cheery too. I hope so, because much of the rest of it is fairly unimpressive. So, I am afraid, were we. Whether the missionary zeal poured out in the performances in Belfast had left us depleted, or whether the gloom of our surroundings of the last six weeks, culminating in this depressed town, had finally dampened our spirits, I cannot say. But Middlesbrough certainly did not see us at our best.

I decided to make one of my overnight dashes home after Middles-brough and indulge in a comforting hot bath, yoga and therapeutic discussions with my husband. Well, they were more harangues really, with poor John taking all the flak for the state of the nation. I purged myself of a lot of bile and girded my loins to confront the ogre I had been dreading – Workington, and thus the fact of Sellafield.

To reserve my strength, I decided to take the train rather than drive since, to be perfectly honest, I had never even heard of Workington and, judging by my maps, motorways did not think it worth going there either. Yet when I looked it up in my father's old Harmsworth encyclopedia, circa 1900, it was obvious it had once been a thriving industrial centre, manufacturing steel rails, boilers, motors and ships, as had the adjoining town of Maryport, with the addition of mills and coal. Yet when I looked up the latter in a current Encyclopedia Britannica it did not merit a mention – though Mary Poppins did. I was later told that someone had telephoned the job centre in Workington asking for a town called Cumbria and, bewildered to discover they were talking to a place *in* Cumbria, continued: 'Well, does a Mary Port live there?' So it is obvious I am not the only one a bit vague about Cumbria.

Trusting that British Rail knew the way, I settled in at Euston in the hopes of a nice sleep. Anyone who travels by rail on Sunday will know that the timetable is apt to go awry as that is the day they do their repairs. It used to be said that only actors and fish travelled on Sundays but the fish have now been replaced by the odd hungover football fan. The somewhat erratic journey that Sunday 27 November was considerably lightened by the virtuosity of the guard. He was obviously a frustrated disc jockey and used the tannoy system as an outlet for his ambitions. Before we set off we were welcomed aboard in his Newcastle/West Indian accent and warned that we had better use the buffet before Crewe as he did not know if the new staff due to join us there would turn up or not. Presumably they did not, for the passengers at Crewe were greeted aboard with the courteous message: 'For those passengers who have just joined us at Crewe – welcome. The buffet is closed.'

As the journey progressed the passengers united in their delight at his running commentary and could not wait to meet him. He did not disappoint as he progressed down the train like Liberace doing a curtain call, a real artist at his job. So despite delays I was in good spirits when I changed at Carlisle to the funny little two-coach diesel-type train that chugs round the coast to Workington.

As I have mentioned, there are many towns on the tour that I have revisited and will again, but if I were asked to name my favourite it would have to be Workington – which only goes to show that life can reveal hidden pleasures in the most unexpected places. Heaven knows what it is that makes one town appeal to me more than another. Workington is fairly unprepossessing. Take the town hall. No Gothic wonder, no grand flourish of municipal pride here, just a rather ordinary two-storey detached house. I suppose it is quite grand compared with the rows of cottages in the town or the windswept pebble-dash council estate on the outskirts. Maybe that is it – nostalgia for pebble-dash. The house I lived in at Bexleyheath, Kent, had walls clad in these vicious little stones, and absent-mindedly picking them off as I stood talking to a boyfriend at the back door was as satisfying as biting my nails.

The walls of the old cottages in the town are made either of this, to me comforting but, let's face it, ugly finish, or a bulky stone cut into strips that seems too heavy for the size of the houses. The stone is actually rather a nice purply-brown colour but this is not set off to advantage by the inhabitants' choices of colour for the paint on the stone round the windows and the front door. Try as I might I cannot defend the Workington colour sense. In one road I saw a particularly nasty battleship-grey alongside a shoe-polish tan colour, which in turn clashed with a vicious sugar-pink and a deeply depressing maroon, which was only slightly less offensive than the pillar-box red next door; the funereal jet black next to that was presumably a refusal to compete. After my OU course on 'Art and the Environment' I should have been appalled, but I loved every clumsy brush stroke. I even like the dogs in Workington. They are ratty little animals, but I love the way they are pampered like posh poodles because they are used by the men in events at the local track.

Our venue was the leisure centre at the end of the council estate which, with its brown wood and black iron exterior, was in keeping with the area. The other side was a vista of rather nasty fields. Well, nasty to me but not to Jimmy Dummigan. Jimmy counts himself lucky that his house on the estate looks over 'the country', and he gets much pleasure from looking at the green from his windows. The salt of the earth, as my father would say. And that is why I like Jimmy – he is like my father was.

About two years before we arrived in Workington, a decision was made to close most of the steel works and thereby virtually close down the town. Rationalisation again. Jimmy was a union official at the works and fought tooth and nail to stop them. Apparently, some of the tactics he used caused questions to be asked in high places but he was convinced, with all the experience of a man who had spent a lifetime in the industry, that they were wrong. Just before the closure they had spent millions on modernising the plant and he was sure that it could be economic. Even if it were not, there were the questions of weighing profits against a whole town's livelihood and the resultant costs of supporting the unemployed community. Indeed, it is the dilemma, which no political party will confront – that of a second Industrial Revolution. Progress.

Jimmy felt that until some of these questions were answered they should at least keep the plant in moth-balls.

However, never one to give up, when he lost he did the next best thing and tried to organise something to restore the pride of his redundant workmates. They took over an old library, did it up, acquired various machines and equipment and set up a centre where they could learn new crafts as well as use their hands and minds. At Christmas, for instance, they could make one toy for their own kids with free materials as long as they made one for a children's home. One man invented a security lock for an old woman who came to the centre after being burgled – now they do hundreds. Another devised a truck for a disabled child to get around in.

Contrary to general opinion, Jimmy is convinced that the old are more affected by redundancy than the young so a real effort is made to mix the age-groups. One lad discovered a talent for painting at the centre and wanted to learn sign-writing but could not afford the fare to Carlisle where the nearest classes were held. So the centre found an old man who lovingly imparted his skill to the younger. Jimmy remembers that when he started work as a lad he instantly had 'five hundred fathers' who taught him what was what in life as well as a trade, and he thinks that society will suffer from the loss of these contacts at the workplace. He cares a lot about society, does Jimmy. He is no Luddite either, like I am. He is a forward-thinking socialist but firmly rooted in the old belief: 'From each according to his abilities, to each according to his needs.'

He has a scheme to make Maryport into the lovely beach it apparently once was for the locals. 'Children have got to have memories,' he says. Remembering warm sand in my toes, ice-cream cones melting on to salty hands, concert parties on the pier, my dad's white body in drooping swimming trunks prancing next to me on the edge of the sea, I know what he means. Treasured moments on pub doorsteps clutching fizzy lemonade and bags of crisps with salt hidden in a twist of blue paper, whilst watching strangely carefree parents carousing inside – all valuable lessons in enjoyment. It may be an uphill battle creating a usable stretch of sand on that coast, just upstream from Sellafield, but if there is anything that will stop their polluting of the sea it will be Jimmy's determination to create his beach. I pin my hopes on that, never mind Greenpeace. In fact my hopes for Britain in general are considerably brightened by my friendship with him. Yes, along with the pebble-dash, he is why I like Workington.

And Frank. Frank Orr is one of Jimmy's most ardent admirers and is often to be seen plodding alongside him. A short, round chap with a semi-circular bald pate, bordered with sandy hair, pixie ears and bright blue eyes, framed by sandy lashes and pink rims, he wears heavy boots and always sports a cloth cap, which he doffs to ladies. The state has not been kind to Frank. His lovingly cared-for house was compulsorily purchased and his job taken away from him, and fate dealt another vicious clout when he came across his twin brother being taken away in an ambulance after dying in the street of a heart attack. Frank is one of those men who accepts what is handed out to him with resignation. I only once saw him really upset, when I tactlessly offered to pay for a newspaper he bought me.

All his awkwardness with me disappeared on my last visit to Workington in 1986 when he got me into the now nearly completely obliterated steel plant. He was like an aristocrat in his stately home as he led me round, pointing out where the furnaces had been and describing how the slag-heaps glowed red hot and cinders from it exploded as they hit the sea behind. He showed me an overgrown lane that had been thronged with bicycles. He knew what every brick and mound had once been. He did not mourn, though. At least, not so as one could notice. His big moment of the day was when he came upon the only part of the works still in operation where a huge crane contraption was loading railway lines on to trucks. He took me up a rickety iron ladder to the top of this, and I could feel the sense of power one must get handling these great machines. How men must miss this trial of their strength and skill, outside in all weathers and dependent on each other for their safety in dangerous operations. Afterwards, as we sat chatting by the still, black cooling pool, Frank was surprised and pleased that I, a mere woman, could understand his feeling for this deserted place.

Later we were in my car at some traffic lights when somebody recognised me and shouted a greeting. As we drove off Frank said shyly, 'I've never been in a car with nobility.' It wrenched my heart. I had seldom met people more noble than Frank or Jimmy and they do not realise they are. I am proud to walk through the town with them and bask in their reflected glory as they are greeted by every single person that we pass.

Yes, that's why I like Workington. Jimmy, the pebble-dash and Frank.

And the audiences. The first night was another standing ovation. The workshop, led by the indefatigable Kath Rogers and James Simmons, was a joy. Initial shyness and inhibition was overcome by my pleading

1959, and my first attempt at a cheesecake picture. I had a lot to learn about the press

In the Swinging Sixties I was photographed in curious poses by curious young men.

Above left: Twisting with Victor Spinetti in *Make Me An Offer* at Theatre Workshop, Stratford East, 1959

Above right: The role of the refrigerator escapes my memory, but the other motley members of the cast of the ill-fated *Here Is The Nose*, 1960, are Cleo Laine, me, Valentine Dyall, Kathy Keeton, Richard Goolden and Lance Percival

Below: Kenneth Williams causing me to hesitate as he repeats some deviation to me during a charity show in the 1960s

Above left: During *The Rag Trade*, 1962: is Little Lil (Esma Cannon) weighing up Miriam and my anti-fear formulae?

Above right: My friend Dilys Laye backing me up in *The Bed-Sit Girl* in 1965, somewhat less wholeheartedly than she has always done in my private life

Below: Derek Nimmo steals my usual sit com reaction in *The Bed-Sit Girl* whilst Hy Hazell wishes she were somewhere else

Jack Hedley and I are nervous of Bette Davis in the film of *The Anniversary*

With Wallace Eaton and Arthur Lowe in classical full-flow in *The Soldier's Fortune* at the Royal Court Theatre, 1967

to the potential Franks of the world: 'Oh, don't be shy – it wastes so much time. You're lovely and special and you can shout if you want to.'

But if they will not, I will let out a little squeak on their behalf. It has not been disproved that the high incidence of leukaemia in children living around Sellafield is caused by the plant. Nor that people who work there are not equally at risk. There have been three hundred accidents in thirty-five years, some serious enough to warrant Nuclear Fuels paying large sums in compensation while still disclaiming responsibility. The fall-out from the nuclear plant explosion in Chernobyl has ironically polluted the hills of Cumbria, making their lamb uneatable and further demonstrating the potential for worldwide disaster. Since Chernobyl, Nuclear Fuels have done everything they can to brush up their image. When we went in 1983 the private police force prowled round the exterior with alsatians, the latter alone being enough to put the fear of God into me, without the weapons which the police discreetly carried. Now smart invitations are enclosed in magazines to participate in guided tours. Adverts on TV make the plant look like a sort of Disneyland set in idyllic countryside. It does look quite pretty across the fields, with its silver and blue, and, I understand, now in 1987 new three-million-pound pink buildings.

Around the time we were there, there was a flurry of adverse publicity about levels of radiation in the waste pouring into the sea from the plant, so our visit turned out to be a bit of an embarrassment at a moment when they would have preferred to lie low. They had obviously tried to keep it quiet. The few workers we bumped into seemed very surprised to see us and knew nothing about the performance, so our audience was just a few officials and stray people we had managed to round up plus a school party from Carlisle who could not get into the two main plays in Workington. This small group in the vast canteen grew smaller as several people walked out during the play, more I suspect from boredom than anger.

I had never been happy at the prospect of doing *Derek* at Sellafield, but now I was sick to my stomach. The presumption of coming to preach to people who have no choice but to work in this hideous place appalled me. In the discussion afterwards I was much more entertained by their jokes about how they light up at night and the canteen serves fish in radiation sauce than they were by our stark little play. I wished we had offered them something lovely and escapist, since they clearly knew they were being manipulated and trapped and they certainly did not need a group of actors swanning in for a few hours to point it out. I would never make an agitprop actress.

Derek is a powerfully felt piece, but in Sellafield the sentiments in it suddenly felt ridiculously naive. What the hell are people meant to do when they need work? Now there is talk of Nuclear Fuels starting up other industries in the area so their stranglehold would be complete. Of course this is how big business thrives but, when you actually see the power of it, a pathetic ballot paper seems a feeble weapon. As did our finger-wagging play. And those bloody petitions.

The policemen outside 10 Downing Street must groan when they see me approaching with yet another armful of papers. Ironically, whilst I was in Cumbria I had to dart down to London to deliver yet another anti-nuclear tome to overwork the dustmen of Westminster. Ever since the 1950s, when I was beside myself at the thought of Ruth Ellis hanging for a crime that, in my passionate youth, I identified with absolutely, I have rushed round pressing pens into people's hands and marched my feet off.

It was sobering for me to come face to face with people who are less able to be fastidious than me because their way of life would be disastrously affected by idealism. The same applied to our next town, Barrow-in-Furness.

I fortunately do not have to live in a town that builds its wealth largely on weapons. The voters of Barrow-in-Furness used the ballot box, turning from a Labour seat to a Tory one, when they suspected the Labour Party's Trident policy might threaten their prosperity, and never mind the debate about how best to keep the peace. During the Falklands War, I am sure the men who did lots of overtime working on the submarines for the battle did not share the media's view of themselves as heroes or villains: they were merely earning a crust. There are other reasons I am not keen on Barrow, however. It seems so stark in comparison to Workington, with its pompous statues to people no one in the town has heard of, its wide streets and sprawling docks. Some of the houses near the docks are nice but the outskirts of the town where we were in digs are suburban and boring, though I might have felt better about it had my bedroom been more than a tiny cell.

Although the town hall we performed in was a nasty modern place, the interior of the Victorian town hall opposite has to be seen. It is beautiful. In the room used for the Mayor's party, the grey stone walls are a perfect setting for the exquisitely carved wooden table and elegant chairs upholstered in red to match the carpet. There is a big bookcase with leather-bound minutes of past meetings, and stunning stained-glass windows. There are also some wonderful paintings and wood-carvings, but it is difficult to find out the artists' names as the brass plaques nearly all pay tribute to the donors. It is a monument to past glories and craftsmanship that must have given more satisfaction to its creators than building a killer submarine.

The unfriendliness of the environment and the industries belie the people, who gave us a great welcome. It is nice to think that by 1986 they were looking forward to building a spectacular new town centre and had a very low unemployment figure. Given the chance they would, I am sure, prefer not to make their money out of the world's quarrels, as the people of Workington would prefer to work somewhere safer than Sellafield, but one can only cope with the world as it is, and in Cumbria that is how it is. They cannot eat their own fish or lamb because it is contaminated; after the fire in Windscale in 1957 they could not drink their milk either; they cannot swim in their sea or play on their beaches; there are nuclear warheads stored under their hills and nuclear waste trundling round their railways and streets; sinister black fighter-planes shatter the silence over their beautiful countryside and they are fighting a losing battle against the army buying up more and more land from hard-pressed farmers to practise their war games on – 24,000 acres so far with another 800 threatened.

One day in 1986 I was joking with Jimmy and Frank and a few other people on a street corner in Workington about Ian MacGregor's knighthood. Tory and Labour alike, they felt this ill-timed honour was a further wound to the thousands of men his actions, right or wrong, had put out of work. As they moved off down the street, Jimmy said: 'Nice people, aren't they? They deserve better.'

They do.

7 : Roots
Bridlington, Wisbech, Milton Keynes, Woodbridge

HOLIDAY HOTELS – CLASS – WORDSWORTH – OLD AGE – MY GARDEN – THE FENS – WISBECH – ELY CATHEDRAL – NUNS – MILTON KEYNES – WOODBRIDGE – THE COUNTY SET – BRIXTON – COMPETITION – MY FATHER – MY MOTHER – MY GRANNIES – THE WAR

Several weeks' exposure to our threatened environment, the miseries of unemployment and the injustices of a divided Britain finally got the better of me. Or maybe it was, more prosaically, my miserable little bedroom in Barrow-in-Furness. Anyway, my analyst would have smirked as I ran away seeking solace for a couple of nights in one of those sybaritic hotels in the Lake District. The food in these places is nectar for fat gods and goddesses, the walks (or rather waddles) are beautiful and one is cushioned from reality by the loving concern for detail: well-chosen books and home-made biscuits in velvet boxes by the bedside, thick towelling dressing-gowns and fragrant toilet preparations in the bathroom. All of which usually soothes my troubled brow in no time. But not when I visited one in December 1983.

I made the mistake of visiting Workington before I set off for the Lakes and happened to see Frank Orr. He asked me to stay for a drink, but so anxious was I to escape to my luxury weekend that I pretended I had a pressing business engagement. As I drove off, leaving him standing on the pavement waving his cap, I felt like Judas.

The memories of the last few weeks were not as easy to dispel as I hoped and when I got to the hotel I spent a miserable twenty-four hours chewing over my curiously split life.

The tour made me acutely aware of the class differences in England. The boundaries are usually defined by money, but with Yuppiedom pushing them up and unemployment throwing them down, people are nowadays constantly moving between the classes. Yet the structure itself shows no sign of erosion. Maybe others who shift class are more able to assimilate comfortably into their new setting than I; so they settle in and maintain the boundaries. My problem may be that I do not really know what pigeon-hole I belonged to in my childhood; my roots were not very firmly planted so, being a bit feeble, they do not take kindly to transplantation.

I usually claim that I am working- or lower-middle-class because that is what I feel, but I did not really grow up in any particular category. When I was born my parents were working for a brewery. This meant the family moving from a hotel in Blackgang on the Isle of Wight to a small country pub in Berkshire, followed by the Carpenter's Arms in King's Cross. Eventually, the appalling hours and barrel-heaving for other people's profit made my father weary enough to stop that way of life and we settled in Bexleyheath, Kent, where he was employed at Vickers Armstrong as a checker – whatever that is – and my mother worked in her shop in Erith. To add to the confusion, I was evacuated for a while to Berkshire during the war and later to Somerset, and my parents ended their married life together near Eastbourne in a caravan christened 'Half Hour'.

In addition to this rootless background, as an actress I have often found myself observing life rather than participating. I can be in the middle of a dreadful row or sobbing my heart out with grief, yet part of me will be filing away gestures or inflections for future use. Similarly, I scrutinise the people around me and note their clothes and behaviour in case I should want to copy them one day. I nearly always carry a camera and, rather guiltily, a little tape-recorder that records conversations without people knowing. This is primarily to keep a record of accents, but on the tour when I had been commissioned to write this book I used it all the time, which is why I can 'remember' dialogue verbatim.

I was listening and looking a lot at dinner that night in the hotel. I did not like what I saw of my fellow guests and, what is more, I did not like what I saw of me, sitting dolled-up in the dining room greedily ploughing my way through a meal that cost enough to have fed a family in Workington for a week. And they would have appreciated the food more than the couple hating one another in the corner of the hotel restaurant, he behind his *Telegraph*, she her *Daily Mail*, forking the meticulously-prepared delicacies round their papers into indifferent mouths. As I gourmandised, I tried to concentrate on the vision through the window of the sun setting over the lake but instead became alternately hypnotised by the American on my right, who preferred to see it through various elaborate lenses of his Leica, and the elegant English gentleman withering his wife with cold looks and sharp remarks on my left. On the table behind was a local lad made good in America, returning with his wife and daughter to show them his native country and his relations back home how well he had done. And me, judging by the furtive looks to see if I was listening. He will never know how well, thanks to my trusty tape-recorder.

HUSBAND: We saw Shakespeare in Los Angeles. You know how you usually go to sleep, but this was good. *Much Ado About Nothing.*
WIFE: Oh, the one with Viola.
DAUGHTER: No, don't be silly – Rosalind.
HUSBAND: No – it's two servants.
WIFE: Oh, *Hamlet.*
HUSBAND: No, the other one.
(Puzzled pause. Me forcing a pompous interruption back in my throat with a mouthful of hazelnut meringue gateau.)
HUSBAND: That Howarth place is open tomorrow.
WIFE: Oh, where Jane Austen lived.
HUSBAND: Don't be silly. Emma Bronte. Jane Austen was a character in her book.
WIFE: Oh, what did she write then?
HUSBAND: *Little Women.*

This was the final *petit four.* After a sleepless night full of food and self-disgust at my critical attitude towards people who on acquaintance would probably be perfectly nice, I decided to move for my second night off to a cheap guest house in Derwentwater, which I also visit occasionally. Although I miss the luxury of the other hotels I am more at home with the guests there.

They take me back to the only two weeks' holiday I had with my parents as a child. The guests in those boarding houses at Ramsgate and Herne Bay then were exactly the same as those at Derwentwater now. One sits in a small dining room in awkward silence as the nice landlord proudly serves his wife's cooking, and the highest compliments he receives are, 'Blimey, that's too much for me,' 'What are you trying to do? Make me fatter than I am?,' 'Go on then – if you want to get rid of it,' and all the other things that people unused to the good life say to cover their embarrassment at indulging themselves. Anyway, the men do not feel too happy in their new short-sleeved shirts, nor the women in their floral prints and dirndl skirts: the couples do not talk a lot, except in whispers; there is often an old husband and wife with a middle-aged single daughter or son (why have they never left home?); and there are frequently lone men of indeterminate age who go off with their packed lunches in knapsacks on endless hikes in heavy boots and well-worn shorts – I wonder if they like it or are too chronically shy to ask someone to go with them. Certainly they redden and back off if anyone talks to them.

The guests in Derwentwater are mainly from Frank's world where you do not complain – the silent majority, I suppose. When I went back in 1986 I noticed the superb bronze beech in the garden was withered. The landlady explained it had started dying after the rain in May, the time of the Chernobyl fall-out. My suggestions of protest and demands for compensation were greeted with resigned shrugs and smiles. That is the trouble with the world today, I urged – too much shrugging, too much silence from the majority. But I recognised the pattern. After a lifetime of being bombarded with phrases like, 'Don't step out of line,' 'Keep your head down', 'Don't blow your own trumpet,' 'Blessed are the meek,' and 'Little girls should be seen and not heard,' they have learned to 'Know their place' and 'Be thankful for small mercies.'

The two-day break did not do much to improve my jaundiced outlook. I found it difficult to 'look on the bright side' as I drove away from the Lake District in 1983. I tried to make light of the planes sweeping overhead and the notices warning about 'Shelled Areas'. Stopping for a while, I strived to recapture the joy of Wordsworth and his friends as I surveyed his 'valley, rock or hill'. But I could merely spew up a parody of the only poem of his I know by heart.

ON WESTMINSTER BRIDGE

Earth has not anything to show more dire:
Dull must he be of sense who cannot be
Depressed, appalled by its sordidity:
This city now doth like a giant drain
Swallow the small grey people; antlike, plain.
Ships, towers, domes, theatres and temples lie
Open unto the fumes that choke the sky;
All dull and crumbling in the acid rain.
Never did sun more miserably steep
In his first splendour rocks and crevices
Never say I, ne'er felt a grief so deep

At what a disgusting pigs' trough this is.
Dear God! we cannot live in this dung heap
So all of London's turned to offices!

Mercifully, the route I then took towards our next venue, Bridlington, is a certain cure for pessimism. A tape of anything by Elgar, the A684, the B6160 plus detours down various lanes into the fells and dales could put Librium out of business. I defy anyone to have a cup of coffee from a thermos, leaning against a dry-stone wall, surrounded by nature's slag-heaps, listening to a clear stream eddying over white stones, a lark ascending, and not be convinced that, despite everything, one is truly blessed to be born in such a country.

The blowing of dirty cobwebs from my mind was furthered by the sea breezes – well, gales – of Bridlington. Usually the English seaside town out of season is not the most uplifting place, but I welcomed the huge, empty beach and echoing hotel where we stayed. With the crashing sea and buffeting wind outside, we huddled together in the hotel and I realised how truly fond I had grown of my little band of hopers; any disaffection lingering from Belfast disappeared into the ether.

I feasted on the windswept freshness of the young members of the company, which contrasted sharply with the looks of the residents in the hotel who were patiently sitting out their old age with library books and telly in the lounge. Robert looked like a boy in comparison and I decided there and then that I would not grow old gracefully. If, unlike Robert, I get too gaga to learn lines any more I shall be a bag-lady and trail round shouting obscenities at people, laughing raucously at secret jokes. I have practised the part. In 1959 I was in a revue at the old Lyric Theatre, Hammersmith (and, later, the Apollo, Shaftesbury Avenue) called *One to Another* in which Beryl Reid and I did a sketch about two old lady tramps in a cafe. It was one of the first pieces written by Harold Pinter, with whom I had acted in repertory in the 1950s at another seaside town – Torquay. In my research for this sketch I went regularly to a stall down on the Embankment, near Charing Cross, where the homeless congregate. I got quite fond of the old woman I found to base my characterisation on for the sketch and, despite the appalling deprivation, I think I would be better cast as her when I am old than as a lady sedately waiting to die in some seaside or spa town.

When you pass the fifty mark you do start thinking of things like that. Either you accept old age and plan to enjoy it or you fight it tooth and nail. I periodically tackle those books like *Ageless Ageing, Stay Young For*

Ever, Wrinkles Away, and for a few weeks rattle with vitamin pills, walking decreasingly briskly to Chiswick High Road and back. But eventually I get into the car and let everything sag, only putting it all into place with make-up and will-power when I perform. I cannot actually believe I am getting old anyway. It is only when I catch sight of my reflection in a shop window that I realise I am not the same as I was ten years ago. I equally find it difficult to believe that one day I shall not be here at all. But my children will. And my garden.

On a visit to a house of friends in Ullswater I was wandering alone in the garden, calmed by its camomile lawn and nooks and crannies with statues and rare plants, when I clearly felt the presence of another woman. Just a warm friendly feeling that she was there. When I mentioned this, I was told that the garden was indeed created by a woman about a hundred years ago. Deciding I would like such pleasant vibrations of myself to be left behind, I asked my husband for a garden for my fiftieth birthday present. I like to think that some space-age Chiswick native around the year 2200 will know that a frightened woman in 1983 wanted to give them a present. When they read the inscription on the mosaic grotto: 'The best in this kind are but shadows,' I hope they will know their *Midsummer Night's Dream* sufficiently well to know that the woman was an actress. I may drift about a bit but my plants' roots are firmly bedded. My mid-life garden is my gesture towards posterity. As I sow and nurture defiantly, I convince myself that the world will have to go on so that my seeds can flourish. And what about the withered beech tree at Derwentwater? Ah, well, yes – shrug, shrug.

The grafting of my touring company on to the main tree of the RSC was proving at this point more difficult than any transplant in my garden. (My devices to link back from my ramblings to the main story have not improved as this book continues!)

One of my conditions for withdrawing my resignation had been that the company should form a part of the next Stratford season. This was to ensure that the public were seeing a true RSC company and not one formed for the tour and then disbanded, and also to make sure the actors had a taste of the comparative luxury of the main company after their travels. Nasty rumours began to reach us in Bridlington that casting was going on in London and I suspected we were forgotten. I sent some melodramatic memos and got some angry ones back. The usual planning muddle was going on back at base, and my protests that the touring company should be playing all the parts were not a lot of help.

I suspect it is very easy to get things out of proportion in the Fens, through which I travelled after a quick run home to our next venue, Wisbech. For a start there is the sky. When you are used to cities you do not notice the sky a lot, and even on my recent journey over the Dales it was broken by hills, but in the Fens the sky engulfs you in its grey or steel-blue from horizon to horizon. Winter is the best time to go there when the absolutely flat countryside is a murky palette of midnight blue, blacks, greys and purples, occasionally arched by a technicolour wide-screen sunset. It is awe-inspiring and sinister, this relentless landscape, only softened by the sinuous whistling sedges that wave by the straight roads. Every spring millions of elvers, after their two to three-year journey from the distant Saragossa Sea, make their way up the long, straight, man-made rivers called uncompromisingly Twenty Foot Drain or Hundred Foot Drain, or more colourfully Bevill's Leam or Crescent Ouse – fitting names for these strange waterways raised in banks above the roads and writhing with eels. There is nothing but the odd, straggly black tree and isolated harsh, square house or chapel above ground level, but what squirmings and oozings go on below the surface on this reclaimed swamp.

As I drove around on my first day, with Britten's *Les Illuminations* on my tape-recorder, I conjured up visions of strange happenings in Prickwillow, Walsoken, Uggmere, Witchford and Grunty Fen. Occasionally I saw a small group of figures, made heavy by layers of woollens and gumboots and strange black plastic aprons, with the only apparent difference between the sexes being the women's headscarves. Work in the fields would stop as they glowered at my alien MG cackling along the deserted single tracks I strayed on to and, curious though I was about their lives, I was glad it did not have one of its turns and chug to a halt in this weird landscape. They probably go home after work and watch *Coronation Street*, but it is difficult not to think of *Cold Comfort Farm*.

The weird landscape does not prepare one for Wisbech. It seems incongruous to find elegant eighteenth-century houses alongside a gentle river built on an ancient bog. Just as the ordered architecture seems to be trying to suppress the mire beneath, so too do the natives – from Squire Clarkson, a resident of 1760, who fought against slavery, to Victoria Gillick in the 1980s with her fight against contraceptives for young people. As one of the first girls I saw there had a T-shirt with 'LUST' emblazoned on her wobbling bosom and Wisbech has trouble with gang warfare, Mrs Gillick's campaign to reassert parental authority seems less than successful in her home town.

This was the only town where the local residents who acted as ushers wore evening dress, and very nice they looked too. But the one image I recall when thinking of Wisbech is of a couple who were dining in our hotel one night. She had many chins, metal glasses, newly set hair and was wearing an over-tight dress in black voile with large pink roses. He had ears that stuck out as if the Fen gales had always been behind him, and was wearing a spacious ginger rough tweed coat. They were having none of the problems I have in adjusting to up-market surroundings. Both their faces were red and blotchy with wine and they gleefully told me that a man for whom he, Jack, did odd jobs had treated them to this unaccustomed night out for their wedding anniversary. As I bade them goodnight I had little doubt they would have one when I saw her little fat naked foot edging up his trouser leg while she stated firmly for all to hear, 'I wanna go to bed.' A sexy place is Wisbech. Believing as I do that environment is bound to influence you, it is interesting to speculate on the effect of the pulsating place which men and women have fought for generations to control.

No greater symbol of this battle is to be found than the great Ship of the Fens – Ely Cathedral. From miles away you can see this sturdy giant squatting in the waves of rustling grasses and black furrows, its heavy exterior belying the soaring delicacy inside. The highest point is the four-hundred-ton wood and lead octagonal tower, seemingly suspended on nothing; six hundred years ago craftsmen managed to invent and raise this miracle. The removal of the stone Norman choir in 1769 may have been a bit crass, but it leaves a stunning long high nave topped by a colourful ceiling, painted by 'two amateurs in 1858-61', as the brochure scathingly reports. It looks all right to me, but then I quite like a touch of the amateur in great buildings – for instance, the two dopey faces in Joan Littlewood woolly hats who stare in blank amazement from the corners of an arch by the Prior's door.

The people who run the church now are far from amateur. You cannot enter God's house without paying one pound fifty, plus eighty pence to see the stained-glass. As you wander round this ancient heritage a tannoy raucously drums up trade by reminding you, 'There are still a few tickets left for the tour', and counting it down like a theatre-call system. 'The tour will start in half an hour, fifteen minutes, ten minutes, a few minutes, is about to . . .'

All told, the atmosphere is not conducive to reverence. The sound system, combined with the electric polisher at work on the floor, probably drowned out my laughter, albeit wry, at the hideous wrought-iron table-lamps that stood in niches built to house holy statues in one of the chapels. I also chortled a bit at the thought of a Bishop Hugh, and even more at a Bishop Nigel who saw to it that he was comfortably settled by sending to Tourai for a sort of carved soft feather blanket on which to lie on his tomb. Bishop Gunning, leaning on one elbow, legs delicately positioned, is one of the campest stone gentlemen I have ever seen. It seemed to make absolute sense that he is credited with inventing the prayer, 'For all sorts and conditions of men'. By this time, in this unquiet place, everything began to seem ridiculous. Even the huge bell, brought here after it fell from its tower in 1898 in a place called Feltwell (which presumably anybody standing underneath it had not). By the time I reached a certain William Hodge Mill, crammed in between the shop door and the postcards, lying, hands desperately clasped in prayer, I was convinced that the two young men kneeling at the bottom of his bed were poised thus with heads fastidiously averted not so much because they were engrossed in the gospels, but rather because his feet smelt.

Since I was myself being sacrilegious it was strange that I was so shocked by the decapitated angels and sword slashes in the stonework of the Lady Chapel, violated by other disbelievers in 1539. I was equally appalled in 1986 when the Dean and Chapter of Ely were only just prevented from becoming property developers by Paul Getty when he discovered they were about to obliterate the centuries-old view of the cathedral by building houses in a field nearby. You cannot have your wafer and eat it, Sheila. The building costs money: they have to raise it. And if that offends your atheist sensibilities, hard luck. The acid rain eating away the ancient stones does not bother about taste. Yet surely we owe it to our ancestors to respect their work. They built a place of stillness and nobody should spoil it. We should not make it tawdry.

According to my dad's encyclopedia, that word – tawdry – is derived from the cheap goods sold at the fair, held in the religious house for men and women founded by St Etheldreda, ie St Awdry, on the site of the cathedral. The 'ie' seems a bit far-fetched, and my father's encyclopedia also says that she was renowned for her love of chastity; which, as she had two husbands and a rather suspect 'faithful' steward called Ovin, I think we can take with a pinch of Saxon salt. One of her parents, however, was definitely Anna, King of East Anglia; which would account for a lot. Anyway, Ethel or Audrey sounds rather jolly with her mixed monastery but, of course, the men soon put paid to that and in 970, after the Danes had knocked it down and killed them all off, the Benedictines moved in and it became men only. Things have not changed much in the Church since then.

I have a soft spot for Ethel as I went to her convent in Ely Place in Holborn when I was a child. My first school was another convent in King's Cross where the nuns frightened me so much that, after several attempts to drag me physically up the hill to school, my father gave in and sent me to St Etheldreda's instead. I do not know quite why they chose a convent for their daughters as we were not Catholic, but the nuns in Ely Place were great fun and would cuddle me on their laps in the glass booth at the back of the chapel during services because the incense made me sick.

I am still intrigued by nuns. Indeed, I am intrigued by any women who want to belong to a Church that so obviously thinks we are inferior, or whatever it is that makes us unfit to give the sacraments. There is an enclosed order of nuns called the Barefoot Nuns in Jávea, Spain, whose convent is right in the middle of the busy town, but they are not allowed to see anyone. You can only glimpse them when their black shapes flit across an iron grille as they receive the wine during communion (from a man); and only talk to them through a wooden wall, below which is a revolving counter on which they will send round delicious almond cakes and invitations to join their order. I have been sorely tempted, if only to find out if they are cavorting not merely barefoot but bare everything else in the dark recesses of that secret place. No one will ever know, but they sound quite content with their female world of devotion. The builders of Ely had the same dedication when they sweated over their magnificent cathedral, putting to shame our fee of one pound to photograph it on a tripod and the need to charge it. One way and another our history has become a sad burden to us – what with Ireland, our colonies, an outmoded Industrial Revolution and our ancient buildings too costly to maintain. (All those good men and true, full of enterprise, striving for progress and excellence. Is it worth it, Maggie?)

It was refreshing after Ely to go to a town with no history before 1971 – blatant in its modernity. Milton Keynes makes no ancient bones about it: it is new, new, new. They cock a snook at the past by calling their wide functional streets in the town centre Saxon and Silbury, but they also have the practical names of V1-10 and H1-10 for the grid system in which the roads are designed. The houses are grouped in districts off these main thoroughfares so that only local traffic enters them. And what houses. No mock Tudor or Regency and very little uniformity. Original and daring designs abound, set always amid luxuriantly planted trees and shrubs. Milton Keynes is one of those names like Scunthorpe and East Cheam that prompts snide jokes. Scunthorpe nowadays belies its name; I cannot answer for East Cheam, but Milton Keynes certainly wiped the sneers from my lips.

When we went it was just before Christmas, and I even ate my words about shopping complexes when I sampled the joys of getting all my presents in the comfort and, yes, beauty of the one in Milton Keynes. Its soaring windows and wide marbled arcades lined with cacti and perfumed plants give the impression of being outside, whilst you remain warm and comfortable. There is an attractive outdoor eating place in the centre and little groups of tables throughout the arcades that are rather like French pavement cafes. The designers of Milton Keynes have obviously incorporated ideas from other countries, including calling their streets in the city centre boulevards. Avebury Boulevard says it all, I think. And they have a Buddhist Peace Pagoda in memory of the people who died in Hiroshima. Any town that has that and concrete cows has got to have my vote. Their architecture is superb, their horticulture magnificent and they have just built a stunning entertainment centre that has ten cinemas, bingo hall, disco and a nightclub, but significantly no theatre. We performed in a sports complex and Milton Keynes was the only place in Britain where the public were not falling over themselves to see us.

This lack of interest in a new and lively town made me think. Perhaps it has some message for the future of theatre, not to mention our society. Maybe when you are young and upwardly mobile you have no time for Shakespeare (although there is no indication that they have more time for the modern plays either). When a Government is leading the way by putting more money into technical colleges and science whilst starving the Arts, you will eventually end up with a society that follows suit. Maybe it does not matter. I like to think that Shakespeare will still be played somewhere in the world long after Milton Keynes is another Silbury or Avebury mound, but that is only my choice. Anyway, probably the lack of interest was because the local promotion was lax. On my arrival a miserable girl on the desk of the leisure centre where we were to appear did not know which part of the building the RSC were in or, indeed, what 'club' they were. Moira then told me that *Derek* had been cancelled 'for lack of interest', as I scowled at the palm trees in the leisure pool.

Much as I liked modern Milton Keynes, it was quite a relief to move on to Woodbridge where things were less flashy and more welcoming. The pace here was comfortably slow. Woodbridge has been there for several centuries and this farming community is used to working to the timetable set by the seasons. In every regard it is the antithesis of Milton

Keynes. Its roads wind up and down hills. No special 'redways' for cycles and pedestrians here, just four-foot-wide pavements and cars with good brakes on busy days. Nothing so vulgar as a shopping precinct, just a group of elegant boutiques round a fountain. It is a very pretty town, with houses from all periods so immaculately painted in soft pinks, yellows and Wedgwood greens and blues that it looks like an advert for Snowcem; they could give the natives of Workington a tip or two – or a bob or two. People do not walk purposefully, as in Milton Keynes; they stroll in their green wellies – and green trousers and green jumpers with leather patches.

My digs were a small hotel frequented by the horsey and boating set and I spent many happy hours hidden in a corner listening to their conversations. Earwigging being my favourite occupation, I picked up some gems in Woodbridge:

'I say, you've been working our Tim a bit hard.'

'Have to, old boy. He thinks manual labour is some president of a South American country.'

And:

'I hear your gardener broke a couple of fingers at the match this afternoon.'

'Did he? . . . Oh my God, I hope it's not his weeding hand.'

Queen Victoria's statue that overlooks this hotel must have blinked a bit at some of the stories about 'Good old Gloria' and other colourful boaters and gallopers. There was one particular saga involving two couples and the movement of a yacht in rough seas that made one wonder about Mrs Thatcher's Victorian values being upheld in this Conservative stronghold seat of John Gummer, no less.

I have always been suspicious of the horsey set since I encountered a Major Trumble at Ventnor, who tried to teach me to ride whilst I was appearing in concert party at Sandown in the 1950s. He had a broad-buttocked assistant who nursed a lust for the Major under her hacking jacket and a consequent growing resentment towards me as he flirtatiously tried to teach this useless actress how to master her mount. I reasoned that if I was nice to the horse it would respond in kind, like any normal human being, so I let it have the odd nibble of grass and tried not to wallop its belly too hard with my heels. Three-year-old children cantered past me as I vainly tried to lift my munching horse's head from the ground. As they disappeared into the mists of Ventnor downs, I would hear the Major bellow: 'Imagine there is a forest fire and r-i-i-i-i-de.'

My steed had no sense of the dramatic and one day on top of the Ventnor downs I was, as usual, muttering, 'Come on – nice horse – you've had enough now – trot on or something,' when suddenly, from out of the low-flying clouds, appeared Major Trumble's secret love. Without a word she gave my horse a wallop on his bum that sent him hurtling off at a gallop. Which I had not yet learned. That vicious animal took me through overhanging branches, down a perpendicular hill, through a stream and over a gate and finally threw me in a mangled heap at Major Trumble's feet, to the mocking cry of, 'Well done, girl' from his love. Horses went on my list, along with dogs, from that day forward.

I simply cannot understand the devotion people have to brutes that only respond to force, and take advantage of the weakness of others. But devoted some people are. I never, when young, shared my daughters' and other little girls' love of ponies and pretty donkeys. I was, however, when grown-up, fascinated by the tales told in my Gloucestershire village of whips, spurs and frilly knickers found under the ancestral beds of the local gentry. It is usually impossible to know what is going on in 'the country set' unless you are part of it, and for that you have to be born into it. No class is more difficult to penetrate. The horse trials at Badminton and the polo at Cirencester are like vast club outings. The local papers' wedding and engagement pages show the interbreeding between the horsey set and the occasional change of partners among polo players. The huntin', shootin' and boatin' brigade of Woodbridge, like those in Gloucestershire, have the same determination to cling to their life-style as any mining community. Witness how the residents of nearby Fulbeck have picketed and demonstrated when threatened with nuclear-waste dumps. Anyone would want to preserve the charm of Woodbridge, too. Not all, perhaps, as short-sightedly as my landlady, who said: 'Yes, it's a nice little town. Unspoilt. No high-rise, no vandals, no graffiti and, I'm not biased, but no blacks swamping us.'

However, the residents seemed to welcome the Americans from the local bases swamping the town on occasions. (The estimated $222,000,000 they contribute to the local Suffolk economy probably has something to do with that.) Yet I remember a time during the war when the GIs' presence was deeply resented. 'Over here, overpaid and oversexed' was the phrase, I believe. I thought they were lovely with their gum ('Got any gum, chum?') badges, nylon stockings for my sister and life-savers, precursors of the polo mint; but most grown-ups treated them with suspicion as well as derision for their sloppy marching and uniforms. There were no black soldiers round our way, so I too had never seen a black man until my teens, except being servile or ridiculous in films.

While I was shopping in Woodbridge one day a black woman and child walked down the street. Watching people throwing curious, furtive glances at them I was reminded that there are still parts of England that hardly ever see other than a white face. Their perception of our black population is obviously therefore going to be what they read or see in the media. The children will not have been educated like Joanna in a multi-racial school. I got to know a lot more about Brixton when I spent a month – day and night – filming on a council estate there, and it would be difficult to find more different roots for children than pretty Woodbridge and that neglected place.

The country folk would not relish the pungent smell of disinfectant trying to mask the smell of urine in the stair-wells. The garages in the middle of the rubbish-strewn courtyards, with metal doors jagged as if broken into with tin openers; the piles of garbage spilling out of the dustbins that are hardly ever emptied, for which the rats and mice are truly grateful, not to mention the marauding packs of dogs; the appalling lack of privacy, where walls are so thin you cannot make love or go to the lavatory without your neighbours knowing and where you listen to the man in the top flat's reggae all day long whether you dig it or not. The protection from the outside world in Woodbridge is all-over net curtains. In one of the flats in Brixton in which we filmed it is nails below the skylight, a driving mirror strategically placed and a sharpened knife stuck in the door jamb.

Although the country set seems to dominate, it is of course only a part of the population of Woodbridge. We were told of the 'Yob and Snob' element, meaning the state and independent schools, but both were equally charming to work with and perform to. The plays went wonderfully, particularly *Derek*, which I put down to more resentment of the surrounding bases than was obvious on the surface.

The beautiful environment was reflected in another project I had set up for the tour – a poster competition. In every town we asked the children to design advertisements for the plays, and it was extraordinary how they varied from town to town. By far the prettiest pictures were in Woodbridge. The standard was excellent, the colours pleasing and tasteful like the town. Quite different in style, for instance, from the equally good but strident pictures in the Castleford competition.

There is much talk nowadays about whether competition is bad for children. It did not seem to do much harm to the delighted and proud winners of the competition in Woodbridge (nor to the intensely competitive Peter Hall and Trevor Nunn, both Suffolk boys). I would venture to suggest that competition is fine as long as everyone wins at something. At school I could not cope with any sports. I could hack my way up the left wing via other girls' shins in hockey, but in netball I hardly ever touched the ball. Also, in those agonising tests that pubescent girls put themselves through – even, I believe, in these liberated times – such as who has got the best hair, eyes, legs, nose (oh help), teeth, knees, I was lucky to win on eyebrows. But I won friends and influenced people by inventing good games for the playground and improvising plays and wild dances when rain forced us indoors for 'wet break'. I would strip off my tunic and, in regulation green woollen school knickers and white liberty bodice, whirl into frightening excesses inciting my overexcited fellow pupils into accompanying me with clapping and desk-banging. Maybe that was why my school report one year said: 'Sheila is a born leader but must be careful to lead the right way.'

I was reminded of all this when I drove up to our next venue at Margate via the Dartford Tunnel, passing one of my old schools on the way. I remembered my father's ecstatic reaction when I rushed to him outside the factory gates at Vickers Armstrong in Crayford to tell him I had won a scholarship to the grammar school. He was a great one for competition. If I told him I was second in an exam there were no congratulations, merely, 'Who was top?' Not first – top. But I would never have achieved even the little I have without my father's blazing belief that I could do anything and his incitements to 'Show 'em, girl.' Both he and my mother seemed to have no personal ambitions at all. They were still under the rule of the Derwentwater code themselves but, however fearful they were for us in the big world, they were determined that we should break it. So they pushed us hard. When I *was* top in anything there were kisses and tears and cuddles aplenty. Which is probably why, when my father died in 1965, the bottom fell out of my world. I felt there was no one left to please. Everything I ever did until I was thirty-two was mainly to see my father's pleasure. More than my mother, because her reaction was more restrained.

Maybe it was because he was born and spent his young childhood in Italy that he was far more effusive than other girls' dads. He laughed till he cried and cried till he laughed. He seldom finished a joke, so convulsed would he be with the telling of it. The sight of him spluttering and weeping with laughter, doubling up and groaning weakly, 'Oh Christ', would have my sister and I rolling on the carpet. Equally would we laugh when, particularly after a few drinks, he would get incoherent with sentiment and yet more tears would cascade into his sodden overworked cotton handkerchief. After every first night I would wait with bated breath for his tear-stained face to burst into my dressing room – the bigger the success, the more he cried. After *Rattle of a Simple Man* he hung himself round the elegant shoulders of my startled producer, Michael Codron, sobbing, 'Well, boy? What about my girl? What about her, then? Aren't you lucky?'

His rendering of 'Pale Hands I Loved' at family parties, with my mother at the piano holding long pauses and ritardandi while he emoted, left not a dry eye in the room – particularly his. And frequently duets with her, such as 'If You Were the Only Girl in the World', would peter off into maudlin silence, causing my mother to break off, mid-melody, with, 'Pull yourself together, Rick'. He did have a fine voice, which he put down partly to the fact that Caruso was supposed to be his godfather. This also accounted for his exotic first name, Enrico, which went uneasily with the second, Cameron, particularly mysterious there being no more Scots than Italian blood in his veins.

When he was behind the bar in the pubs he had a good outlet for his exuberance, but I think working in a place like Vickers and living in a road of identical semi-detacheds in Bexleyheath must have come hard to him when ill-health forced him out of his limelight. But he still lived his life at full tilt, and his originality shone through. Whilst every other garden in Latham Road, Bexleyheath, in those days had a neat lawn with regular flower beds, Daddy devised a remarkable sunken affair, all crazy-paving and irregular shapes and angles. I was his willing labourer as he broke up pavement slabs and dug up holes and sifted earth, the better to grow unusual plants. I loved the squelchy puddings of sand, cement and water and the to-ing and fro-ing with wheelbarrows. His passion for his garden drove him to the only relatively dishonest act I believe he ever committed. In the next street to us was a big empty property, rapidly going derelict, which had a beautiful stone bird-bath – unusual, ornate and a perfect centrepiece for Dad's Bexleyheath Tivoli Gardens. Uncharacteristically, he must have stolen it in the dead of night before somebody else did. I do not think he was ever too happy about it, though. Two years ago I returned to No 58 to try to get it for my new garden. There was my father's creation as perfect as the day he finished it. All that hard core and spirit levelling had stood the test of time. But the bird-bath had gone. The present inhabitants had thought it a bit of an eyesore and, only a few weeks before my visit, had yanked it out and sent it to a tip. I went back to my car and cried my eyes out. I did not risk asking if the rest of the garden would later follow suit and I shall never dare to go back and find out.

Tastes change. It is all patios and space to park your car now. Subsequent residents of No 58 were not to know when they got rid of the shed in the garden of the happy hours we spent together there, repairing things, cleaning shoes daily with a neat collection of brushes and dusters and pungent polishes, silently enjoying each other's company. I have since wondered whether the elation I felt with my father in that womb-like retreat was anything to do with the glue that was frequently bubbling away in the black iron pot, but I am sure it was more to do with my young awareness that here was a good man, gentle and true.

His temperament would, I suspect, have been more out of control had it not been for the check of my mother's stability. I took part in a series of TV programmes examining the relationship of mother and daughter, and, under expert grilling from Bel Mooney, discovered how little I really knew of my mother. She was always there, caring, picking up pieces, utterly reliable. But, looking back, I realise that the beautiful young girl in the photos had her youth blighted by one World War and her married life by the other. She worked in a flower shop and as a barmaid as a girl, and there was talk of a boyfriend killed in the First World War. There was a first baby that was born dead. I only discovered this when I asked her to attend a concert in a church hall in Bexleyheath where she had also spent the early years of her marriage. She calmly refused my invitation, explaining that when she had lost her baby she had gone to some ritual at the church for women called Churching. The other mothers were there with their new babies and one can only imagine the pain of this young, empty-armed girl when the vicar gave her no word of comfort. Like the Derwentwater guests she did not complain. She just never returned.

I know nothing about her education but she was skilled at many things. She made most of our clothes, cooked well, played the piano and sang, and was a superb organiser. She had to be – keeping a house with no modern machines, only a mangle and a washboard, as well as working from nine to five six days a week in various jobs and, of course, much longer hours when she ran the pubs with Dad. On top of that she looked after both my grandmothers.

In our small house in Bexleyheath when they were both alive, Nannie Woodward had the box room and the lounge was turned into a bedroom for Grandma Hancock who had ideas above her station. It was an endless bone of contention that, because Nannie Woodward had been careful with her meagre earnings and had a little 'put by', she received no help from the state, whereas Grandma Hancock, who had never worked in her life and sailed around in a rather moth-eaten fur tippet, did. On top of that Grandma Hancock was forgetful. She would go to the cinema every afternoon to see the same film, behaving like visiting royalty with the manager; he would relate all this to Nannie who would in turn report the latest madness of that 'silly bitch' to my mother. Grandma Hancock was also apt to do stately dances with the children in the streets and announce to all and sundry that my mother was poisoning her.

I do not know how my mother bore this turmoil. There was no TV or car to take her mind off things. The wireless and piano were some solace, but she must have been damn glad to get to work where she had her own identity and could laugh with her friends. She did have Daddy, though. He must have been hell to handle but he worshipped the ground she walked on. The few times my father hit me were because I had worried or hurt my mother with my superior grammar school ways. It was a true love affair. When my father died suddenly of a heart attack, my mother had one brief anguished weep, then got on with arranging the funeral. But despite the cheerful surface I am sure that the cancer that was to kill her two years later started eating away her life from the minute he went. She hardly mentioned my father after his funeral, but a few days before she died she sat up in bed and said in her old firm voice: 'Now wait a minute, Rick – I have things to do – I'll be with you as soon as I can.' I would like to believe it was not just the drugs that held out this promise of a reunion.

I only once saw my mother less able to cope than my father. I was six when the fatal 'No such undertaking' announcement was made over the wireless. The lurching siren that followed immediately after the declaration of war made my mother grab my sister and I and rush around in an untypical panic. Mummy had always spent thunder storms trembling in the cupboard under the stairs, so for her the thought of air-raids was horrific. Daddy had only got as far as digging a hole for a bomb shelter and obtaining some railway sleepers. He sat us in the hole, dragged the sleepers over by some superhuman effort and started to pile earth on top of them. I have never been so frightened in my life as I was sitting on that wet soil with earth and stones raining down on my head, watching my mother cry. Even at six years old, the fear of the unknown was worse for me than the reality. Although that was pretty grim, I suppose. Being in close proximity to Vickers and Woolwich Arsenal, as well as on the route to London, Bexleyheath was in the midst of the defence system. The sky was very soon grey with barrage balloons, there were strange black tubes down the road that were supposed to send up smoke screens, and searchlights and a mobile gun were stationed near us. My poor mother preferred the intermittent bombs to that 'sodding gun'. My father was in the ARP, not being fit or young enough for the services. He prowled the streets with his shaded torch, bellowing, 'Put that light out' to any trespasser of the black-out rules. That inky blackness was very ominous to me as I stumbled down the garden to the shelter with my siren suit over my pyjamas when the warning went. Even now I leap out of bed in those towns where the old air-raid siren is used as a fire alarm, and am dressed before it has even started its first glissando. There is a sort of purr that happens before that which links up with some antenna in my guts that sends messages to the rest of my body, before my brain has a chance to reason that the war has been over for forty-two years.

When we eventually got a more comfortable Anderson shelter made of corrugated iron and equipped with bunks and a wooden floor made by my father, and the raids became more frequent, we slept down the shelter all night and did our lessons down big shelters all day. In fact, for one period during the war the only time we surfaced was to scuttle in crocodiles to school with our helmets and gas masks on our back, guarded by a teacher or parent.

I did not mind the raids very much. I enjoyed the singsongs we had down the shelters to drown the sound of the bombs and guns. I used to entertain my class with impersonations of Evelyn Laye, Ciceley Courtenidge and Suzette Tarri, none of whom they had heard of, nor I seen. But I had seen Florence Desmond impersonating them. I was on safer ground with Vera Lynn and Petula Clark. I also loved collecting shrapnel, especially when I found machine-gun and shell cases. When the doodlebugs started I enjoyed taking my turn on watch, ready to blow my whistle if one was approaching. I liked less the deathly pause when the engines cut out and everyone ducked, fingers crossed, waiting for it to land. I liked watching the dogfights in daylight, with Spitfires ducking and weaving and little puffs of smoke dotting the sky. I did not mind at all that our roof kept being blown off and the windows shattered. The night before I sat my scholarship exam, after an all-clear had blown on a dreadful raid and I could not sleep, my mother took me indoors, shook the debris off the dusky pink eiderdown and cuddled me in her double bed, stroking my forehead as I stared at the stars through a hole in the rafters. In those days, just before the Education Act, I had to pass that exam to get the education she dreamed of for me but could not afford.

I was inordinately proud when my sister joined ENSA and felt then I could hold my own with my friends whose fathers and brothers were away in the forces – and her uniform was nicer too. When any of these brothers and fathers were reported missing I thought it was only temporary, like the fountain pens and rubbers I lost. They would turn up again.

One did – after the war. We had the street parties, and on VE night my Auntie Ruby took me up to Shooters Hill and I saw the flickering lights all over London. Our parents danced round the bonfires in the streets, people wept and laughed, the bunting was stretched between the lamp posts and the Union Jacks hung out over the pebble-dash. A little while later the Fricker boy came back from a Japanese war camp. He had been fond of me as a little girl and I was asked to talk to him. He sat, staring at me blankly, a silent stranger, and I saw with my twelve-year-old eyes that there was really nothing to celebrate.

There is no doubt that these six war years left scars on all of us, of whatever age. They are probably deeper than I care to think. Superficially, I have a facial twitch, acquired during the bombing, which still returns when I feel insecure. I know my NHS number off by heart because it was also my identity number during the war. Logic and liberalism apart, I can never altogether love the Germans or Japanese and I always sleep with my right hand above my head as a result of having it constantly on the escape hatch spanner in the shelter in case a German bailed out in our garden. On the positive side, I have a strong streak of self-preservation and a firm belief that little people can take on mighty powers and survive more or less intact.

All this childhood reminiscence has managed to leave me stranded between Woodbridge and Margate, but at this half-way mark in the book I find my thoughts more often wandering away from the tour.

8 : Bullies and Comforters
Margate and Tiverton

BULLYING – ECCENTRICS – CASTING FOR THE MAIN COMPANY
– CHRISTMAS – THE COUNTRY – EVACUATION – WALLINGFORD
– CREWKERNE – DANCING LEDGE – TIVERTON – DARTMOOR –
DAME CICELY SAUNDERS – MY MOTHER'S DEATH – ALEC'S
DEATH – LOSS OF FAITH – GREENHAM

As I have gone round the country I have become uneasily aware that there are some people who are being, for want of a better word, bullied. Maybe it has always been there – this bullying. Maybe because of my determination to see for myself some of the things I was reading in the papers, I was picking brains and accosting strangers even more than I usually do. So, maybe I was just more aware of it. But I do not think so. At least, I do not think that in my parents' day bullying was admired. Not like now. By some.

'I will do anything to make their lives hell,' bayed Thatcher, when a pathetic group of drop-outs tried to reach Stonehenge for some silly ceremony in the summer of 1986. We were all outraged when they damaged another Englishman's castle. Laws were changed, squads of police descended. Good old Maggie. Teachers and miners that I met were amongst those branded 'The Enemy Within'. I talked to men and women with a sincere dedication to the socialism we are now incited to 'eliminate' because 'it is alien to the British way of life'. I have seen people described in a paper as 'middle-class, middle-aged hooligans' when they peacefully demonstrated against the dumping of nuclear waste under their houses in Fulbeck. It is only too easy to agree that the DHSS fiddlers are despicable and should be hounded; that drunken drivers are 'a menace to society' as the hoardings proclaim (an interesting shift this from the pitiable widow in the poster who used to invoke our social conscience in days of yore). The British self-righteousness is easily unleashed. It is not difficult to hate what is alien and alienate it, if that is what you are told to do – like me and the Germans, except that now I am supposed to like them. And I do like those I have met. People that met the hippie convoy tell me that they were actually no more menacing than I assume I was when I trekked barefoot round Europe, a Union Jack sewn on my knapsack, and sat in Damm Square and on the steps of the Sacré Coeur daftly singing Ewan Macoll songs to an ill-played guitar. Despite this assault on European eardrums, I received much kindness then in 1948. There was more of it about in those days, I think. Or perhaps we were allowed to show it more without feeling 'wet'.

No, it *is* still there. When the marksman shot the criminal who was holding out in a van in Philbeach Gardens last year, it was there in the little pile of flowers I saw as I passed the place of his death the next day. While the world heaped praise on the authorities that had saved society from this 'animal', onlookers were moved to pity. Surely a society is no longer civilised that cannot embrace, or at least feel compassion for its outsiders and nuisances? Which is why I like my own profession. It is made up of a motley crew, but I have never seen anyone ostracised for being odd. And quite a lot of us are. Or seem to be when we are let out on the streets.

The venerable Dame Athene Seyler, as I gave her a lift home from the theatre, would wave her fist and shout from my little Morris 1000 to big cars that passed, 'You are very vulgar'. Sir Ralph Richardson talked loudly and affectionately to his huge motorcycle as he rode round the West End. Most people being dragged dangerously along by a moving bus would shout, 'Help!' – Ernest Milton trilled, 'Stop, stop, you're killing a genius.' We are no worse than other people really. We just project better. Every walk of life has its diddle-ohs and drunks. It is just that the Richard Burtons, Brendan Behans and Wilfred Lawsons do it more spectacularly, more amusingly and, of course, more publicly. Unfortunately there is a tendency in the big companies to be less tolerant of the mavericks. The phrases, 'a good company person' and 'he's very humble' or 'a darling', would come up frequently as recommendation in casting sessions at the RSC. Big businesses and governments alike run more easily without gritty foreign bodies getting into the complicated machinery. Even in my little tour set-up I sometimes would have preferred to wash away the irritating agitators: so how much more irksome our rattlings must have been to the complex main operation.

The memos and phone calls were still ricocheting backwards and forwards between Margate and London, where casting was continuing for the 1984 Stratford season. In response to an accusation by me of disloyalty to my company, a long angry memo from Joyce Nettles outlined the problems presented by the promise of parts for the tour actors when they had not even finally decided the shows, or found the stars to lead the 1984 Stratford company. My riposte was that the shows could be chosen to fit *my* actors and that *they* should be the stars.

I actually had no real right to be included in the planning discussions, particularly as no offers were being made to me personally to continue with the company; but I felt responsible for the promises I, in the RSC's name, had made to the actors. My hectoring, and the directors' essential good intentions, eventually bore fruit and while we were in Margate letters were sent to every member of the company – except me – containing offers of parts. These were received with varying degrees of outrage or pleasure according to how good they were, the best news being that Robert Holman, author of *Other Worlds*, was to be commissioned to write a play especially for the company, which resulted the following year in the highly successful *Today*. But, at the time, this was an unknown quantity.

After all the suspense a sort of hysteria set in when the offers arrived. The unhappy ones became very grand and all the habitual face-saving exercises were gone through – talks of other offers, not wanting to be stuck at Stratford, need for a rest, and how they were not really concerned for themselves but thought it was disgraceful how darling so-and-so had been treated. One man with family responsibilities was openly grateful to get any job at all, but this on the whole is an unusual attitude for actors. Even the lowliest is choosy about the quality of the work rather than the salary. And most of them were not too over the moon with the stature of the roles on offer.

Being in another rain-lashed, out-of-season seaside resort was also not uplifting to the spirits, although Margate's regency streets are surprisingly attractive without the holiday crowds. The audiences smoothed our egos by responding joyfully to the shows there, little realising how painfully insecure were the underlying feelings of some of the performers. Or my own, as I gave one of my chats to theatre-goers on the glories of the RSC.

It being just before Christmas, we drowned our doubts at a party we had in the beautiful Winter Gardens, during the course of which various actors cornered me for advice on their futures. I was torn between my loyalty to the management and the actors as individuals, and ended up doing my Martha Graham act on Margate beach at four o'clock in the morning. I felt a lot better after that. I was confident the company was destined for good things in the long run – and I was right. Penny Downie and Roger Allam, Polly James, James Simmons and Simon Templeman became major leads with the RSC; Kath Rogers was soon to do some stunning TV performances; Amanda Root did well with the company, but even better when she left, as did Dan Day Lewis. Indeed, nearly all of them have subsequently proved themselves as good as I had proclaimed them; and those who have not yet, will.

Still hungover from the party, I bade farewell to drizzly Margate the next morning and left the company to mull their wine and their offers during the Christmas break. Fortunately, I did not have any time to worry as I organised the food and presents and Boxing Day party for the family. This is an annual event of some notoriety in Chiswick, including as it does a treasure hunt with clues laid in the street as well as the house. The Thaw family, plus sundry Briers, are to be seen in curious outfits from the previous dressing-up games rampaging along Strand-on-the-Green, fighting savagely. Despite my erudite clues, my family is stronger on brute force than intelligence and my ex-miner/lorry driver/social worker/Mancunian gem of a father-in-law raises sophisticated Southern eyebrows with his violent, diversionary tactics. I once had to rescue his ten-year-old granddaughter from hypothermia when he locked her outside the house with a peremptory, 'Stay there, you little bugger.' Considering the prize is usually a liquorice whirl, the passion is somewhat excessive. But then, as one of my neighbours observed, we are 'theatricals'!

I cannot deny, though, that I miss the religious emphasis of my childhood Christmases. To attend the midnight services on Christmas Eve and Christmas morning would now be hypocritical, but I remember fondly my father's joyous rendering of the descant to 'The First Noel' in our Congregational church. I would glow with pleasure at his side in my new gloves or scarf (and once in a furry-lined velvet muff), full of anticipation for the chicken and Christmas pudding ahead. The afternoon was spent getting mouth ulcers from eating wet walnuts dipped in salt, and further exploring the goodies from my pillow case, which a rather tipsy Santa Claus had filled the night before, muttering, 'Happy Christmas, Bum Face', with surprising familiarity as he stumbled out of my bedroom. My presents were usually made by my parents. One Christmas a carved wooden sewing box on legs, lined with pink satin, explained why I had been locked out of our shed rendezvous for some weeks. There was always a new dress and apron, made by my mother, and dolls dressed in knitted take-offable knickers, lace petties and frocks, coats and hats made from scraps. It is no wonder I have ended up a somewhat torn feminist with all that early conditioning.

In 1983 we had a proper Christmas for once as my husband also had a few nights off from his Cardinal Wolseying and Toby Belching in Stratford. It was a rare pleasure for us all to be free together, so it was particularly hard after the week's break to leave the comfort of home and family to brave the wilds of South-West England on the last lap of the tour. The weather was freezing, so I was lucky to have Joanna as a hot-water bottle during her Christmas holidays. The farm outside Tiverton where we stayed was icy cold and surrounded by a forbidding moat of mud and cow-dung. I suppose the undulating green velvet hills of Devon, dotted with woolly sheep and pink and white thatched houses, make up an archetypal English country scene, but a little of it goes a long way for me. Especially in winter. I love visiting the English countryside, but I am a town person really. Even when looking at beautiful scenery I am scanning it for traces of human life, whether houses, dry-stone walls, old workings, bridges or, best of all, ancient remains and stone circles. I soon tire of peopleless landscape. The most boring holiday I ever spent was a week in Austria where there was nothing but mountains and smelly bath-salty fir trees. The monotony was only slightly relieved when I strode into an inn, demanding hot chocolate, only to discover, after I had drunk it and offered to pay, that it was a private house and the nice couple who spoke no English but nodded and smiled a lot were the owners trying to eat their lunch.

We never saw both the owners of our farm in Devon. The farmer served our meals and did not talk of his wife, though we did hear a woman's voice coming, we decided, from the cellar in which she was locked. We went for walks, but once you have seen one green hill you have seen them all, and my treks in the country are apt to be rather circuitous as I am frightened of cows as well as horses and dogs, which means a long detour every time any one of these species heaves into sight. I am not too keen on rabbits either. But that is not due so much to fear as fearful memories connected with them when I was evacuated. In fact, I put my ambivalent attitude to the countryside in general down to that period of my childhood.

When war broke out and invasion threatened, my parents contemplated sending my sister and me with other evacuees to the USA. But it was the example of the Royal Family keeping the little princesses in England that prevented my becoming Elizabeth Taylor. That and the violet eyes, I suppose. Anyway, I was first evacuated to Wallingford in Berkshire, managing to return to London in time to catch the full brunt of the Blitz. Then I went off to Crewkerne in Somerset, returning yet again in time to experience the V1s (doodlebugs) and V2s (rockets).

Although I had lived in Wallingford as a small child, when my parents ran the pub, I did not remember much about it. I had a vague recollection of packing my cardboard attaché case to leave home after some affront and, following an agony of indecision round the corner, toddling back shamefacedly, yet defiantly assuring the tittering customers in the public bar that I had only come back because I had forgotten my gloves. When I returned in 1939, life in the country proved a novel experience.

Smells, textures and sounds of my first day in Wallingford remain with me vividly to this day. Arriving, bewildered, clutching my gas-mask box, I had a halting conversation with Mrs Giles, after which she suggested I go out for a breath of fresh air in the fields while she prepared some tea. The first gate I came to opened into an expanse of yellow flowers. I remember the ache in my throat as I lay face down on the damp grass and breathed in the unfamiliar earth, and the feeling of the sun on the back of my knees, and the sound of insects and grasshoppers. I picked a bunch of cowslips, a flower I had never seen before. I grow this endangered species in my Chiswick garden now to make up for this sacrilege; it is my favourite flower. Clutching them in my hand that day, I ran as fast as I could down a steep, grassy hill, and suddenly from the depths of despair my spirits somersaulted up into orgasmic ecstasy. I tore down that hill many times later, and other hills since, but have never recaptured that feeling.

Returning to the tiny cottage where I was billeted, I found Mrs Giles had prepared an egg custard. I had not had a real egg for ages, and the slippery texture after dried eggs unfortunately made me gag and I had to rush down the garden to the lavatory. Its scrubbed, white wooden seat concealed the mouth of hell and I didn't dare to sit above it. I stood for a while retching in the dark cell, which I shared with several large fat spiders. After a decent interval I scurried back to the house to my made-up bed on the brown leatherette sofa. Mr and Mrs Giles awkwardly retired and, as the latch clanked down on the door at the foot of the stairs, I looked out of the window and willed myself under the same stars as my mother and father. My pillow became sodden either side of my head.

The Gileses were always caring and kind to me, despite being unused to little girls – which is more than could be said for some of the hosts of the evacuees, or 'the bloody vaccies' as we were often known by the local children. The only kids who really seemed pleased to see us in Wallingford were the orphans from the local cottage homes in their long navy three-pleat tunics, who went to the same village school and ceded to us the privilege of being bullied. Especially me. I had already developed my facial twitch, which was a hideous circling of my nose followed by a stretching of my open mouth. Not pretty, but something over which I had no control.

In my class at the village school there was a certain girl with many brothers who bewitched me with her toughness. Suffering as she, and indeed her whole family, did with impetigo, her face was a woad-like vision of gentian violet. This only added to her desirability, and I longed for her friendship and approval. One day in art class I made an approach. Art class consisted of drawing with rulers versions of the Union Jack – a shape I absent-mindedly doodle to this day – and sitting with your arms folded when you had finished. No talking allowed. The Jones girl and I were sitting like this when I caught her eye and attempted a smile, which was distorted by one of my spasms into what looked like pulling a face. I was unaware of this at the time and was therefore disappointed that my friendly approach received a scowling response. That afternoon we had flea parade, and since I was discovered to be contaminated I had to stay behind to have my hair washed in vinegar, following a caning of my hand for nervously giggling at my sin. When I emerged from this humiliation, I went to cross the crinny – a large field outside the school – only to be confronted by the glowering purple Jones family *en bloc*. They slowly encircled me and silently punched me from one side of their ritual ring to the other. I did not cry, they did not speak and the other kids, even my fellow evacuees, did not dare to intercede. The mob were blindly accepting the judgement of the mighty on the twitching outsider. Eventually an angel of mercy in the shape of 'a middle-class, middle-aged hooligan' rescued me and walked home with me. But I went in fear of my skin for weeks, until I used my usual weapon of clowning one day to make the youngest Jones boy laugh and was adopted as their cap-and-bells gang member. It was not a fun gang to be in, but sometimes I did manage to talk them into some more harmless games. Years later, I found that the ghost of that wretched little school has been laid for me by its conversion to an arts centre. So, 'Up you, Miss Greenbum', as we vaccies used to mutter to the headmistress who hated us. The root of this nickname is clouded in time, but her mean face and caning hand are not.

I have happier memories of my second exile into the country during the war, when I stayed with a distant relative who fancied herself as a medium. She hardly noticed my twitch because of her preoccupation with my 'lovely aura', and she got me a part-time job working on a farm. This proved to be the same mixed blessing as the countryside always presents to me. The bleak side was the rabbits. I used to go gleaning and stooking – stacking the bundles of corn or wheat or whatever it was into piles of three after they were dropped by the reaper. As I had no wellies, my ankles would become scratched and bloody from the stubble, a pain which was nothing to that suffered by the rabbits that huddled into the ever-decreasing shelter of the tall crop, from which eventually they broke cover only to be beaten to death by the locals who gathered to catch their dinner. But this brutality was counterbalanced by the sweetness of my love for John Chapman.

I honestly cannot remember what this object of my passion looked like, but I know he was considerably older than me and very, very handsome. He must also have been a rather simple boy as I kept up a tortuous pretence with him of being twins, and he never saw through it. It started when I discovered he loved me in a game of 'Truth, dare and force' we played on a haystack one break when we ate our sandwiches. This revelation so amazed and frightened me that I jumped down and ran home at top speed, nearly knocking myself unconscious under an iron barrier on the way. Desperate to make amends for this mawkish behaviour, I invented a more poised identical twin sister, Carole, who had arrived from London and duly apologised for her sister's lack of grace. In this performance of the sophisticated city girl – a bit of a hussy – I inveigled myself into John Chapman's affections, and he was soon slagging off his last love, my shy twin Sheila. Undaunted by his two-faced behaviour, I felt free to express my affection while pretending to be someone else and had a whale of a time for some months. Perhaps this was my first realisation of the release of acting, although my strict moral code, not to say my age – I was only nine – did not permit any great erotic experiences.

When my parents visited me for a week my mother was shocked at this duplicity, but my father joined in the pretence with gusto when he met my poor, deluded boyfriend, complaining to him what a scallywag that Carole was compared to the lovely Sheila. Dad and I plotted scenarios as we rode our borrowed bikes down country lanes in search of bluebells.

We cycled for miles during that idyllic week, my father fuddled by Somerset cider, until he ached too much to lift his leg over the saddle and had to dismount by throwing himself, choking with laughter, on to a grass verge. Choruses from 'The Student Prince' and 'Desert Song' reverberated round the hills of Somerset, and the natives were startled to hear savage renderings of the 'Riff Song':

> Ho, so we sing as we are riding ho,
> When you hear our bells a'ringing so
> It means the Ricks are abroad.
> Go before you've bitten the sword.

At nine years old, if blessed with loving parents, your overriding fear is that you will lose them. Death is a terrible ogre. My pain when they left me after that week to return to London was probably about as bad as theirs. They arranged, as solace, for me to visit my best friend, Brenda Barry, who was billeted in a cottage miles from anywhere on the Isle of Purbeck in Dorset. This smugglers' countryside entranced me, and I was yet again consoled by an experience matching that in the Wallingford cowslip field.

There is a place on the coast where, crossing fields, you come to a steep cliff. Clamber down and you find an enchanted rock pool on a shelf – just the right size for swimming. Dancing Ledge, it is called. The tide fills it, and after a sunny day it is warm and velvety. You have to swim naked for the full bliss. Then, to float with your best friend in the soft water, looking up at a starlit sky and listening to the sea lapping the rocks beyond and the seagulls calling, is to be absorbed into the universe. I curse the oil prospectors and Ministry of Defence camp-makers and the nuclear experimenters in nearby Winfrith who threaten to pollute that enchanted area. Children need memories like this, as Jimmy pointed out.

For want of a better link back to the subject of the tour, I will observe that fortunately there are in Tiverton, the next town on the tour, many people who care about their children's futures. It is at a dangerous crossroads just now. I imagine it is quite a nice little town, if you could see or hear it for the huge lorries that are tipped into it from the M5 link-road, and it is on the brink of a big development. A new station, six thousand new houses, growing industry and tourist attractions are gathering pace, and local residents are fighting to see that the necessary development is wisely done. Deeply involved in this battle are Nevill and Elizabeth Ambler, who run the mouth-watering restaurant, Henderson's, that threw open its doors at all hours for our company and was my chief

Above: The intrepid RSC Touring Company, 1983/4, before they set out

Below left: A visit to Greenham for some inspiration

Below right: Friends from Workington

The Company on tour

Above left: Pennie Downie after a few weeks' travelling

Above right: Sue Jane Tanner using her waits more energetically

Below: George Raistrick, Robert Eddison and Daniel Day Lewis trying to relax in a table-tennis room somewhere in the North of England

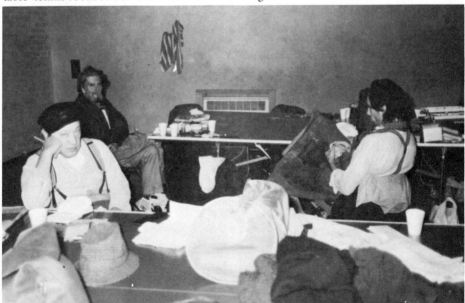

The Power of the Media 1: Dennis Waterman, John and Garfield Morgan trying to satisfy the customers whilst shooting *The Sweeney*

The Power of the Media 2: This photograph appeared in the *Daily Mirror* above a caption suggesting John and I were at loggerheads. In fact we were simply on our way out of the Haymarket Theatre after seeing a show

Above: The Ian McKellen/Edward Petherbridge Company at the National Theatre, 1985/6 in *The Cherry Orchard*. 'We should be doing a pantomime'

Below left: Edward and Ian posing for publicity in Chicago. I was presumably in the gym

Below right: My non-Oxbridge Madam Ranyevskaya

reason for liking Tiverton. Milton Keynes aside, I had become shamefully blasé about the invariably eulogistic reaction to the plays, and towns were now apt to be judged for their creature comforts. Appreciation of the food at Henderson's, together with the hospitality of the hosts, was unanimous – as was approval of the local launderette and the week's late night movies. The dressing-room arrangements were passable, too. We had to have a larger space, usually in toilets or cloakrooms, allotted to the actresses to accommodate overspill of non-smoking actors who needed to escape from the eye-watering poker school the male area invariably became – modesty by this time being irrelevant. The completion of Robert's *Times* crossword was a major objective of the day. Hotels were assessed by him on the merits of the toast, by Penny Downie on the coffee, and by me on the availability of porridge. On all counts Tiverton was a success. So, after all this comfort I was in good spirits as I set off with Jo, still on her holidays, to cross Dartmoor via a friend in St Austell, before going on to our next date in Redruth, Cornwall.

The weather was bright as we drove higher and higher, passing yellow, oil-skinned Hiawathas canoeing down the rushing River Dart. But as the hedges gave way to dry-stone walls near the top, then to no enclosures at all, the weather clamped down into *Great Expectations*-like mist and rain. From the back seat Joanna read out the obligatory guide book that I inflict on family and friends wherever I visit, and it was easy to believe its tales of devils and hairy hands. Not as frightening to me, however, as the wild-eyed horses and sheep, outrageously blazoned with rampant red and blue patches on their shaggy coats, suggesting much more bawdy sex lives than the neat blobs on their lowland Devon cousins. From time to time the mist would clear to reveal blazing rust and orange splashes on the black landscape, and sometimes a sweating boy soldier was seen crossing it with huge packs on his back, oblivious to the splendour around in his panting struggle to keep upright. We moved on, encountering the even stranger moonscapes of the china-clay pits of south Cornwall. If horned club-footed satyrs would come as no surprise on Dartmoor, neither would little green men with inverted goldfish bowls on their heads in the grey and white curves of the clay pits. It was quite a relief to see the comforting human face of Enid Dalton-White in St Austell.

I am fortunate to count several older women as good friends, two of the best of whom I met through the hospice movement. Enid had been a tireless fund-raiser for a hospice in Cornwall, for which I had turned the first shovelful of earth the year before. She is a witty, lovely woman with a colourful past and an energetic present. I know that in every organisation similar to this there are these tireless women, selflessly, joyfully working for charity. To move amongst them is an antidote to the bullying.

Much has been written of the doyenne of them all, Dame Cicely Saunders, the founder of St Christopher's Hospice in Crystal Palace. She comes over as a sort of saint. I know her and she is much better than that. She looks awfully grand in pictures, sporting various honorary doctorate sets and medals and chains. But I have seen her light up like a child at the sight of a rare bird to add to her bird-watching list or merrily singing her heart out in the hospice choir or firmly holding the wasted hand of my first husband when she had only just met him. I have sat on committees with her when the hospice has been in dire financial straits, and her calm assertion that something will turn up has almost made me share her steady faith in God. Instead, I have found myself armed with figures and five minutes in which to convince Barbara Castle (the then Minister of Health) of the need for more money from the Ministry. Which is where Cicely and I differ. She is inspired by God; I by her. It is strange that I should finally lose my faith when close to this splendid God-fearing woman.

All my Christian life I had battled with the old chestnut, 'Why suffering?' I read the books and listened to the sermons. But every time I witnessed more pain, I wondered at the incompetence of this supposedly all-loving God. I had already become resentful of the Church's insistence on the unworthiness of us miserable offenders and the diminishing of our self-esteem. I gradually stopped going to church on Sundays and began to switch off droning broadcast services. I had tortuous arguments about faith with that jolly Welsh disbeliever, Victor Spinetti, which he won hands down. I was also deeply influenced by a correspondence with another older woman, Kit Mouat, which started when she wrote to me after I did a radio chat show with Pete Murray, sending me a book on Humanism. An atheist to the end, she fought off her death from cancer, against the prognosis, for ten years, during which time she formed support groups and natural-health cancer clinics.

I clumsily nursed my blameless mother through her wretched terminal illness, clinging to the belief that someone up there must like us really. Even when I hurt her with injections and witnessed her humiliation as I changed her incontinence pads, I tried to believe it was a penance for past sins or a necessary journey towards a better world. The fact that my friend, Dilys Laye, and my Aunt Ruby were a damn sight more helpful in the nitty-gritty daily horror than the recipient of my nightly prayers still did not stop me kneeling humbly by my bed as I had been taught. And when my mother died I duly knelt and gave thanks for her deliverance.

No such offering passed my lips when a year later I stood by the body of my first husband, Alec, who also died of cancer. Through his last illness, he and I had been supported by St Christopher's. Doubting, I suppose, my ability to cope so soon with another stretch of terminal nursing, my GP introduced me to the hospice. It was with great reluctance that I inspected this place for the dying, thinking that I could never subject my husband to such depressing surroundings. The airy building, covered in bright paintings by Cicely's husband, the sounds of children in the creche and the peaceful gardens were an uplifting surprise. At my first meeting with Cicely, when she told me with confidence that Alec would not suffer and that we might even discover death was a positive experience, I could have kissed her. Indeed, I think I did.

At that stage Alec had been given a few weeks to live. He was racked with pain and could not eat without vomiting. Still exhausted from watching my mother's illness, my resilience was at a low ebb. Alec and I could hardly speak to one another; I for fear I should disclose the gravity of his illness – 'Don't worry, darling. The doctor says it's only a rather nasty ulcer' – and he because every ounce of his strength was concentrated in fighting the pain and staying alive.

After one week as an in-patient in St Christopher's he was pain-free and happy. He came home with his drugs, and with regular visits from nurses and doctors from Crystal Palace he remained home until he died nine months later. Life was not particularly just to Alec. A promising career in the theatre was ruptured by the war. A mere boy of eighteen, he saw friends killed and was forced to kill others himself. He sat aside, frequently unemployed, whilst his young wife had lucky breaks and successes. But thanks to the hospice's expertise he was able to enjoy in those last months the fruits of the one thing at which he was truly successful – friendship. People came from far and wide to sit with him and chat. Relatives, friends from the RAF, from our repertory days; old drinking companions like Patrick Magee and Ruskin Spear rocked the tiny house in Hammersmith with laughter, and only as they left would I see the tears in their eyes. Frankie Howerd would clown, then in the hall clutch me in anguish. This is why Cicely says a dignified death is so important. Things can be said before it is too late, values realised, tributes paid. I remember at the hospice once a worn little cockney woman saying that day had been the best birthday of her life because her awkward great sons and husband had been encouraged actually to tell her out loud that they loved her. One day, when I was doing a particularly squalid bit of nursing to Alec, he said, 'Oh you are an angel,' to which I said in apology for a host of past unkindnesses, 'I've always meant to be an angel.' In joking forgiveness and understanding, he replied, 'Yes, but such a militant angel.' We had several such exchanges. Many wounds were healed. I was again proud and full of respect for him. None of this would have been possible without the support of those deeply religious carers. With my mother, my bungling helplessness permitted only one similar moment of understanding. One day as I washed her I commented on her lovely nose. She looked at me in amazement and told me she had always thought of it as ugly. I could not believe she was capable of such insecurity and being so wrong, and I said what I had never realised needed saying, 'You are the most beautiful woman I know.' Her suffering was undeserved and bewildering to me. Yet, in spite of this, I had still struggled to believe. Alec's death was less harrowing, but ironically my faith died with him.

On the night Alec was dying a nurse from the hospice came and sat with us. He fought to stay alive and during that struggle, knowing of my growing disbelief, she asked if I minded if she prayed. As she knelt there I felt a calm resolve; a sort of revelation, I suppose. Alec died and she left the room. I did not kneel, I stood. And I said aloud 'There is no God.' It was so simple. That nurse is now a nun in an enclosed order while I am one of the vice presidents of St Christopher's Hospice; she went her way, I mine. What has replaced my faith in a loving God is a belief that I, unaided, have to do everything I can to make this life good. Full stop. This is all I can be sure of. It was the practical example of St Christopher's that got to me, not their prayers. Their skill, their doing something about death and pain. To me, it is now a waste of time and an irrelevance to ponder on the whys and wherefores of life and suffering. Here it is, this is it, let's get on with it. I do not make a habit of brandishing my atheism because I know how some people need their faith. When I do mention it, I have letters from people trying kindly to restore mine. But I no longer have any need of religion. The struggles and failures are over and it is such a relief.

Perhaps the change would not have been so easy without the chain of events that followed Alec's death. First of all, I was committed to go straight into a play at the RSC by Edward Albee called *All Over*. Not only was it about a man dying (and like a psychiatrist's couch for me), but the cast, especially Dame Peggy Ashcroft and Angela Lansbury, were endlessly loving. I was allowed to talk, emotionally if I liked, about death and religion and Alec in the rehearsal process. Too often bereaved people are asked to forget too soon. I was able to use our experience constructively. And laugh if I liked. Again, the world often expects a consistently grief-stricken performance from widows, and is shocked by the occasional flashes of humour that the most dire situation can encompass. Death can be very funny.

My mother died in the middle of the night. The very next day I had to be in a TV studio to rehearse all day, and that night record a silly situation-comedy in front of a studio audience. I told no one what had happened as I knew it would make the day even more difficult if people were sympathetic. The usual badinage went on at rehearsal and I got through the performance, but after the director had said, 'It's a wrap, it's in the can', I crept behind the set and sunk in a heap, sobbing, completely out of control. I was discovered by a stagehand who put his hand on my shoulder and said, 'Oh come on, Sheila – I've seen worse shows.' I told him what I was crying about and, to his eternal credit, he did not allow embarrassment at his inadvertent gaffe to stop him from having a good laugh with me. It was what I needed without feeling guilty about it. Similarly, on the day after Alec's death I had to go to the office of the Registrar of Births, Deaths and Marriages to inform him of it. I was accompanied by my dear friend, Tony Beckley, both of us wrung out with exhaustion and grief as we slumped in the waiting room. Suddenly, in breezed the registrar, rubbing his hands in anticipation of a wedding fee, and chirruped, 'Hello. Are you the happy couple?' Our laughter was more of a relief than our tears.

I have made use of these two incidents in subsequent speeches I have made about bereavement – and I have made quite a few. I badly needed some practical exercise to substitute for religious solace in my new godless world. A few months after Alec died, Cicely asked me to make a speech at a seminar on the care of the dying to be held at the Royal College of Physicians. Being the only layperson I was daunted, but determined. I contrasted in the speech the illness of my mother with too little professional support or careful drug therapy and that of Alec with the hospice approach. Lambasting the lack of communication skills in surgeons, I suggested that they could be taught them like actors. Lessons in how to break bad news. When and what to tell patients. How to treat them with respect. To be the inert subject of a specialist, talking to medical students over your bed while he sweeps magisterially round the ward, is to be set back several weeks in your recovery. Equally, to be hidden behind curtains in a general ward, because dying people are an affront to a profession trained to cure, is a lonely way to end. I spoke about nurses bustling my mother heartily, as if she were a backward child with no awareness of her individuality. Not their fault. Their training did not encompass death. One way or another, I let rip a whole lot of pent-up feelings and the speech made headlines.

As a result, I was inundated with letters from others pouring out their worries and hundreds of pleas for help from those as lost as I had been. So, straightaway my new found determination to use suffering constructively found an outlet. With the help of the hospice and Cruse (an organisation for widows and widowers), I became a sort of unofficial advice centre. I made a film on bereavement and gave lectures at home and abroad. I put myself about as a telly personality for fund-raising events and served on the management committee of the hospice. My life was filled with this work, in addition to trying to support myself and Ellie-Jane at the same time. It was a salutary and releasing period, made doubly precious by my relationship with Cicely and her assistant, Tom West.

I hope during those five or six years I was helpful to the growth of the hospice movement, but eventually the time came to pull back and continue my other life. These days I do not involve myself with such a frenzy. My dedication was always more selfish than charitable. I needed to make those two deaths mean something valuable. It is incumbent upon a Humanist to try to make the here and now better for everyone in the belief that it is all you can be sure of having. Life has become so precious that I spit with rage at spoiled lives or anything that endangers future lives.

As a Christian, I involved myself in the beginnings of CND. As a Humanist, my involvement has become more urgent. The horror of Hiroshima and Nagasaki and the new possibility of the annihilation of God's creation stirred me into marching and sitting and signing. (I made an LP with Sydney Carter, full of anti-bomb propaganda. Disconcertingly, the song put in at the eleventh hour to fill the record, called 'My Last Cigarette', is the only track that people remember.) It was as a Humanist that, on the Sunday between Wisbech and Milton Keynes, I took part during the tour in a big demonstration at Greenham Common.

I joined with tens of thousands of other women in 'embracing the base' and decorating the wire fence with webs and pictures. As the helicoptors clattered threateningly low, I heard for the first time that unearthly keening which women have used down the ages gradually spread right round the perimeter of that obscene place. No wonder the men froze in their tracks. I felt, as I always do when I go to Greenham, sorry for the civilian and MoD police, the British soldiers and the Americans behind the wire. The women have such a good time at the demos that they must feel left out. On 12 December 1983 there were bands and performances and dancing inside the base, on the silos, as well as outside. It was a day of great gentleness, and I was appalled when I read the misrepresentation in the press and heard the attacks in the House of Commons – no mention of the women whom I saw being roughly handled or of the staggering numbers present; only the fifty arrests and thirty 'injured' police and, most heinous of all crimes, one horse hurt. Which is worse, I wonder – the non-reporting in Russia, or the selective and distorted reporting in England? The tens of thousands of women from all walks of life, from all parts of the country must have been as angry as I was at the distortion of that extraordinary day.

Greenham Common is a grim place, but only on one occasion have I not actually enjoyed myself there. Visiting Main Gate one day (the other gates have been called after the colours of the rainbow) when Greenham was at its lowest ebb, out of fashion and ignored, I intruded upon a group of women who expressed their resentment at my casual visits, accusing me of exploiting their suffering by participating in the recent Quaker record, 'The Gates of Greenham'. Upset though I was by their anger, I could well understand it in the light of the daily harassment I had witnessed from the bailiffs with eviction orders, tossing the women's belongings into crunchers, dousing their fires and destroying their shelters so that they were reduced to sleeping under the bare sky in freezing temperatures. At various times over the last six years the women have endured prison sentences, foul language and abuse, pig's blood and maggots tipped over them, cars driven at them and one of their number murdered. Even the local Newbury paper, not known for its sympathy towards the peace women, has objected to the obscene graffiti against them on the army vehicles. Only a tiny proportion of the bullying they have endured has been publicised, but they are still there and will be, I am sure, for 'as long as it takes'. And I, for one, who has not got their guts, am in their debt. If, as seems likely, Cruise missiles are at last removed from this country it will be very much due to their relentless pressure.

They are an enduring symbol of protest. When the Libyan raid happened I could think of nothing better to do than to go to Greenham and stand, willing it all to stop. I was not alone. There is a tangible feeling of strength to be found in simply staring in unison at that scar on our common land. The use of primitive sound, or alternatively the silence of the Quakers, to combat brute force is strongly potent when you are participating, though I admit it looks pretty silly on the telly. The men behind the wire rush round with walkie-talkies and the police ostentatiously take videos for their criminal records, but they look pretty daft too. I have an idea that, unlike us, they feel it.

It refreshes me to talk to the Greenham women. They are creative and original, their scrapbooks and songs and systems of efficient organisation without leaders or male structures being evidence of new systems being evolved by women. In the tenacity of this tattered, assorted group I see hope for resistance to the bullies of the world. We are constantly told that the bomb has prevented wars for forty years. In Europe. But can we really discount the other thirty million people killed in over a hundred major wars in other parts of the world during that period, often using weapons supplied by us, the USA and Russia – not to mention lives lost in the Falklands? Have we already forgotten them? And Ireland? Politicians talk of deterrents as though the prevention of war involves rational behaviour. Isn't war just the same cock-up as other disasters, usually involving the odd madman who would not be averse to getting rid of a whole race? One of them had a go with six million Jews. And, unpredictably, did not invade England although we only had a few blokes like my father with a few guns waiting this side of the Channel. Maybe if we had had an atom bomb his maniac ambition might have been tempted to outwit us. If he had dropped one he could have used the argument that it was justified in order to bring the war to an end quicker. Others did. Twice.

If all the money spent on weapons could be diverted overnight to enrich people's lives worldwide, it would be the best and safest defence strategy possible. And I do not think my 'idealism' is any more ridiculous than clanking weapons containing two hundred and fifty-six Hiroshimas'-worth of annihilation round the streets of England, supposedly 'melting into the countryside' so incompetently that they can be detected and stopped by a disorganised chain of protesters. A mistake with a nuclear warhead is potentially catastrophic. And mistakes get made. Look at Flixborough. I believe it is time we took away these dangerous toys from the boys. And girls.

Mrs Thatcher, on a children's programme on television, was teaching the children that you have to fight bullies with threats. She did not say anything about trying to turn them into friends. This little girl, many years ago, used laughter, helped by timely adult intervention. She got a few bruises but peace was finally achieved – without annihilating the whole of Wallingford.

9 : Loners and Groupings
Redruth and the Isle of Wight

CORNWALL RULES, OK – MY FAVOURITE SMALL HOTEL – BRIT-
ISH RAIL BUREAUCRATS – NEWTON ABBOTT – MY BIRTHPLACE
– PROPINQUITY – BOYS – REASONS FOR GOING ON THE STAGE
– GREEK GODS – JOAN COLLINS AND DIANE CILENTO – ALEC
– VARIETY AND 'LEGIT' – COMICS – PUBLIC AFFECTION – FANS
– LONG LARTIN PRISON – PARKHURST – OU SUMMER SCHOOL
– GREENHAM UNITY – EDUCATION– TEACHERS – SWET AWARDS

Much is made of the North/South divide in England. That is nothing
compared to all the other chasms. The more I travel around the country,
the more I marvel that we ever see eye to eye over anything. How on
earth does any television programme become universally popular with
such diverse viewers? How, apart from the dread Milton Keynes episode,
did our plays have such appeal in all parts of the country? In the South
West, as well as in the Midlands and North, many people I met had
never left the place of their birth. We are not merely insular but townsular
and villagesular as well. My father-in-law from Lancashire has not a
good word to say for Yorkshiremen. What is more, being a Manchester
City man, he is vituperative about United supporters – and that includes
his own son.

I suppose the world is such a frightening place that we huddle into
groups for protection. There is a strong nationalist movement in Cornwall
to preserve their celtic culture, and even to separate from the rest of the
country. Never mind the blacks – keep out the English. And it is not
difficult to understand the separatist movement as you drive down to
Redruth on the south-west tip of England and see how remote it is. It
is always further away than I expect. The people even *look* different.
There are a lot of men with beards and big, brown, staring eyes. The
landscape is a perfect combination of wild nature and ruined buildings.
I doubt if the unemployed share my relish for the derelict tin mines with

their sturdy chimney fingers pointing at the sky, or that the house owners are particularly delighted with their gardens disappearing into one of the mines that honeycomb beneath north Cornwall; but I love the feeling of danger there, particularly in St Agnes Bay where I had my best digs of the tour. The Trevaunance Point Hotel is set on the edge of a steep cliff, overlooking a thunderous sea, where men have tried to build a harbour five times and five times the sea has destroyed it, leaving just a few lumps of granite lying in a heap when the tide goes out as evidence of their failure.

When Joanna and I got out of the car on arrival there was a howling gale and lashing rain, but through the salt we could faintly smell woodsmoke. Shouting to one another over the barrage of wind and sea, we clambered down the steep stone steps and entered what used to be the old dock office and store but is now my favourite small hotel. It is probably the contrast with the ferocious elements outside, but the interior of the low-beamed bar with its roaring log fire and three-foot thick walls is a most welcoming place. Not that the landlord over does the hospitality. He is a man of few words himself, but with that best of all attributes for a landlord, a good ear. In fact, he is prepared to stay up all night listening to you. Which went down very well with the company. We had a lot to discuss.

About this time a big regional theatre offered me funding and facilities to set up a company and I was sorely tempted to steal this one. Several of the actors were keen on the idea, and I pounded the beach and the cliffs trying to pluck up the courage. Together with my stalwart team I felt I had made a success of the tour, but organising does not come easily to me. I worry and fret and find the endless rallying and responsibility onerous. Always surprised to find myself in authority, I do not relish the isolation that being the final decision-maker sometimes forces upon you. Having had quite a lot of that I could not face the thought of more, so I finally decided to turn down the offer.

Despite this agonising I was enjoying my visit to Redruth, tucked away in the Carn Brae leisure centre, built on a site rich in legend, backed by ruined mines and castles and overlooking South Croftie, one of the few active tin mines left in Cornwall. Then I was summoned to London to a planning meeting.

The tedium of the journey was not helped by the train juddering to a halt in the back of beyond and all the heating going off while we waited for rescue. It all might have been bearable if it had not been for the presence of an officious British Rail bureaucrat, who happened to be travelling on the train and took it into his head to organise us. But the British do not like being *forced* into groups. He rushed up and down, instructing us on how to keep warm and imparting communiqués of campaign progress. He bullied the guard and generally made a thorough nuisance of himself. This was treated with the usual British mocking indifference. I think everyone shared my fear that he would suggest a singsong any minute, so we tried to ignore him. Eventually he got out a notebook from his briefcase and started asking each of us in turn our destination – presumably with the intention of working out how British Rail would get us there.

'Basingstoke.'

'Right you are.'

'Stroud.'

'Yes, right.'

'London.'

'Right.'

'London.'

'Right you are.'

'The Caribbean.'

' – '

I need never have left St Agnes since I eventually arrived in London too late for the planning meeting, but was told that the powers-that-be were beginning to get annoyed by my company's choosiness about parts and ultimatums were threatened. The company by this time had moved on and were sampling the joys of Newton Abbott, so I left a few memos and went to join them.

My first image of this town was of the tower, all that remains of the ancient church of St Leonard's which is now marooned on an island surrounded by swirling traffic. Silhouetted in a window was a group of bell-ringers, labouring to produce their changes. Absolutely no one was taking a blind bit of notice. Familiarity breeds contempt, I suppose; or maybe they thought it was canned. Or perhaps the inhabitants of Newton Abbott were just too busy chatting, which they seem to do a lot. They have to shout as the traffic noise is almost as deafening as in Tiverton.

Unlike rugged Redruth, Newton Abbott is a cosy town. It abounds in tea-shops full of ladies in Gor-ray skirts and quilted jackets: Martha Mellor's, Sarah's, Mr Bumble's Eating House. One bold creature tried to open up a cheeky French bistro called Franglais, but Newton Abbott was not having any of that camp nonsense and it went bust. The inhabitants of Newton Abbott just politely reject what they do not like.

On a visit last year to the town, when some aberration on the part of W. H. Smith's had prompted them to set up a display of Joe Orton's obscene diaries in their branch there, I lurked for ages, hoping to witness some irate matron or colonel making a scene. A few people merely flicked through a copy, raised a surprised eyebrow and neatly put it back in its place, moving sedately on to the Jeffrey Archers or the cookery section.

In spite of this self-control and being just up the road from the taciturn Cornish, Newton Abbott is as friendly as a Northern town. People are apt to chunter to you as you pass – 'Oh lordie, I'm always in a rush!', 'What a life, eh?', 'Nice day en' it?' They received the shows warmly, too. We performed in a school built of grey bricks and slate, which must have seemed a good design idea until they saw it in the rain, but the children had jollied it up with murals and graffiti.

Lulled by our warmly cheerful reception in Newton Abbott, we were quite startled by the hysteria of our reception on our second overseas date, the Isle of Wight. This was the most insular place we went to, in every sense of the word, and we were received like visitors to a desert island.

It is nowhere near as cut off these days as it used to be. I was born there in the Blackgang Hotel, and my mother later told me dark stories of entwined families and incest. In the 1950s, when I went on the ferry to bury myself in the three summer seasons of repertory theatre with the Barry O'Brien company in Shanklin and later one in concert party with Cyril Fletcher on Sandown Pier, I used to feel a mild dose of the isolation that the inmates facing life sentences in Albany and Parkhurst Prison must experience as they watch the mainland disappear behind them. The islanders treated us artists with suspicion then. In 1954, when one of our number was arrested in a public lavatory in Ryde, the whole island nearly sank with the reverberations. Queen Victoria's shadow still hung over the place from when she retired to Osborne House after Albert's death, and I was even reprimanded by a member of the town council for wearing too short shorts in the High Street. The local shopkeepers knew about my fellow actors' carryings on before they did themselves. It was a fair assumption that a bit of extra-curricular activity went on. We clung together in self-defence. Also, prior to settling on the island for a few months each year, this same company had been nomading all over England with one play, usually by Agatha Christie, so we were thrown together over a long period. Propinquity was the excuse. That and the cold.

Oh, those freezing digs of my touring youth with one miserable little coal fire in the parlour and ice inside the bedroom windows. The only way to cope was by seeking out the Turkish baths in every town that had them, spending as much of the day there as possible and finding someone to cuddle up to at night. All except me, that is. I went to bed wearing winceyette pyjamas and bedsocks knitted by my mum, plus the beaver lamb fur coat inherited from my sister. Much as I envied all the romance around me I was far too shy to join in. I was better at worshipping from afar.

In my formative years I had very little contact with boys. In my teens I outgrew my mixed streetgang games, and at grammar school I always had too much homework. Occasionally I did go to socials at the Congregational church, but these were models of decorum by today's standards. The most daring game we played was called Winking, in the course of which you sat gingerly on a boy's lap and that was as far as the vicar would allow us to go. Sometimes the customary 'Valetas' and 'Dashing White Sergeants' were punctuated with a jitterbug – shock-horror from the adults as the more extrovert of us did our ungainly dance, whirling around, and even over our partners with serious abandon. But after these eruptions we returned to our seats along opposite walls – girls one side, boys the other; each group desperate to cross the divide.

The agonising moment of every social was the last waltz. Would anyone ask me? This meant you would be walked home by a boy. He might even hold your hand or, more awkwardly, put his arm round your waist, in which case it was tricky to synchronise your steps with his and know what to do with your own inner arm which was now squashed between you. And finally the torture on the doorstep. Would he kiss you goodnight? If so, should you open your mouth or not? And again, where should you put your arms and hands? (This was where the pebble-dash came in.) It all looked so easy in the pictures: they never bumped noses or missed mouths. Anyway, you could hear Dad coughing in the kitchenette and knew it was more of a warning than his TB playing up. The next day at school there was much whispered discussion as to whether the escort was 'a good kisser'. I dread to think what the topic is nowadays. Truth to tell, I did not get walked home a lot anyway. But these solitary walks gradually led to a resolve to go into the theatre. Most comics will tell how they went on the stage because making people laugh was the only way for them to attract attention. That was certainly how my theatrical ambitions started.

When I was five I used to force my one-woman version of *Snow White and the Seven Dwarfs* upon the poor old girls having a quiet port and lemon in the Ladies' Bar of the Carpenter's Arms in King's Cross. They smothered me in praise, doubtless hoping for a free drink from my father. Not long after this small debut I did my first proper public performance in the same play in Bexley.

This was at Upton Road Juniors, yet another school I attended (I went to six all told before I was eleven). I coveted the role of Snow White but, of course, that went to the pretty child with black hair and blue eyes who had a pushy mother, and I was relegated, to my chagrin, to the role of Dopey. My sister, Billie, tried to cheer me up by creating a lovely costume out of my red dressing-gown, on to which she sewed a red flannel train like the figure in the cartoon. This, together with my cotton-wool beard, was my downfall. In every sense of the word. Still seething with jealousy at the first performance, I managed to entwine myself in my skirt as I mounted the wooden steps on to the platform on my first entrance with my fellow dwarfs, singing 'Heigh ho, heigh ho, it's off to work we go.' The laugh this provoked from the audience as I fell flat on my face stopped Snow White in her tracks, and she had to shout her next speech over the laughter as I pulled down the beard which had sprung on its elastic up to my eyes during my fall. This, I decided, was a very good game. I essayed another little trip during her next speech. That went down well too. For the rest of the play I improvised train and beard business that would have warmed Joan Littlewood's heart with its ingenuity, if not its economy. My teacher was not best pleased. Neither was Snow White's mother. But I had made the invaluable discovery for any little girl that beauty is not necessarily the only way of grabbing attention.

I was frequently asked on the tour why I went on the stage. The eager young questioners expected some noble answer, but I fear my motives were more basic; I wanted to be rich, I wanted to be admired and, if possible, I wanted to get a man. If challenged to pinpoint one particular event it had to be my performance as St Joan at Dartford County Grammar School for Girls. Not that I enjoyed it very much, encountering as I did my first taste of nerves manifested as chronic wind (for which I took packets of Rennies, causing myself to froth at the mouth on the first night). But it lead to an event that decided my future.

The boys' grammar school round the corner (which Mick Jagger later attended) was surprisingly not as well equipped in chemistry laboratories as the girls' building. Therefore a small group of boys, known as the Science Sixth, visited our school. Amongst these worshipped male interlopers was a veritable Greek god called Alan Coast. With my acne and my twitch I was not in his class, but this did not stop me from fighting to be bell monitor so that I could clang my way past the laboratories for a glimpse of this paragon. Needless to say, he scarcely glanced in my direction – even when I managed to time my duty to coincide with sports and swung my bell vigorously enough to afford him a glimpse of green woolly knicker under my short, flared gym skirt. All to no avail. Until the school play.

I frothed my way through Shaw's masterpiece, but all the praise heaped on my head after the performance was but nought compared to the momentous happening the following day. As I rang past the glass windows of the chemistry laboratory, the beautiful blond head lifted from the bunsen burner and tilted back to signal the door. Dumbstruck, I nodded acceptance to his curt invitation to the school dance and there and then decided on a life in the theatre. How could one resist an endless vista of Greek gods and glamorous nights? Perhaps I should have heeded the warning note that he never asked me out again after the dance, but the die was cast. In fact, we did meet again thirty years later when he was dragged back to England with his wife and six children from his tea planting in Rhodesia to appear on my *This is Your Life*. Slightly paunchy and balding, he was visibly shaken that his invitation, which he did not even remember, had been responsible for my choice of career. He and Dopey.

My early years in the profession proved a sad failure in the Greek god department. There were one or two around, but my sheltered upbringing plus my feeling of inferiority did not make me much of a raver when I started working as an actress in the provinces, and I affected a rather superior 'I-want-to-be-alone' act to cover my embarrassment. During my time with the Barry O'Brien company, on our one day off, Sunday, I would go to church twice and take solitary walks; but I really ached to join in. And thanks to two people, I eventually did.

The first was one of the most glamorous women I have ever met – our leading lady, Moya Fenwick. She is one of that rare breed of actresses who never reach fame but has grafted away for years bringing pleasure to many audiences with absolute dedication. However dire the backwater we played Moya would stun it with her elegance. She had style – something I was lamentably short of, and miserably aware of it. To hell with talent and cleverness and nice natures, I just wanted to be beautiful. I have always envied beautiful women. Whatever people say about skin-deepness and not being loved for yourself, beautiful women always seem to have a damn good time to me. When I began at the Royal

Academy of Dramatic Art in 1949, Joan Collins was a finalist and her looks then were a legend. It was a perfect face and I would cast jealous glances at it. Her face did not, however, give me such a thrill as the totally different beauty of another student – Diane Cilento, a radiant creature with natural blonde hair, green eyes and a glowing golden skin, all of which she was totally unselfconscious about. Maybe I coveted her face more because she bore a vague resemblance to myself. In fact, the man who served our food in the canteen used to say we were like two versions of the same face, good and evil. That the world preferred the good was later to be proved when she was given the lead in a film version of *Rattle of a Simple Man* in which I had had such a big success on stage. I was not terribly upset; in those days it was just accepted that you did not play leads in films unless you were pretty. And by this time I was less insecure about my appearance – thanks mainly to Moya.

She taught me how to make the most of what I had got. This is not that sort of book (so do not worry, chaps), but I have subsequently managed during my life to catch the eye of one or two fairly desirable males and Moya's pep talks and face-packs were a huge help. In Shanklin she took me in hand and cleared up my acne. She did my hair, boosted my morale and the improvements she generously wrought attracted the attention of the second person who drew me further out of my loner's shell.

Alec Ross was ten years older than me and a dish. He sported navy blue blazers, nonchalant scarves tucked into the neck of open shirts, had thick curly hair, bedroom eyes and a debonair way with a cigarette. He was very, very smooth. I had played several romantic parts opposite him but it had not entered my head that he could possibly be interested in me. He went through all the pretty actresses that joined the company, and all the local women in every town we visited, married or single, queued for his favours. Maybe the novelty of this gawky girl appealed to him, but during one blissful season in Shanklin he began to woo me. It was a bit of a game to him, I think. But not to me.

I had only had one fairly serious boyfriend before this, when I was nineteen years old. He was not an actor and I think he was on the verge of proposing when we went to see *Porgy and Bess*. He did not like it. I walked away from him outside the theatre and never saw him again. He probably liked Gilbert and Sullivan too. Anyway, we were plainly incompatible. But Alec was everything I could wish for, and he was fool enough to take notice of me. I honestly think he got more than he bargained for. In fact, he got seventeen years of marriage.

On the Isle of Wight I worked with one of the happiest show business couples I know, Cyril Fletcher and Betty Astell. In the theatre on Sandown Pier I had the difficult task of replacing Betty when she became manager of, instead of performer in, the concert party show, *Masquerade*, which she and Cyril had done together for many years. Cyril would stare at me reproachfully as I lost laughs that Betty had created in the sketches. We did five changes of programme during the week and I never knew where I was. I once mistakenly rushed on after a quick change, dressed as an Indian squaw, to find myself singing 'My Old Man Said Follow the Van' in a cockney scena (pronounced shayner).

It is no wonder that I was lost as I had never done anything like it before. Trained at RADA, no less, and thinking of myself as a 'straight' actress, I was not too sure about the switch into revue. There used to be a big divide between variety and what was known significantly as 'legitimate artistes' which has now virtually disappeared, but when I first worked with Cyril (and still thought of myself as a potential Hedda Gabler), all this larking about was a bit shocking. I later contended with Tommy Cooper, Kenneth Williams, Dickie Henderson, Norman Wisdom, et al, but it was a novel experience this ad libbing and fooling. At first, it did not seem quite right to make things up in front of an audience but I soon got into the swing of it. Only in revue and concert party, mind you. I was still not prepared for Frankie Howerd's treatment of a straight play a couple of years further on.

On the first night of *Tons of Money* at the New Theatre, Bromley, we 'legits', Nigel Hawthorne and I, were astounded when Frank came on in best Ralph Lynn manner to deliver the first scripted line:

'Good morning all, good morning fish, good morning rolls, good night bills, good morning Auntie Ben.'

No laugh. So he turned balefully to the audience and said, 'What a load of old rubbish.' From then on, every time I tried to keep to the script – particularly if I got a laugh – Frank would interrupt with something like:

'No, don't laugh – she's from the RADA you know [pronounced radar]. No, no, she doesn't like it. Have a bit of respect. Poor soul.'

During one of my soliloquies one night, he rode on through the french windows on a bicycle sucking an ice-cream cornet, glared at me reproachfully, then, without a word, rode out.

Starting with Cyril, I have had my most enjoyable moments on stage working with comics. They give the impression of relishing being up there, but with most of them this is just an act and they are usually deadly serious. A lot of them are unhappy, often drinkers, and it is curious that they, who unite their audiences in laughter, can so often be loners themselves. With Kenneth Williams, Frankie Howerd, Max Wall and others there is a feeling that if the laughter stops for a second a terrible anguish will be revealed; there are unguarded moments when their faces in repose chill the soul. They would, I suspect, love to be part of a warm circle, but something in their natures seems to forbid it. Tony Hancock gradually got rid of all his artistic team and friends, of which Kenneth was one, and eventually got rid of himself.

I have seen these men struggle against their instincts to try to behave in public as they are expected to, sometimes at cost to themselves. I was at a function with Eric Morecambe after his heart operation and he was gallantly bantering with the crowd, showing his scars and making the jokes whilst his anxious wife tried to tear him away to go home and relax. Perhaps they know how easily audiences can turn on any clown when the laughter stops. I cannot claim to be a comic, but during Alec's illness I was appearing in a comedy show on television. One day, after I had done a personal appearance, I was slouched on a seat on Swindon station dreading what new horror awaited me at home, when a porter shouted across from the opposite platform, 'For Gawd's sake cheer up, Sheila. Give us a laugh.' I could not respond and in no time he and his mates were making loud comments: 'Who does she think she is?' 'I don't like her show anyway.' 'We made her, we can break her.' And, of course, they can. Max Wall spent years in the doldrums, deserted by audiences, when he left his wife and children to live with a beauty queen and the press whipped up a hate campaign against him.

It puzzles me, this knife-edge attitude of the public. I fear that at heart they do not really like performers very much. Some of them do not think of us as real people, or do not want us to be, maybe because the real people in their lives are so unsatisfactory that they need fantasy substitutes. One of *The Sweeney* fans who really believes my husband is Jack Regan has utterly destroyed her marriage and family unit by her obsession, not with John, but with the fictional character he plays. Having a crush on my husband's screen image I can just about understand. I find it less comprehensible that a man became obsessed with actor Brian Ellis while he was playing a rat in pantomine, completely covered by a furry skin. Brian thought it was perceptive appreciation of his jumps and squeaks until the letters took a strange turn: 'Do you wear Y-fronts under your ratskin?'

I have several fans whom I count as friends and who have seen all my shows over the years, and they are quite a different kettle of fish to these people who quite often do not want to meet actors face to face; the letters are enough. Others do not want to make any contact at all, even by letter. I discovered this in Long Lartin Prison which I visited while acting at Stratford in 1982 to take part in a poetry recital called 'Groupings'.

Amongst the crowd of men who perched on windowsills and sat on the floor, drinking in our every word, was someone who had made a beautiful collage on the wall out of photos, drawings and paintings of me. There were old, yellowing newspaper cuttings from years back and stills from films and television appearances which he must have sent off for from various studios. He had asked for his identity to be kept secret and I still worry that his image of me was shattered when he saw me in the flesh. We did some pretty heavy poetry – T. S. Eliot and so forth. I hope he enjoyed it as much as *The Bedsit Girl* and *Cary on Cleo*.

I had my second experience of working in a prison when I and some of the touring company did a workshop in Parkhurst while we were on the island. As in Long Lartin, it was a new departure to have actors in the prison and one which the governor was not a little nervous about, there having been recent riots. For this reason we were only allowed to work with nine of the inmates.

We requested not to have guards in the room, feeling their presence would inhibit us all. The first prisoner jogged in wearing over-long shorts and dripping with sweat having just finished a weight-training session. The other eight drifted in one by one – some silent, some giggling – all embarrassed. We dealt with them in the usual way of playing games to unite the group. Sitting cross-legged on the floor, we did rhythmic word-association games, hummed yoga mantras and then danced and did some movement exercises. Once the weight-lifter decided he had nothing to lose and began to join in with gusto the others followed suit, except one man who hung his head and kept silent. I used my usual approach of physical contact with him and started to massage his shoulders in the hopes of relaxing him. I am rather proud of my 'healing hands', but on this occasion my method failed lamentably and the man visibly tightened. One of the others drew me aside and whispered that the day before another prisoner had thrown scalding water over this man's shoulders and he was a mass of blisters under his shirt. Although my kneading hands must have hurt him dreadfully, he had understood my intention and made every effort to join in after that; he has used part of his precious letter allocation to write to me since.

When we were all relaxed – indeed, by this time I had completely forgotten where we were – we turned to working on the text of *The Dream*. I had asked that they should be given copies before our arrival and read them with their English tutor, Carol Martys. They confessed they found it incomprehensible and utterly unfunny. None of them had ever seen Shakespeare, or indeed any play, on stage. So we tackled the Mechanicals' scenes first. We urged them not to bother about thinking that the scenes were meant to be comic, but just to try to understand the urgency and effort these working-class men were putting into presenting a play for the toffs. Not unlike themselves, really. Gradually the titters started and very soon we were roaring with laughter. They thought up bits of business which we put into the show later and they ended up unanimously voting the scenes 'bloody funny', and we agreed that they were the best cast for the play we had ever seen. It affirmed Joan Littlewood's belief that anyone can act.

By the time we moved on to the more difficult task of tackling the poetry of the play, they were prepared to have a go at anything – even a man falling in love with a fairy. Our weight-lifter eventually played the meeting of Bottom and Titania with Penny, who found new depths in her interpretation by her passionate desire to get through to him. As she promised him all the soft and lovely gifts that Titania offers Bottom, 'to purge thy mortal grossness', Shakespeare's spell fell upon a roomful of united rogues and vagabonds. I wept – of course. Then we were told it was time to go and the hugs we exchanged on parting told of the bond we had forged.

On my way home on the ferry a couple of days later, I was approached by a guard from Parkhurst in civvies. He was a tough nut. Told me he believed in capital punishment. An eye for an eye was his credo. It's them or us. Anyway, if they topped some of them it would prevent overcrowding in the prisons. Less work for us. Half of that lot would get the chop. For instance, the bloke who had tenderly played one of the love scenes had thrown his wife to her death over a balcony; you had to keep your distance from them or they took liberties.

After a couple of drinks he suddenly said, 'You did well – you lot. Do you learn that, then – how to deal with people?' It dawned on me that, like doctors, the guards were given no training in communication. It was not considered a prime requirement for the job. Why should it be? He kept control in his own way – most of the time. He told me that a big posse of guards had been stationed in the corridor whilst we did the workshop – their 'fingers on the button', using mirrors to see what was going on without us or the inmates seeing them. They had all been ready to burst in when I massaged the man's shoulders. As the session went on, he confessed, they had all become engrossed, and he admitted he would not have thought it possible for anyone to get that group doing what we did. The guards had been uneasy that the men would cause trouble the next day, but apparently they had been still excited and full of it. One had proudly told Reggie Kray that he had been acting with the RSC, and another had come out of his cell next morning shouting, 'To be or not to be', to which the warder had replied, 'Yes, that's the bloody question, isn't it?' and they both had a laugh. In other words, he conceded, we had done nothing but good.

I firmly believe that uniting people through creative pursuits is beneficial to both individuals and the community in general. We all need to express ourselves. On one of the OU summer school weeks I went to, it was lovely to see people, hitherto unaware that they had any talent, turning out wonderful pictures and sculptures from found objects. No ballet at Covent Garden was deeper felt or more engrossing than a dance by a fat little woman who had started the week barely able to say hello. The discos at summer schools are rip-roaring occasions, with child-bearing hips gyrating amongst the pot-bellies with explosive abandon, frequently outlasting the younger dancers. The divisions are inevitably there; in the OU as in the country in general. North/South, good/bad, upper/middle/lower-class: but we manage to reach across the barriers. Class, regional, political and religious divides are completely swept away at Greenham too.

I am sure this is mainly because they express their protest very largely through their talents. The poems, the paintings, the music they create is what distinguishes one woman from another, not their education or their class. The punk with blue hair from London and the lesbian separatist from Wales would not normally have much in common with each other, let alone with the local Newbury woman who periodically joins them in her neat tent, and climbs daintily over the wire with them, clutching her good leather handbag and wearing her smart fur hat; yet here they are friends. The youngsters were full of admiration when this woman was caught red-handed in the camp but shook off the arresting soldier's hand, indignantly protesting, 'Don't be a silly little man – do I *look* like a Greenham woman?' The working-class women roar with laughter as she sloshes round in the mud with middle-class disdain, and the vegetarians never protest when she eats Marks and Spencer's Chicken Kiev, fastidiously cooked over the bonfire next to their vegetable stews.

The group that could not cope with this particular lady were the authorities at Holloway Prison, where she was taken having not been able to convince the policeman of her innocence. She treated it like a hotel, demanding her full quota of rights: visits from all denominations of padres and a full medical (usually avoided by the women), including a smear and breast cancer test – 'Cheaper than BUPA, darlings.' Eventually, she was turned out before her sentence was up on the desperate pretext that she had paid her fine from money found in her purse. She protested violently that Her Majesty had invited her to stay for a week, but they could not take any more of her. Complaining that they make her house smell dreadfully, she continues to open her doors to the camp women for baths and the occasional warm-up.

I suppose the single most unifying device is a good education. The quickest way to remove divisions would be to give everyone the same opportunities. And, after my tour of the nation's schools, let no one dare tell me they have, or utter the old canard that some very successful men and women have had poor educations – they were exceptional or lucky. How many others have slipped through the net? It is usually the educated that are disparaging about the value of knowledge. (I got a lot of that when there was publicity about my OU course. 'Why do you need a degree with your life experience?', 'You must formulate your own views', 'Life is the best tutor.' When I pursued the points they made, I discovered that *all* the antis had come from people who had in fact been to university themselves.) I had not the slightest idea of what university was like as a child, so I did not go to one then. The only people I knew with degrees were my teachers, and I never met a single person who had been to university other than them until after I was eighteen. I envied my teachers their impressive gowns on Speech Day, but they seemed from another world to me. Because my sister was already in the variety theatre the stage seemed more accessible. So, despite matriculating in seven subjects with five distinctions and two credits, I left school at fifteen and, funded by the first Kent Education Scholarship in Drama, I made my start on a theatrical career. I probably would not if I had my time again. Despite Alan Coast and Dopey.

It would be nice to think that that kind of unawareness was a thing of the past, but it isn't. The options are still not properly presented to everyone. People who have grown up surrounded by books and music have no idea what it is like when you have not. I was lucky to have an Auntie Ruby and some good teachers to enlighten me: above all, Miss Winifred Scott, LRAM, my piano teacher, a pale, frail lady who placed her hankie, smelling of sweet violets, on the treble clef while she manipulated my fingers with her soft cold hands. I enjoyed my visits to her but I never practised. One day in desperation she put on a record of the orchestration of Grieg's Piano Concerto and thundered out the piano part of the first movement in her Bexleyheath front parlour. I could not believe my ears. I wrote down the title and composer and rushed straight round to the post office, took out my savings, and tried to buy the record for my father's wind-up gramophone. They had not got it and suggested some Tchaikovsky instead, but I had never heard of him and could not imagine that anyone else wrote stuff like that. Miss Scott and a teacher at school, Miss Tudor Craig, gradually taught me about the others that did.

How *can* we not realise the vital importance of our teachers? How have teachers, so respected when I was a child, now become the villains of society? Why have we reached a state where many of them feel they are fighting a losing battle against cut-backs and criticism? And how can we believe that the Arts only merit 0.003 per cent of our national expenditure? By the Arts, I do not mean just the RSC and the National, but Gazebo and all those TIE and community groups, and new approaches not even dreamed of yet. In 1987, they held the first Government-sponsored debate on the Arts in the House of Commons for thirty years. At the end of it, only a hundred-odd MPs remained in their seats – and this at a time when people are increasingly forced to fill non-working hours. The Arts are at the bottom of the country's priorities, yet the Mechanicals in *The Dream*, the men in Parkhurst and Long Lartin, the dancer in the OU workshop, the sign-writer in Workington, the young painters in Castleford and Woodbridge all discovered how fulfilling using a talent can be, as well as learning to admire those of others.

While on the Isle of Wight I had to dart up to London to make a speech at the SWET Awards. Two things occurred to me. First, how much these publicity junkets contribute to the false impression of actors. No wonder people do not think we are human. Nearly all of us loathe these occasions: dolled-up to the nines, putting on a good loser's face, making the ghastly thank-you speeches, and smiling and smiling and smiling. The second thing was prompted by a speech from Joan Littlewood. She stood, clutching her prize, next to Peter Brook, clutching his, looking like a cruet set, and made her usual speech about acting whilst he nodded benignly. Everyone can act. Get rid of religion and politics, let's have the clowns. Although perhaps she overstated her case, I know what she means. We need the politicians to provide the jobs to eliminate that aspect of the North/South divide, but it is the clown, the artist in all of us who can break down many of the other divisions without sacrificing the uniqueness of the individual.

10 : Bridges
Thatcham, Stroud, Stratford

HUMBER BRIDGE — ACCESS TO HIGH PLACES — THATCHAM — FEMININE INTERPRETATION OF SHAKESPEARE — WOMEN'S GROUPS — *THE FEMALE EUNUCH* — *NOW SERIOUSLY, IT'S SHEILA HANCOCK* — TOKEN WOMEN — WOMEN DIRECTORS AND WHY THEY ARE NEEDED — WHY THEY CANNOT GET IN — WOMEN AND HISTORY — MEN'S CLUBS — MARGARET THATCHER — PREMA PROJECT — LAST NIGHT OF THE TOUR — REHEARSING AGAIN — STRATFORD — CRITICISING THE CRITICS — UNEMPLOYMENT — SECURITY — THE ACTORS CENTRE — ARTS FOR ALL

I love bridges. When I was evacuated to Wallingford I played under the mysterious arches of the Thames Bridge there; whenever in Newcastle I enjoy walking by the great iron structure over the Tyne, and from Bridgnorth I visited the cradle of the Industrial Revolution at Ironbridge, and admired the Brunel invention that the Victorians thought so stunning.

What would they have made of the Humber Bridge? It blew my mind when I first went over it earlier in the tour on my way to Middlesborough. If one's life is low on thrills, a trip over this wondrous structure is highly recommended. When I nosed my MG on to the start, the old heart was pumping as I looked at the thin ribbon of road ahead, suspended on a cobweb of wires hanging from two slender towers, and as I crossed my stomach lurched when I peeked to my left at the chasm of water below. Then my fear gave way to exhilaration and I whistled, spluttered and laughed out loud at the sheer audacity of crossing these sinister depths on a piece of gossamer. How did they *do* it, never mind the Pyramids, and Stonehenge? I confess I turned round and went back, then crossed again. It was worth every penny of the £3.60, and I was delighted to help them pay off their £259,000,000 debt.

Yes, men can build beautiful bridges. But they seem to have problems in finding the new skills needed to build some metaphorical ones. They talk a lot about bridging the gap between men and women's positions in society, but talk is the only thing that has radically changed in the last decade. The bra-burning jokes would be considered bad taste now, but with only two top companies out of one thousand having a woman in the chair and only 6.2 per cent of managerial posts in industry held by women in 1986, not to mention all the current frantic machinations to prevent women entering the Ministry of the Church, I do not think we can claim to have crossed the drawbridge into many hallowed citadels. As I write this, the Director General of the BBC has just resigned and lots of men are pontificating about who should take over. It did not even enter their heads that it should be a woman, despite the huge female TV audience. I believe that men's sympathetic words about equality cloak their absolute disbelief that anything would improve if women played a greater part in public life: they still believe that it would be unnatural and to their detriment. Exactly the same reasons still stop most men taking over their share of domestic chores, even when women are working as many hours outside the home as they.

The opportunities for actresses are admittedly better than for, say, surgeons or MPs, for the simple reason that there have to be some women for the female roles. The increase in women playwrights is beginning to alter things, but in most plays there is still a preponderance of male parts, especially in those by Shakespeare. The men far outnumber the women in the acting company at the RSC, and the men also usually have louder voices so the women can easily be shouted down. As in Thatcham, our next tour venue.

Since I commuted from London, I remember little of Thatcham except a standing ovation on the first night that warmed the cockles of our hearts, and a splendid banquet, cooked by the school's domestic science students, that did much for our stomachs. But our extremities were frozen. A nasty fire inspector made pointless restrictions on our lighting and dressing-room heating arrangements with the result that Thatcham audiences were treated to a shivering Oberon, who had to be restrained from covering his bare torso with a decidedly earthly overcoat, and a frozen Puck, who wanted to wear Doc Martens on his bare feet. Also, the cold didn't help the rehearsal I had called because one of the actresses was worried about a duologue in the play which wasn't working well. Throughout the rehearsal, the young actor involved in the scene suggested that if she did such and such, he could do this, and every criticism I had of his approach to the scene was diverted into complaints about her. Her interpretation was unconventional but truthful, and had he listened he could just as well have changed to fit in with her as she with him. As things got heated the woman gave up, being less articulate than he, and the morning ended in tears. When I spoke to her afterwards, she admitted that it had got to the stage when she would rather do what he wanted than suffer further aggro – the cry of women down the ages, whether faced with physical or mental violence. The rather uptight young man had reverted to type by finding it difficult to accept a radical change suggested by two women, especially since the new interpretation we were putting forward was one which made his character look ridiculous – and some actors are not too keen on that. In his view, it was more natural that the woman should end at a disadvantage in the scene; weeping, in fact.

Even the most liberated of men have received images of women that they mistake for reality, usually involving a lot of gentleness, a lot of charm and a few tears. It is not that actors or male directors deliberately distort the portrayal of female characters, but it is obviously difficult for them to comprehend our behaviour as well as they do that of their own sex. The new young actresses like Juliet Stevenson or Harriet Walter, who were acting with the RSC at the same time as me, were beginning to challenge the male perception of Shakespeare's women, but it was hard going. Not only the directors but our fellow actors were apt at best to tolerate, but at worst to ridicule our contributions. I had difficulties rehearsing the scene in *The Winter's Tale* where Paulina confronts the men in Leontes' court, seeing them all as weak idiots and Paulina as the only honest person there. I was making a generalised judgement of the male characters' behaviour, but equally so were they in perceiving her as simply an interfering nag.

The actors took more kindly to suggestions Gemma Jones and I made to explain Leontes' seemingly unreasonable attack of violent jealousy against his wife, Hermione. We tried to explain how, in spite of ourselves, pregnancy had made us almost cruel in our self-absorption, preoccupied by pleasure in our own bodies; how, in the latter stages, we probably had not needed or wanted our partner's attentions and could understand them feeling left out. Further, we confided how we had several times been on the receiving end of thoroughly nice men's romantic attentions during their wives' pregnancies, which proved Leontes was not the first man to be driven to ignoble behaviour at that time. One or two of the married actors shifted uncomfortably at this revelation, but the women's viewpoint was genuinely helpful. On this occasion the actors had everything to gain by listening; an explanation of seemingly inexcusable male behaviour as being caused by a woman's unthinking neglect. It is less easy to convince some of them when it might lessen their impact or switch sympathy away from the male character.

In *Titus Andronicus*, I thought much more should be made of the murder of Tamara's son and her humiliation in the first scenes to explain her own later savagery, and that the Romans should be shown for the murdering guttersnipes I thought them. But, once the men had weapons in their hands, there was no restraining their 'honourable soldier' approach. Male actors do love swaggering around with swords and have far more empathy than women with codes of honour and the right of kings. They can justify the most appalling atrocities by a king's duty to honour his family, or some such rot which I cannot comprehend. But, on the other hand, I could have explained Tamara's motives if they had wanted to listen. Sadly, like the actress at Thatcham, I did not put my arguments very well and ended up doing more or less what I was told.

In 1981 some of the women at Stratford formed a weekly discussion group to give one another moral support, groups that women are increasingly discovering they need to find their own voices. The Greenham women, the miners' wives, the 300 Group and various others are helping women disprove the old myth that we hate one another, do nothing but bitch when we are together, and that our loyalty to our friends is a secondary consideration to our pursuit of the male. At Stratford that season it was comforting to realise we all felt similar frustrations and we gave one another the courage to speak up.

I need all the help I can get in sorting out my tangled attitudes. My daughters have grown up holding all the new feminist views, but it is less easy for women of my generation. Despite my parents' ambition for me and the fact that my mother worked all her life, at heart they both still believed that the women should service the men; and they certainly could not wait for me to settle down with a good husband. Vicars, fathers and Winston Churchill knew best. It was not until 1970 that I began to question these beliefs. In 1968 I was appearing in Charles Wood's *Fill the Stage with Happy Hours*; which it did not, for many, in the Vaudeville Theatre. During the brief run, three of the other actresses, Faith Brook, Stella Moray and Helen Cotterill, and I, discovered during dressing-room chats that we formed a perfectly balanced foursome for discussion of our personal problems – which seemed to be manifold. We formed ourselves into 'The Group' and continued to meet after the show closed. In 1972 I read the book everyone was talking about – Germaine Greer's *The Female Eunuch*. It shook me rigid. I passed it round 'The Group' and our meetings over the next decade helped me to cope with the radical rethink my life was propelled into by the book.

Not only did it alter my attitude to men and women, but also my approach to my work. I was no longer happy to troll around as the dizzy blonde I had been lumbered with in a succession of sit-coms: *The Rag Trade, Bedsit Girl, Mr Digby Darling, Now Take My Wife*. She had served me well and was right at the time, but now I wanted to show another side of myself. I turned down various ideas from the BBC Light Entertainment Department until eventually, with generosity or exasperation, they offered me an hour's air-time to do with what I liked. Barry Took and I dreamed up a show called *Simply Sheila* which, in turn, led to a series called *Now Seriously, It's Sheila Hancock* in 1972. It did not quite come off and going out late at night on BBC2 it is long forgotten, but it was quite innovative for its time, with poems, cartoons, songs and sketches built round diverse themes such as the Law, Music, Women, the Arts and the Environment, combined with interviews with the likes of Peter Hall, John Mortimer, Kenneth Allsop, Dudley Moore and Germaine herself. Not bad, really, for a comedy show with a woman lead in the early 1970s.

I received many grateful letters from women, but vile notices from the male critics, and the BBC were uneasy about the programme. For one of the shows in the series I wanted to do a sketch by Ken Hoare about prejudice, in which I played a demented, evil landlady who hated everyone. The department put their foot down as they said they found it offensive and were worried about my 'image'. I took it to the head of the channel and, eventually, the head of the BBC until I got my way. I have seldom worked for BBC Light Entertainment since. To be fair, I think they really felt I had gone a bit odd and were bewildered as to what I was trying to do. I was not quite sure myself at the time, but when I see Victoria Wood and her ilk, doing things that I as a woman find funny in a way that I seldom have in TV comedy in the past, I realise it was probably that. Alas, again I missed the bus, or rather got on it too soon, before it was ready to go.

However, I hope it is not too presumptuous to claim I may have opened a few minds at the BBC for later women (the disputed sketch was a big success). Hopefully the same is true at the RSC. Di Trevis, who declined my invitation to join me on the tour, actually ran it two years later. And there has been a Women's Festival in 1986/7, set up by the actresses and allowed by the management. So, at any rate, I do not seem to have put them off.

Any woman who is a first, or token member has a terrible sense of responsibility. Failure is much more noticed and feels like an act of betrayal to your sex. All the time I was at the RSC, and later at the National, I was at pains not to frighten the horses too much lest they should shy away from future potential mares because they thought me a nag. I therefore did not know whether to rejoice or feel guilty when I was told later that on arrival at Stratford my company, particularly the women, were considered 'difficult' for the directors to handle (domi-nate?). 'You are not working for Sheila Hancock now, you know,' was apparently the retort of one director to an argumentative actress.

Of course, it is ridiculous that I was only the second woman Artistic Director at the RSC since Buzz Goodbody founded the Other Place ten years before, although Penny Cherns and Jane Howell both did one-off productions during the decade. The same paucity of women is apparent at the National. I was the first and, as I write, still the last woman to direct on the main Olivier stage. Only Julie Pascall and Nancy Meckler had been let into the other two auditoria before I arrived (and I make no apology for listing the names of some of my fellow women directors who are mentioned too seldom). I am glad that Di Trevis has since followed me to the South Bank, as well as the splendid Sarah Pia Anderson who directed *Derek* on the tour. Both have gone back to Stratford during 1987 to do a production (not, however, on the main stage), as has Deborah Warner. Things are looking up. I suppose we should be grateful for these small but precious mercies. But it is hard not to feel that this attitude to women is a surprising and nasty blot on the liberal reputation of our profession.

One of the most powerful reasons for getting some female directors into the RSC and the National is nothing to do with fairness or equality for its own sake, but just for the sake of improving the work. I believe we women must stop pretending that we are as good/the same as men and emphasise our individual qualities. I have no doubt at all that women are sensitive to different things in life, so too, it follows, to the texts of plays. Surely it could only enrich an audience's perception to get another viewpoint. In a subsequent rehearsal at Thatcham we managed to shift that one particular actor's resistance; but it is hard for actresses to do that without a director's support. Judging by what I see and hear from other actresses, it is sometimes difficult to get that support from a male director. Sadly, though, the men do not see the need for change. I guarantee not one of the associate directors at the RSC has anything *against* women directors *per se*, but what they obviously do not accept is that our inclusion would be a positive benefit. Otherwise we would be there. It is as simple as that.

On the fringe and in the regions, things are better. Women are regularly crossing the bridges. Or, more significantly, building new ones. To fresh designs. Claire Venables runs the huge complex of Sheffield Crucible with a predominantly female staff; Deborah Warner, whom the RSC has now noticed, set up and ran her own Kick Theatre Company, Glen Walford is at Liverpool, Pip Broughton with Paines Plough, Sue Dunderdale at the Soho Poly, Annie Casledine at Derby – all are proving their unique talents. These new organisations, run by women in the theatre, are changing styles of administration and product. Just as at Greenham, they are shunning established male structures. In the new industries, such as PR and advertising, women are doing well because they have made their own rules. However, change is more laborious in the big London-based theatrical organisations. For a start, there seems no definite policy for hiring and firing; the same directors have been there for years. In addition, women have vacillated for too long, like me at St Agnes, shunning the responsibility. The bus had filled up before we tried to get on.

There is no conscious discrimination against women directors at the RSC (in fact there are probably just as many male directors who feel kept out of the charmed circle). But it is only comparatively recently that women have started knocking hard on the directorial doors. If the women had been there from the start, the pattern would have been set differently and the accusations of sexism would not arise. But the men have got set in their ways now and I can understand their attitude. I myself sit on a very successful board of directors, which we are always reluctant to expand because we are frightened newcomers will rock our nicely balanced boat.

In all walks of life, history, tradition and precedent are the enemies of women – whether it be recent history, like that of the National and the RSC, or further back. So many of our structures and so much of our behaviour is based on it. And, as women have only just begun to count, history works against us. Or at least the way it has been interpreted.

When I was young we only learned about kings and queens; the working-class might as well not have existed. Similarly, the chroniclers being men, little mention is made of women. I was amazed to discover in a TV programme by Edna Healey that David Livingstone was usually

A very, very smooth Alec Ross, 1957

Melanie (Ellie-Jane) jumping all over
me – as usual

Above left: My definitive performance as Mrs Senna Pod in *Carry On Cleo* with Jim Dale and Kenneth Connor

Above right: With Edward Woodward in *Rattle of a Simple Man*, 1962

Below: Sending up the perfect hostess in *Now Seriously, It's Sheila Hancock*, 1972

Above left: Come on Sheila – eyes, teeth and tits. Preparing for a sketch in *One Over the Eight*

Above right: I have no idea what I was watching or where I was when this picture was taken, but I have always liked Salvationists since my pub childhood

Below: For this speech the toastmasters awarded me 'The Best After Dinner Speaker of the Year Award, 1969'. Well, at least the body language was eloquent

Above left: My perfect director who happens to be a woman: Joan Littlewood opening the Manchester Actors Centre in 1986

Above right: The Hampstead Theatre Club, November 1972, in *The Effects of Gamma Rays on Man-in-the-Moon Marigolds*

Below: With Richard Briers in Alan Ayckbourn's *Absurd Person Singular*

accompanied on his expeditions by his wife. It was she who set up the trips, liaised with the Africans and started the schools, as well as giving birth to the odd child. But no one told me about her. Who else has not been recorded, I wonder? Perhaps some of the disciples were women, but the male recorders did not think them worth mentioning. That would make some of the elders of the Church who oppose the ordination of women on historic grounds look pretty silly. They would have to drum up some other reason for their misogyny.

It is tempting for women who gain power to join the male club and fit in with the old world. Any feminist who believes that women could change things radically for the better has to take on board Margaret Thatcher. My only defence is that, as a woman of an even earlier generation than I, she cannot have read *The Female Eunuch*, and she does not know Helen, Faith and Stella. Although, to be fair, no one woman could single-handedly change a country that men in the City, the law courts, the Church, Parliament and the media have had buttoned up for so long. Imagine even trying to alter all those games they play in their funny wigs and outfits with their catch-phrases: ''Ear, 'ear', 'order, order', 'the honourable gentleman opposite', 'through the chair'. You try joining the men in chambers, on the floor, on the bench or benches, on the Woolsack or called to, at or propping up the bar, and see if you can persuade them that their Black Rods and three-line whips are odd. When I was in Stroud, I visited Gloucester Cathedral with Joanna and we were prodded savagely by a man when we were not 'upstanding' for a procession of other men and boys in frocks. In this case, men have got more courage of their convictions than I. They have stopped jumping to their feet, like my father did, for women; they have taken to that new behaviour like drakes to water. But not me in Gloucester Cathedral. When the man prodded me, I stood up for the men. So did Joanna. And so has Maggie.

She can stand up to any man. I cannot fault her courage, patriotism and dedication to her job. She sticks to her principles and says what she believes. I just happen to think that almost all her principles and everything she believes are wrong. (So saying, the story of the old actor in the theatrical club comes to mind who, having listened to a young out-of-work nonentity loudly declaring he loathed Judy Garland, gently muttered, 'Oh, what a pity – she spoke so well of you.')

I have actually met Mrs Thatcher several times. The first was when we appeared on *Any Questions* together at Wotton-under-Edge in 1975. It is a terrifying show to appear on, not least because it necessitates reading every newspaper for several weeks before the programme in order to crash in an encyclopedic knowledge of current world affairs, from the Irish question to the latest pop star's misbehaviour. On top of that, if you have expressed an even mildly liberal viewpoint, the mail after the programme unleashes a fascist diatribe that you would not believe possible in this nice country of free speech. Dare to say you are not altogether keen on capital punishment and the anonymous, 'You should be put against a wall and shot' brigade are out in force.

Disturbing though I find all this, I am always tempted into appearing on the show, partly because it flatters my ego to be asked but mainly because I meet such interesting people on the panels. Some that sound interesting turn out to be amazingly mediocre: the self-made millionaire whose main preoccupation seemed to be how to pinch my bottom, the ex-Prime Minister who was much more interested in gossip and bitching than the fate of the nation, the newspaper magnate with dyed ginger-brown hair who picked his nose. More intriguing were Jeffrey Archer, Anthony Crosland, Dennis Potter, Lord Robens, Ernest Marples and, above all, the Right Honourable Margaret Thatcher.

When we appeared together she had just been made Leader of the Opposition and was radiant with confidence. The supper before the show is always infinitely more interesting than the broadcast when public figures temper their opinions for the air-waves. She was no exception and I found her pretty alarming. It is the custom to listen to the news on the radio during the meal in case something has happened which may prompt a question. There was reference to something frivolous and David Jacobs said that it might come up. I was piqued when she said jokingly: 'Well, Sheila can answer that one.' The usual assumption. Actress – daft. Looking back at the transcript of the show it is nice to discover I did actually score a few points over her, usually with well-placed laughs, but I fear my constant, 'I mean, I means' compared unfavourably with her calm, 'Well look nows.'

She has got the better of me on three other occasions. When I was appearing in *Annie* at the Victoria Palace in 1978, we had more than our fair share of Royals and public figures in the audience, usually roped in for some charity benefit. Night after night, the tannoy would inform us that His or Her Majesty/Excellency would be coming on stage after the show to meet the cast so would we wait in a line after the final curtain. We had had several evenings of this in a row and my baby-sitter was getting pretty fed up when we were told to await the Leader of the Opposition. I put my foot down. I informed the company manager I was prepared to be polite to Heads of State and Royals but enough was enough, and I went straight to my dressing-room to change after the curtain-calls.

I had a wonderful dresser, Ann Hoey, whom I have to compete with Miriam Karlin and Judi Dench to get to look after me. Annie was not best pleased with my behaviour. In fact, my dressing-room performance in general is not up to any good dresser's standards. Ever since Athene Seyler told me off for staying drinking with friends in my room after the show: 'It is not a bar, dear, it is your workplace,' that is what I have tried to make it – functional and spartan. Similarly, my gown is more of an overall than a negligée in which to receive back-stage callers, a faded towelling number, smeared with greasepaint on the shoulder where I wipe my fingers between rubbing in the various colours of make-up on my face. I was, therefore, not a pretty sight, standing in my bra, pants and tatty gown hanging loosely over them, when a knock came on the door, swiftly followed by Mrs Thatcher's head round it. 'I did not want to miss you,' she said sweetly, as Annie blushed with shame and I marvelled at her one-upwomanship.

Again, in 1979 when she was Prime Minister, a couple of friends came up to London. After the show I drove them round to see the lights and was gawping at 10 Downing Street when Mrs Thatcher glided home in a limousine. She would probably have given the royal wave to any of her subjects, but I suspect it was with a touch more relish when she saw that I had now come to her door.

The last time I saw her I progressed to be invited inside the door. I had visited Number 10 under Labour administrations, but was surprised to be invited to a party for representatives of the Arts in 1987. Again, I was not at my best. As I stepped out of the taxi the one button holding up my silk skirt burst off, causing it to drop to the pavement. With as much dignity as I could muster I gathered it up, leaped into the taxi again and went back through the surprised barrier of policemen. Rushing into the gift shop opposite the Houses of Parliament, I asked for a safety pin and the shopkeeper kindly took me into his back room and sewed me into my skirt. As I yet again went through the police barrier outside Number 10, I met Sir John Gielgud. When we eventually reached the top of the stairs – Sir John being entranced by all the pictures on the wall on the way up – the Right Honourable Lady all but knocked me over in her rush to appear before the television cameras with our venerable knight.

The room was full of dark-suited men. Doubtless she had not arranged the invitations, but it would have been nice if, as our first lady Prime Minister, she had made sure there were a few more women present than usual. Again, I looked up the transcript of the *Any Questions* I did with her in 1975. In the course of it, she said:

'Well, I don't meet any male chauvinists. They mostly seem to be quite reasonable these days. But there are occasions when in politics you meet someone who looks at you very hard and says, "I believe a woman's place is in the home." And that's quite tricky because, of course, for many women the home is the centre of their lives and what men don't realise is, it's not the limit to women's abilities and we're just trying to make them realise it day by day. But honestly, there aren't many male chauvinists.'

To which one can only reply that we must try harder to make them realise that forty-one women is not enough out of six hundred MPs, and there must be some female chauvinists as there is only one woman in the Cabinet.

But to return to the tour (having dispensed with tortuous links). The leisure centre in Stroud, our last venue, was a lovely design. Built in Cotswold stone, it melts into the surrounding landscaped gardens with restrained charm. We played *Derek* to a great reception at the Prema Arts Centre in the village of Uley. I knew the centre before this visit, having in 1981 opened the upper room in which we were to perform. The place had been started the previous year when the son of a local respected family had returned from his wanderings in India and bought the virtually derelict Bathsheda Chapel. Local children would drift in to watch him painting and turning pots, and gradually they began to join in.

Andrew and his wife Caroline bring to this small Gloucestershire village the most extraordinary programme of events. Our London critics, who always complain about the insularity of our theatre, should pay a visit to Prema Project. A typical choice of workshops for a three-month period in 1986 included Chinese calligraphy, Nigerian dyeing and printing, West African mask-making, Latin American puppetry and the Japanese tea ceremony. The regular ones include all forms of art, contemporary dance, creative knitting, writing and body-popping. There are also plays and films from Russia, Poland, India, the USA and Europe.

It was a joy to do our last performances of *Derek* and our children's play at a place that puts into practice all the things I would like to see happen everywhere else; discovering and developing people's talents, plus the added bonus of building bridges between this tiny Gloucestershire town and different cultures worldwide.

At our last night of *The Dream* in Stroud, I was delighted to see in the audience our Barnsley supporters in their funny hats, along with several others from various parts of the country. Although we were going on to do it at Stratford, it was the last performance with the present cast and we knew it would never be quite the same again. This play about love and friendship at the end of our extraordinary four months together was deeply touching. When Michael Thomas dragged me on to the stage at the end to join in the final dance, muttering, 'Now you can see how embarrassing it is,' and then Robert made a gracious and generous speech, I was beside myself. Clutching my treasured book that the company gave me, after the auditorium was struck for the last time, I went back to my hotel with Joanna and felt the world had come to an end. As I left the next morning, the cheerful landlord handed me a note to give to my husband who had stopped there the previous year when filming. When I got home, I was pouring out my heart to John about the loss of my company and how awful it all was when I remembered it.

John read it to me. The landlord wanted to tell him that his daughter, mother of two young children, whom he thought John would remember, had died suddenly a month before. Before the first night of the tour I had sat outside Lincoln staring at two trees to remind myself there was a world elsewhere: this piece of paper served the same purpose after the last.

*

I was soon thrown back into the old RSC routine when, on phoning the Barbican by chance two days after my return from Stroud, I was told, 'You are holding your first audition in ten minutes' time.' As usual, everybody thought somebody else had informed me. I arrived at the Barbican hot, bothered and apologetic and went through the difficult task of replacing the six members of my cast who had left. One of my biggest losses was Daniel Day Lewis as a perfect Thisbe whom I myself had urged to leave and become a film star, after which I assured him the RSC would offer him better roles. I never gave anyone wiser advice.

Eventually I found splendid replacements. It was strange for the old company to rehearse the play they knew so well with the newcomers. It was actually very refreshing in many ways, but it was sometimes difficult to convince the company that treasured moments that had worked marvellously before were no longer appropriate. One of my regrets during our rehearsal period was a loss of innocence in our approach.

Because, of course, now we were going to be judged by the clever-sticks and the critics. When we moved from London to Stratford for the final week of rehearsal, this pressure became more obvious.

It is a very cloistered world in Stratford. Whilst I was there acting in 1981/2 I had little contact with the townsfolk who, on the whole, do not seem to like the actors very much although we bring them in quite a bit of money. Most of them are so busy making this money that they have no time to attend the performances anyway. So the company are thrown together for months on end, like a huge family not of our own making. Usually propinquity works its spell, a good time is had by all and it is inspiring to be doing Shakespeare's plays in his home town.

The Other Place, where we were to perform *The Dream* and *Romeo and Juliet*, which has in its time mounted some of the best productions at the RSC, is actually a corrugated-iron hut, the same stuff as our Anderson air-raid shelter was made of. Buzz Goodbody, the first Artistic Director, and Jean Moore, the first administrator, had opened the theatre to the public in April 1974, exactly ten years before we arrived with the touring company. One year later in April 1975, just after opening her production of *Hamlet* with Ben Kingsley in the title role, Buzz killed herself at the age of twenty-eight.

She loved the Other Place, as do the actors, despite appalling back-stage conditions. It is difficult to explain its charm. Theatre spaces either work or they don't. It is not just the acoustics or the sight-lines, it is an inexplicable atmosphere that places like the Other Place have and others have not. It is hideously uncomfortable for the audiences, too hot or too cold, the seats cramped and hard, and it is almost better to observe a show from outside the theatre and catch the actors charging round the grounds in all weathers to make an entrance from the other end, often doing a quick change *en route*. The actors have to shout to make themselves heard over the rain beating on the roof. And local church bells or firework displays are a nightmare. But, given all this, it is an example of how the most unlikely spaces can work while buildings costing millions can sometimes fail to gel.

It calls for a delicate approach, though, and the first preview of *The Dream* was not a success. The company misjudged the space and were pushing too hard, as they frequently had to with the acoustics on the tour. The laughs were coming in different places with the new cast, they felt insecure and depressed, and in such a tiny place every emotion is communicated to the audience. We had to work very hard over the next few previews to regain the spirit of the play, but the night before the critics were due we did. It was a magical performance, and it seemed as if the audiences had at last stopped comparing it with all the other *Dreams* they had seen and gave themselves to the play as they had done on the tour. Despite this, however, much as I tried to persuade them it was irrelevant what a handful of scribblers felt after all the people we had already played to, the company were anxious about the critics' reaction. Knowing how difficult it would be to conceal myself in that tiny auditorium, I decided I could do them no good by sitting amongst the first-night audience, particularly as I would be radiating anxiety for them. So, after a warm up and a pep talk, I said goodbye. In our profession you are always saying goodbye, but this one was more painful than most.

I was expecting that the show would not go well on the first night, with the restricted space crammed full of men with notebooks on their knees: theatre is a communal activity and I have seldom known a premiere, particularly in a small theatre, not to be blighted by the critics' breaking of that essential bond by the calculated detachment necessary for their job. But I am told that on the first night of *The Dream* the actors did pretty well, despite the loud whisper from one of the critics when the Mechanicals came on before the show and chatted to the audience of, 'Oh God, we know what this is going to be like, don't we?' They were not even thrown when one of the critics fell asleep. It was, after all, hot with the heaters on and they had been seen having a convivial time in the Duck before the show. I did once sit behind a man who snored through Olivier's stunning *Richard III*, but then he was not going to write a notice about it.

In a way, though disappointed for the company by the bad reviews we received, it was a salutary experience for me. Hitherto I have always believed the bad notices rather than the good; this time I believed the good ones. These dreaded paragraphs are usually the first opinions from outsiders that actors get after rehearsing a play. During previews friends and relatives come, but they are bound to be biased in your favour. But on this occasion, because we had been playing for four months to perceptive reactions, and even children had noticed points that the critics had utterly missed, I knew they were wrong. Indeed, two of the reviews so incensed me that I plucked up my courage and photostated a pile of letters of thanks from all over the country and sent them to the critics in question to illustrate how dull they had been. One of these critics who had, in his notice, accused me, as 'a funny actress' of being a 'wicked' choice to head an RSC tour of the regions, replied condescendingly: 'Of course I would not deny for a minute that your *MND* was a crowd-pleaser.

That was not my point. Your fine swatch of letters indicates that a lot of people had a very nice time. But none, I think, has been written by a poet.' Whereupon he got another earful from me about his utter conceit in assuming he was more of a poet than they were.

It is always difficult to criticise the critics as it seems like sour grapes. But I have had lots of very good reviews, and if I am honest I still think the overall standard of criticism we have at the moment is the lowest I can remember since I started in the theatre; an opinion that is shared by most of my colleagues behind closed doors.

I suppose our poor, jaded critics were bound not to go with any great anticipation to see a play they know inside out directed by a 'funny actress'. It was not a revolutionary production, nor was intended to be. But it had one or two new things to say about the women in the play which were completely overlooked and, above all, it had some stunning performances which were scarcely mentioned. Small, subtle details are overlooked by weary scribes who have been at the job for years and need something really startling to shake them out of their apathy. And that is where the main complaint lies. Most of the critics have simply been at it too long. The good ones like Tynan, Levin and Fenton left when they got fed up, but some of our major critics just refuse to budge.

Blame is laid at directors' doors for the present emphasis on concept and sets. I suspect some should also be laid on our critics. Judging by the way most directors disappear after the reviews, regardless of the state of the show, their sole intention seems to be to please these fellows, never mind the audiences. So it follows that approaches are sometimes taken to please the critics rather than the public, which would be all right if so many of them did not have a limited outlook. Indeed, most of our major critics are from the same middle-class, middle-aged, academic, white, male mafia as the directors.

It is absurd that we have practically no black critics. I am equally sure the lack of female critics is detrimental to the theatre. The male critics wax sentimental nowadays over Buzz Goodbody, but when she was alive they were far less perceptive about her work. They viciously attacked her one main-house production of *As You Like It*, which destroyed her confidence for large-scale work, and ironically she died before her best reviews for – *Hamlet* – were published.

The same lack of understanding of women's roles as shown by male directors is evident in male criticism. I did a play at the Hampstead Theatre Club called *How Gamma Rays Affected the Man in the Moon Marigolds*. (Admittedly in 1972, but I would maintain that little has changed.) In it I played a mother who abused her children, making no attempt to temper her cruelty although I hope I also demonstrated through the script the reasons for her behaviour. The critics were unanimously appalled and hurled insults at the play and myself. Caring deeply for the character, I was shocked at their reaction and my apparent betrayal of the play until Germaine Greer wrote a critique of their criticisms, trying to explain how worried these male middle-class men had been by the shattering of their mother image whereas the women in the audience had been moved by the harsh reality of motherhood. There were no women critics to put forward that view. My performance as Mrs Darling, the archetypal mother in *Peter Pan*, moved them to superlatives whilst driving me to drink with her tedium and unreality. It reminded me of Angela Lansbury hesitating to do *Gypsy* in London because she considered the British critics did not like gutsy women.

I suppose we should try to discuss things more with the critics, but it is usually embarrassing to meet them face to face. Even so, it is a pity there is not more liaison between the good ones and us workers. We should build some bridges there too. There is no doubt that some of them have a broad knowledge acquired by seeing so much theatre here and overseas, and although they cannot do it themselves they have taste and discretion that could be put to good use by the practitioners. My correspondence with the other critic, Michael Coveney, after *The Dream*, was actually quite enlightening: for us both, I hope!

But the company told me on the phone that their anger about the stupid reviews was quickly assuaged by the packed, happy audiences, and my confidence was soon restored by the continuing flow of letters from people as diverse as John Barton (probably the most knowledgeable person I know about Shakespeare's language), David Hare, Tony Sher and an old-age pensioner who, 'at 1.30 am was sitting up in bed with a large brandy and soda, still chuckling'. I soon began to feel less 'wicked'.

It was strange to visit the company from time to time to give notes as an outsider. For, while they went from triumph to triumph as they took on new plays at Stratford, I joined the legions of the unemployed. I was not unduly worried for the first five months. I was used to it. Any actor is. Casual labourers, we do not have the same terror of unemployment as do people who are used to regular jobs. At any given moment seventy-five per cent of our profession are idle, and to be 'resting' is no disgrace, just an occupational hazard.

In the present climate of job uncertainty in the country, actors are probably the only people who feel relatively at home. I suspect there is something in our natures that actually thrives on insecurity. When I see some folk striving to keep up with the boring Joneses, giving themselves coronaries to obtain an apparently joyless life, I can understand theatre-folk's preference for adventure and frightening leaps in the dark. It seems sad that people spend so much energy pursuing security when, in actual fact, it does not exist. Factories close down, husbands leave and there are knock for knock agreements in car insurances. I have seen in the bereavement counselling I undertake the amount of suffering that is caused by the shock of discovering one has been led into believing life can be made safe. So perhaps we actors are more sane than most in not having these objectives. I have a lovely house now, but I would not be in the least surprised if I had to sell it tomorrow and live in a bedsit. I have done it before and can do it again. But what is most important, is that my fellow actors would merely regard it as the normal sort of hiccup that could happen to anyone. There would be no shame.

The main horror of unemployment in the theatre, as elsewhere, is the isolation. That we do feel. To help alleviate this, I have collaborated with a small group of actors and actresses in setting up a thriving Actors Centre in London and Manchester, as dreamed up by Clive Swift, where we can meet, learn and exchange information, whether working or not. There are divided political factions in Equity, but this centre helps to form bridges between them.

I would like to see artists better used during these gaps between jobs. But, then again, I would actually like to see a revolution in everyone's attitude to leisure, which I think is what we have to begin to regard unemployment as. We have to change our attitude towards it, but no political party has the guts to take on board the fact that if people like me have got to be dragged screaming into a robot world then we are all going to have to work less.

Perhaps we should have a campaign like the hugely successful Sports For All, which has filled the magnificent complexes that have been built all over the country: an Arts For All campaign. We do not need specially designed buildings. Quite the reverse. We have had enough of them. Each area could adapt a building that is already familiar and liked by the inhabitants. Some towns already have centres, but nowhere near enough; and those that exist are desperately underfunded. Each centre would develop its own personality according to the local character. The problem is how to legislate for developments in the Arts; the fashionable cost-effectiveness does not apply. Individuals with vision, like Andrew in Uley or Jimmy in Workington and Peter Hall or Trevor Nunn, have to be allowed their heads. If the vision is strange, like Joan Littlewood's Fun Palace, it is difficult to produce feasibility studies on it to satisfy civil servants. But we put up with the experiments of scientists and engineers; why not let the artists have a go at wasting money? At least they will not blow everyone up.

If these new bridges are not going to be built in the orthodox way, then we have to find other ways of getting across to people. As a child, I found it thrilling to be dared to paddle through a pitch-dark tunnel over a stream, going *under* the bridge, and emerging triumphant, blinking at the sun. There are more ways than one of getting over to the other side.

I got across the Thames to the South Bank, for instance, via a phone call on 12 January 1985. After my gloomy period of unemployment, the sun was about to shine.

PART THREE

THE NATIONAL

11 : Fun
At the National

These days I seldom have to audition for a job, although I am quite happy to do so if necessary. I did in 1978 for the role of Miss Hannigan in *Annie* because Martin Charnin, the American producer, did not know me from Eve and the English contingent was not sure if I could sing well enough. (I couldn't, but they still engaged me.) Similarly, I had to go through my vocal paces for Stephen Sondheim before getting the much-coveted role of Mrs Lovett in *Sweeney Todd*. Both these trials were, in fact, enjoyable experiences conducted by sensitive men; but in the bad old days of my youth, auditions were all too often humiliating cattle markets.

As soon as news of an audition got out, a queue would form outside the theatre where it was being held and you would wait, come wind, come rain, sometimes for several hours, before you were herded on to the stage. I was invariably weeded out in first line-ups where you were judged merely on your appearance. A disembodied voice from the stalls would shout: 'The blonde with the legs, the little pretty one, the thin one in the green shorts', and so forth, but seldom, 'the tall one with the spots'. A harassed stage manager then separated out the lucky few, whereupon all the 'sparkle, sparkle, eyes, teeth and tits' would drain from the rest of us, as we shuffled off the stage, dismissed by a brusque 'Next' from the darkness.

Any selection process in such an overcrowded profession is bound to be dispiriting for the rejected, but actors these days usually receive slightly better treatment. Of course, there are still hurts and humiliations in getting work but they are not quite so flagrant as in those days of the mass audition. Now the main problem is getting a good agent since auditions and interviews are usually by appointment only. Without an agent it is very difficult to know that casting is taking place, and some managements will not respond to direct applications from actors anyway. You can no longer just turn up if you hear of an audition; you have to be on the list. If you are lucky you are contracted to an agent who exclusively looks after his or her 'stable', as it is rather insultingly called. They make it their business to know what parts are being cast and contact the managements or directors, suggesting their artists. Without such an agent you have to spend your unemployment money on stamps for hundreds of letters and making dozens of phone calls, hoping to get someone to see you. If your agent is not very *au fait* with what is going on, you have to do that anyway; it is a constant complaint of actors that these middle-men and women do nothing to help them get a job, yet still take ten or fifteen per cent of their weekly salary. As a result many actors are forming themselves into co-operatives, staffing the phones for each other when they are out of work: their names describe their policy – Actors' Alliance, Actors' Exchange, Actors' File, Actorum and, more colourfully, A Narrow Road.

When I was starting out it was very different; there were a few top agents who contracted the leading players, then a myriad of others who were glorified job-sellers – the jobs usually being in one of the many weekly repertory companies throughout the country. These agents ran a free-for-all system of trying to get anyone a job for which they, naturally, took their ten per cent. This meant that hundreds of actors who had no up-market agent had to do the rounds of all the tatty ones, hoping their face would fit any of the jobs on offer that day.

I would come up daily from Bexleyheath in my best clothes, including the hat and gloves which were obligatory in London then, and tramp up and down Charing Cross Road, St Martin's Lane and Shaftesbury Avenue where most of these agents were based, including the doyenne of them all, Miriam Warner. A tiny, fat, Jewish woman who always wore a big squashed hat (rumoured to cover a bald head), she operated from two small rooms in Cambridge Circus (and was said to be in league with MI6 opposite). In the outer office, covered in cigarette ash, worked the faded ex-chorus girl, Pauline, and an ex-comic, Smithie, dispensing tea and a list of Miss Warner's latest faux pas to out-of-work actors. Miss

Warner herself would regale you with stories of all the people she had discovered and guided to fame and fortune, like 'Young Laurie Oliver', before offering you 'a special week of twice-nightly repertory in Upper Drodsmouth – provide your own costumes – salary eight pounds, ten shillings and no pence a week, and I had to fight to get that, dearie'. I have never dared ask 'Laurie' if he ever met her.

When I was still at RADA she got me a job as a Bluebell Girl in Paris and was furious when Sir Kenneth Barnes, the Principal of the Academy, turned down my request to leave my course early. He had never heard of Miss Bluebell and appeared to be under the impression that she was some sort of white-slave trader. With my height and my acne I was not going to be easy to place, Miss Warner warned, and some of those Bluebell Girls married Lords. Despite Sir Kenneth's rebuff she persevered in trying to place me in the theatre. One day I arrived, dolled up to the nines in a new suit and hat with a veil in which I felt quite attractive for once. I was ushered into her office where she somewhat dampened my confidence by announcing triumphantly: 'I've got just the job for you at last. Panto – wolf-skin provided.' In the light of my friend Brian's success as a rat, I rather regret turning down this offer.

She managed to twist the arms of a few repertory companies to employ the nineteen-year-old me as a 'juvenile character girl', as long as I always wore flat shoes and covered my acne with Max Factor pancake. As my versatility became known in weekly repertory circles, in my twenties I added to my CV 'leading lady' and 'character woman', thereby saving the companies a lot of money since I then had to play everything from adolescents to centenarians and they never needed to give me a week out. Miss Warner would encourage me by listing all the plain actresses that had become stars – with her help, of course. 'Look at Flora Robertson, darling – I did all right for her.' Occasionally she took me out to the theatre on complimentary tickets she had wangled. In 1956 we went to Paul Scofield's *Hamlet* which I suspect was not really her cup of tea. Her body overflowed the seat and she wheezed and fidgeted through it all, except the famous soliloquy 'To be or not to be', at the start of which she perked up no end. 'I like this bit,' she said, and proceeded to sing-along-with-Paul very loudly and inaccurately, nodding and smiling at the audience round her, oblivious of their disdain. She gave him a round of applause at the end of the speech, saying in a loud whisper: 'He's very good. I discovered him, you know.'

We older actors tend to laugh at the memory of Miriam Warner, but I have every reason to be grateful to her. In my first eight years in the business she was the only person who got me any work at all. There was so little of it about, apart from the reps and some tours. The bulk of actors these days make their living on television, but there was scarcely any work in that field when I was young. Radio was quite busy but the BBC Repertory Company did all the plays and that was an impossible circle to penetrate. The National, of course, did not exist and the RSC was not the gargantuan organisation it is today; just one company in one theatre at Stratford. Apart from the cattle markets, the West End was absolutely out of bounds too. The exotic Binkie Beaumont seemed to put on all the plays in London, using the same people all the time, and the women were usually Vivien Leigh, Claire Bloom, Coral Browne and their beautiful ilk: I would never have been perfect casting for fey maidens in Christopher Fry plays, even if I had been part of the charmed theatrical West End circle – which I was not. I was never invited to one of Terence Rattigan's parties. I had to wait for the Michael Codrons to come along before I could get a look in. That, and a change of taste.

Tom Stoppard, with whom I was just about to work in 1986, wrote of me back in 1962: 'Sheila Hancock fits into the new clutch of toughened individualists now ousting the tradition of sweet young things who once conquered all with a wistful lift of a false eyelash.' The long years of ousting by actresses like me were not easy. They would have toughened anyone.

The agent rounds were much more fun, however, after I married Alec, since he included several hostelries in his visits. The Salisbury public house in St Martin's Lane was the starting point as it was full of actors passing on casting news. The Arts Theatre Club was more conventional, but nearby was the hard drinkers' hang-out, the ever-open Kismet, these days cowering beneath a health club and organic food restaurant. Modern actors are more likely to frequent those than the gloomy hole that was in those days graced by the regular presence of Dylan Thomas, Peter Finch and the glorious Wilfred Lawson, weaving fantastic spells over more sober mortals. There were several other clubs, all sleazy, noisy and disreputable so that they frightened off proper people, and actors could really let their hair down; stars, about-to-bes, also-rans and has-beens together. Joe Allen's and Langans are really very tame by comparison. Have we become more respectable and conventional, I wonder? As far as I know there is nothing like these delicious theatrical dives nowadays. Maybe it is because we no longer traipse the streets looking for work; most of it is done by phone.

Which brings me – circuitously as is my wont – back to my phone call on 12 January 1985. I was into the 'I'll never work again' phase of unemployment when, out of the blue, in the life-saving way it often happens in our profession, came the much-mimicked voice of Ian McKellen, chortling, 'I'm phoning from a dressing room of the Royal Shakespeare Theatre at Stratford-upon-Avon – would you like to work at the National?' It was not a joke. He and Edward Petherbridge were using the waits in the latter's matinee performances of *Love's Labours Lost* to set up a company to work for a year under their leadership on the South Bank. I did not know Edward at all at this stage and Ian only slightly. He and I had occasionally passed each other in the West End on our motor scooters in the 1970s; we had discovered at a party in 1977 a shared passion for games; he had been involved in the launch of the Actors Centre in 1980, when we had made a lightning tour of pantomimes in Birmingham to recruit Frankie Howerd and Les Dawson, for both of whom this classical actor developed, like me, a deep admiration. Our shared passion for scooters, games and comics probably counted more in my favour with Ian, who likes a good time, than my production of *The Dream* which he had seen in Belfast. But it was my directing ability that he commended to Edward Petherbridge for the production of Sheridan's *Critic* they had chosen as the other half of a double bill with Tom Stoppard's *The Real Inspector Hound*.

Their brief from Sir Peter Hall, Artistic Director of the National, was to present three productions over the year – one for each auditorium on the South Bank – with a company of sixteen actors who were to play all the parts and understudy as well. It would be more economic to have actors working at full tilt rather than coming in for just one or maybe two plays and having lots of paid nights off, as sometimes happened. By breaking into small groups the huge acting company necessary to keep the building operational they hoped it would be possible to prevent the loss of identity that the big organisation was apt to create. The different companies would also provide audiences with a wide range of plays, dictated by the style of their leadership. It seemed a fair bet that groups led by directors as diverse as David Hare, Peter Wood and Alan Aykbourn would cover a broad spectrum of theatre between them.

Ian and Edward were the only actors chosen to head a group. They had good credentials: Ian was already established as a star of the National in such plays as *Coriolanus* and *Wild Honey*; Edward, too, was a highly respected actor at both the National and the RSC, and together they had successfully launched the Actors' Company. I had attended some of the preliminary meetings for this but had had to drop out when my mother became ill. That was the first time – way back in 1970 – that I had ever heard discussed the possibility of a group of actors deciding the policy, choosing the directors and themselves running a company which is now so fashionable, but they actually did it; most of us still just discuss it. The Actors' Company was a triumph and still exists, although Ian and Edward left it as active members once it was successfully on its way.

Possibly because of lack of time, or a dread of more endless meetings with actors going round and round in circles in order to reach democratic decisions (for which the Actors' Company was notorious), this time they had decided to choose two of the productions themselves, designate suitable directors and *then* choose the company. As a compromise, for the third production they would choose the director and then let him or her and the chosen actors decide on the play. They planned to open in the large proscenium theatre, the Lyttelton, in July with *The Duchess of Malfi*, directed by Philip Prowse; to follow that in September, in the huge open-staged Olivier Theatre, with the double bill of *The Critic*, directed by me, and Tom Stoppard directing *The Real Inspector Hound*. They asked Mike Alfreds to direct the third play, yet to be chosen, in the smallest theatre, the Cottesloe, for December. Although they could be, and were, accused of selecting fairly unadventurous plays by the theatre cogniscenti who wanted to see the National do seldom-performed world drama or new work, their objectives as actors were to provide their fellows with good roles and audiences with an exciting display of acting. However, no one could accuse them of being conservative in their choice of directors. It was revolutionary.

Mike Alfreds is best known for his work in fringe theatre with his company Shared Experience, their biggest successes being improvised versions of books, with the emphasis on story-telling. He is a guru figure to many young actors, but had never before worked for the 'Establishment'.

Philip Prowse has done some spectacular opera productions with his own stunning designs, but is chiefly renowned for running the extraordinary Glasgow Citizens Theatre with Robert David Macdonald and Giles Havergal. Here they have proved that, with minimal resources, you can attract regional audiences with a repertoire of world drama, done in imaginative (bordering on eccentric) ways. Their design tradition is much more European than British, sometimes verging on the high camp. Philip is definitely not a member of the Establishment either.

Tom, though a distinguished writer, had only ever directed one production, and I, for heaven's sake, was a woman and an actress. Usually newcomers, especially female ones, are kept in the studio spaces; yet they were suggesting that we two should direct on the largest and most difficult stage in the building.

Though mindful of the honour they were paying me, I did not react to it with immediate enthusiasm. I had decided I had had enough of directing. Much as I had enjoyed the tour, the more selfish enjoyment I had been getting from acting in the television version of D. H. Lawrence's *The Daughter-in-Law* (the one job I had during my recent spell of unemployment) had revived my taste for being part of a team for which I did not carry the ultimate responsibility. Whereas at the RSC I had requested to direct as well as act, I now found myself asking if I could act as well as direct. There was only a tiny part suitable in *Malfi* but, in the spirit of all of us mucking in, I said I was happy to do that. (I was less happy, as were we all, when we later discovered that some of the other groups did not work with quite such selfless dedication, refusing to understudy and bringing in stars for the odd play who had no intention of playing the butler.)

I only knew *The Critic* from hearsay, but Ian with his usual impetuosity put a copy of the French's edition through my door in the middle of the same night. I was appalled when I read it. The situation of professional actors putting on a play written by an enthusiastic amateur was potentially a funny one but, for a writer whom I knew from *The Rivals* to be delicately witty, the writing was crass and unfunny. Indeed, so clumsy were some of the jokes – about turning over two pages at once when reading a script and mispronouncing words – that my suspicions were aroused. The next day I went to the trusty London Library to look through an old edition and, sure enough, it was totally different. When I directed Somerset Maugham's *Constant Wife* in 1979 and Terence Rattigan's *In Praise of Love* in 1980 for the Cambridge Theatre Company, I had similarly discovered gross distortions in the printed editions of earlier productions – presumably rewritten to fit the tastes of audiences, the censor or a director, or to accommodate a star player. Both were much better plays in their original form and were received with surprise in my productions – especially the Rattigan, about which I received angry letters from Aunt Ednas (as he called his public) on the bad language which they could not believe that nice Mr Rattigan had written.

Delving further, I read some contemporary reviews of the original production of *The Critic* in 1779 in the British Library Archives and found references to several scenes originally performed on the first night that had disappeared, even in the London Library edition. The end of the play gives a stage direction indicating a lavish pageant:

> *(Flourish of drums – trumpets – cannon, etc etc. Scene changes to the sea – the fleets engage – the music plays 'Britons strike home' – Spanish fleet destroyed by fire-ships, etc – English fleet advances – musick plays 'Rule Britannia' – The procession of all the English rivers and their tributaries with their emblems, etc. begins with Handel's water musick – ends with a chorus, to the march in Judas Maccabaeus – During this scene, Puff directs and applauds everything –)*

After all this, Mr Puff has the line: 'Well, pretty well – but not quite perfect.' Another mystery. Why not quite perfect? How had Sheridan intended to end the play?

However, despite my increasing interest, I was still uncertain that I wanted to hide myself away for another long term with a national company, particularly given the amount of commitment this venture would involve. I had had enough of commitment, and was ready for a bit of indulgence, a bit of glamour. Quite the reverse of my motives for undertaking the tour; the Lake District hotel part of my nature rearing its disgraceful head. I wanted to earn a great deal of money for doing a job that was not in the least worthy, and have a lot of laughs. If I worked for the National I could forget the money for a start, and understudying and playing small parts, as well as directing in one of the most difficult theatres in the world, did not promise a year of unalloyed joy. However, a couple of weeks after the phone call, a meeting held at my house between Edward, Ian, Tom and I had my nostrils twitching at the scent of possible unexpected pleasure.

It is not just attractive women I admire. I am also partial to glamorous men. And these three were. Tom is always the height of nonchalant elegance. He wears his wildly expensive clothes with superb indifference and has more presence than any actor I know. That night the other three of us disappeared into the wallpaper as he held forth in front of my marble fireplace, black eyes flashing and voluptuous mouth sending forth dazzling verbal displays, only slightly undermined by his inability to roll his 'r's properly. Even Ian, sprawled over an armchair, looked like a rag doll in comparison. Nobody can be more physically electric on stage than he, but it is sometimes difficult to equate the near-naked, taut-bodied sword-fighting actor of *Coriolanus* with the sloppy, uncoordinated creature with over-large hands and feet he is off-stage. The face that can portray a man of any age or class in a play often appears almost featureless in repose. He too wears expensive clothes, but is apt to top a superb vicuña cream overcoat with a ridiculous woolly hat, making him look like the village idiot. But glamorous nevertheless.

Edward was in a Marks and Spencer's V-neck pullover that seemed incongruent with his lank, grey hair and lean aristocratic face. He is neat delicate, elegant, every move of his body displaying his mime skills, but the face can flash in a moment from intellectual intensity to a Bugs Bunny-like toothy grin. In fact, all three men have the most infectious laughs. And it was really that that decided me: those laughs.

The things I saw on the tour made me very, very angry. And very, very boring. My husband became heartily sick of what he called my 'Messiah complex'. Who the hell was I anyway? Of course I could not change everything. Only myself. Well, I could try and start by counting my blessings, enjoy the here and now.

Actors are prize moaners and I have always been top of the league. We moan when we are out of work and we moan when we get a job. I have belly-ached about long runs, audiences, managements, directors, money, dressing rooms – you name it, I have hated it. People have rushed back stage, shiny-eyed and bushy-tailed to tell me how wonderful I am, only to find me snappy and ungracious because I fluffed one of my lines. An entire audience could be clapping and cheering and I will only spot the one person who is sitting indifferently with his arms folded. The national press can be unanimously ecstatic and I will gloomily remind everyone that the *Fishing Times* hated it. However, after the tour I had resolved to try and be more jolly to work with. And that would be easier if I worked with jolly people.

I could not in all honesty feel the same social commitment about working on the South Bank as I did about the RSC tour. There is, of course, a regional audience to serve in London which gets overlooked by it being a capital city. There are arguments about keeping up progress by doing new work and setting high standards in 'Centres of Excellence' from which others with fewer resources can feed and breed; for keeping the classics and world drama alive when smaller companies can no longer afford to present them on a grand scale. And, I agree, Britain should have a national theatre. I know all the arguments, but I am less concerned with Theatre, with a capital 'T', for its own sake than reaching out to audiences, particularly ill-served ones. Idealistically, my desire for a better society supersedes my concern for discovering new theatrical forms. But, in the absence of any concrete offers to change the world, I decided to opt for a bit of fun instead. And I saw the possibility of it with these three. Then the next day I met Philip.

'Saturnine' is the word that springs to mind. To look at, I mean. Always wearing unrelieved vampire black save for an occasional white scarf or T-shirt – even black eyes in a thin white face – but again a laugh that utterly disarms you. He is apt to fold your arm in his while he imparts the latest wicked story. A man of brilliant vision who does not suffer fools gladly, or any other way. When I met him I was finally hooked. By this stage, I would have willingly joined all four of them for nothing. Just to go to the party.

This small group within the National was entirely new and autonomous, so I had no problems of integrating with an established male organisation. We had to set up the structure from scratch. Or rather Ian and Edward did, but they welcomed our contributions. Ian was the golden boy and very good at getting his own way: the National structure was much more fluid than the RSC, having a constant flow of different directors, and the administration was far larger and better equipped to provide back-up. The individual groups were left free to operate as they liked, and ours made up its rules as it went along. For once, I was never aware of being the only woman at our meetings except inasmuch as they were tolerant of my domestic responsibilities. Indeed, Tom and Edward seemed to put their families first too, which was a welcome change from usual male fellow-workers. So it was easily accepted that Joanna's German measles, Ellie-Jane's broken romance and Abigail's car crash in Italy necessitated postponed meetings. Even Ian, who is a workaholic, finally swallowed my reasons for rejecting the offer to take over a large part in *Coriolanus* and play a part in *Hound* on top of my other tasks, on the grounds that I needed to be at home occasionally. We all worked very hard during the four-month preparation period, but as we were home-based it was easier to remember there was a world elsewhere, and the fanatic intensity that can overtake theatrical ventures was noticeably absent. Also, being primarily actors and a writer, we found that directing at the National was nobody's sole occupation; we had other careers to fall back on.

The atmosphere seemed congenial on the South Bank – largely due, I think, to the building and location. People criticise the concrete exterior of the National Theatre complex but I find it majestic, especially when floodlit at night. The foyers are very welcoming with their music and bookstalls and cafes, and with people packed in, sitting on the floor and stairs, chatting and watching the world go by.

My husband John, on the other hand, cannot bear the front-of-house at the National because it was here that he was cornered for his *This Is Your Life*. Thinking he was coming through a pass-door to the car park lift after a meeting back-stage, he was confronted by a waiting crowd of close friends and Eamonn with the red book. Well, not all close friends. The actor John Bluthal just happened to be going to a show that night and was dragged in by some of the others for the booze-up. On the show Eamonn announced, 'And here are all your very good friends – Tony Selby, Dennis Waterman, Ian Hendry, James Ellis, etc.' On the video recording we have, John Bluthal (whom John had never met in his life) is clearly heard to mutter as he shakes John's hand, 'Sorry about this, mate.'

Back-stage is much better than at the Barbican. The people on the reception desk and the security guards are welcoming, and miraculously seem to know everyone by name. They even send all the new shows first-night cards. The security men in their lookout box outside the Barbican, on the other hand, make the place seem like a well-guarded fortress. I was reminded of the difference whilst I was at the National when I went back to the Barbican in March 1986 to appear in a concert to raise funds for Ethiopia, organised by the RSC. A few of us were sitting in the stalls after a rehearsal when a security man rushed in and demanded to know who we were. An actor who had been there for a year told him: 'The RSC.' Whereupon the guard wanted to know what right we had to be there and said into his walkie-talkie, 'I've got a group of people here who say they are the – what was it again?'

'The RSC.'

(With disbelief), 'The R-S-C, and they won't leave or explain their presence.' There was a lengthy wait, presumably while headquarters checked us out. Then the reply came back: 'It's all right – they are the lessees.' With conferences, concerts, library and God knows what under one roof at the Barbican Centre it is difficult to keep tabs on everyone I am sure, but even so . . .

The dressing rooms at the National are pretty cell-like but at least they encircle a courtyard where the banter shouted between windows can be very entertaining. As can the tannoy. Non-stop stage management instructions and actors' calls for all three theatres go out constantly in the dressing rooms, but you can also turn to a relay of any show you choose. I always thoroughly enjoyed listening to *Yonadab* by Peter Schaffer, which I never saw for fear of spoiling my imagined version. It sounded like one of those religious plays you hear on Radio Four in

Wednesday Matinee, and the mental picture was enhanced by the stage-management calls of 'set rape platform', 'strike orgy light'.

My favourite tannoy voice was that of Diane Boddington. This legendary woman has stage-managed for the greatest in the land, so no one would dare to object when she shows her distaste or pleasure for the plays she works on in her announcements. The weary, 'This is your half-hour call', on her misery nights told it all, as did her joy on saying, 'The next performance of such-and-such will be in *three weeks' time*' (sigh of relief). Similarly, she would sweetly say, 'Mr Hopkins, you are usually here by now', yet snap, 'So-and-so, *you're off*' to less favoured creatures, usually contriving to leave the mike open long enough for us to hear chunterings about not knowing what we were coming to and the odd 'Oh, fuck.' One night she graciously announced that *Yonadab* wished the *Hamlet* company a 'Happy Last Night Performance'. This was followed by some wag whispering into another mike: 'The *Hamlet* company wish *Yonadab* a Happy thirty-second Performance;' and then another voice: 'The *Yonadab* company wish *Malfi* a Happy twenty-three-and-a-half Performance;' then another: 'The *Malfi* company wish they could all go home;' and finally, from someone: 'Mr X wishes everyone would shut up so he could go to sleep,' and so on throughout the evening. These send-ups were interspersed with heavy groans and mutterings from Diane.

Unlike me at the RSC, Ian and Edward did not have to fight for an office. Admittedly it was minute and labelled 'Michael Bogdanov', but it had a phone and some chairs. From here we started casting at the end of January 1985. Edward had to leave for New York where he had a previous engagement to do *Strange Interlude* on Broadway, and Mike Alfreds was tied up with his company, Shared Experience, so it was left to Ian, Philip, Tom and me to conduct the auditions. It was not easy to find leading actors prepared to understudy – a job that is traditionally undertaken by newcomers or actors who specialise in this rather frustrating area. It was also difficult to find a group of sixteen people with sufficient versatility to encompass Jacobean tragedy, modern sophisticated comedy and eighteenth-century farce. And we were all looking for different things: Tom wanted people who fitted his writer's view of his parts; I wanted people with comedy instinct; Ian, people who handled language well and Philip people who would look good in his 'cozzies'. We all threw in suggestions of actors we had worked with, which led to a motley parade of eccentrics from Glasgow Citizens, classical actors, boulevard performers and light entertainment artists, and we ended up with the oddest company I have ever worked with. When eventually the names were finalised over the phone to Edward in New York, he remarked that perhaps we should forget about *Duchess of Malfi* and do a pantomime instead.

We started rehearsals for *Malfi* on 7 May. If the Arts Council should still be in doubt about my earning my money during the production period of the RSC tour, perhaps I can further plead that at the National I earned not a penny during the four months of research, design and casting. Because of the recent witch-hunt of Peter Hall and Trevor Nunn in some of the press, there is an impression that all directors are millionaires. In fact, unless a director is lucky enough to have a long-running success for which he receives a weekly percentage, they are very underpaid and consequently often have to take on more work than they can reasonably cover. The same applies to designers. Which is why Bill Dudley, who was to design the double bill, was simultaneously immersed in the intricacies of getting the musical *Mutiny* on the road (or water).

This made him a bit elusive at the beginning, but I was very happy digging up old prints and descriptions of the work of an incredible eighteenth-century scenic artist, Philip de Loutherbourg, who worked with Garrick and Sheridan at Drury Lane. I rifled through dusty boxes in the Theatre Museum collection waiting, ready packed, at the Victoria & Albert to go to its new premises in Covent Garden. I eagerly devoured every scrap of information I could glean about theatre costumes and acting styles in the eighteenth century, and I ended up, as I always do when I direct, liking the author as a person very much. In Sheridan's day design, as in the 1980s, had begun to dwarf the actors, so, with Tom and me, Bill worked towards a set that would comment on this (as I suspect Sheridan did when the play was first produced). I recruited my RSC team of Geraldine Stephenson, choreographer, Malcolm Ransome, fight arranger, and Illona Sekacz, composer, and together we devised and wrote a fight and finale for the omitted ending that was the satire of nationalism and excess that I believe Sheridan intended.

I wanted the show to end with our group of sixteen actors, who would have to play all fifty parts, standing in the modern Olivier stage with no set at all. Working backwards, Bill and the engineer, Peter Kemp, devised a total, breathtaking collapse of the eighteenth-century theatre which would happen round the actors as they valiantly continued their patriotic finale – ending with Claire Moore as Britannia singing 'God Save The King', suspended on a cloud in mid-air over a smoking, deserted wasteland. The gritty symbolism which we intended I am afraid was subsequently overlooked in the general hilarity (until, that is, we took the show abroad, as I will come to later). But the final line when Ian, as Puff, emerged from under a flat to say cheerfully, 'Well, very well, but not quite perfect', never failed to bring the house down.

Many of these plans were made while rehearsing my small part in *Malfi*. Fortunately I had to lie down dead for quite a long time, so I managed to cram in some reading while being a corpse. But the part, or rather Philip's interpretation of it, presented me with quite a lot of unimagined problems. Having just got used to the RSC way of dissecting a text and building a character from inside, here was this director saying: 'Oh, ducky, I hate all that RSC acting – it's too poetic, too expressive. I don't want sub-text. I want a fishwife, a nasty old whore. She should sound like a peacock.' And the next day when I came in making squawking noises, he decided what he really wanted was the Duchess of Argyll or Mrs Simpson.

Some people get tetchy about his tendency to describe a finished product rather than helping you to achieve it, his belief being that we were the actors and that it was our job to do it by ourselves. There is truth in what he says. An awful lot of time can be wasted with endless chat and analysis when going for an effect can actually get there quicker. As a director I have frequently gone into tortuous discussions with an actor over a speech or scene, when I would really rather have just said, 'Act better.' He made it very clear what sort of result he wanted. The design alone showed that. A bleak grey box, everybody wearing black with just the occasional red stocking or heel, and gold jewellery. Evil, harsh, decadent, but ravishingly beautiful.

When I thought my part would give me lots of time with my feet up, I reckoned without Philip's costumes. I spent far more time in my dressing room being laced and unlaced, buttoning boots and putting on layers of petticoats than I spent on stage, and the costumes were torture to wear, too. My first one had a vicious high ruff and a long, savagely-corseted bodice. The centre bone pushed my chin up in the air and then went down to dig in my crotch. It was impossible to sit down, so if the curtain-up was delayed I had no choice but to stand in my dressing room, hardly able to breathe. I could not go up on stage as the show began with a procession in heavy veils which squashed my bright red, high wig if I wore it too long.

My second costume was a Spanish man's suit, except that my boobs half-poked out of the top. And my final costume was a totally transparent, voluminous chiffon number, hanging off one shoulder, over which was draped one of Philip's famous duvets. These are huge quilted garments in luxurious fabrics that he likes you to drape and swish about you. I had occasion to be grateful for this adaptable cloak when I walked up the long, trailing front hem of my dress, pulling it down to my waist and thereby exposing even more than the costume intended.

But, once I got into the swing of it, I loved rushing around posing and primping and squeaking. Philip was delighted when I invented a particularly nasty sexy bit of business with Ian against one of his grey walls, which unfortunately decided to move on the first night on 4 July 1985. It was not the only thing that went wrong. Philip could not get over the fact that his small theatre in Glasgow managed to cope technically so much better than this huge organisation with all its gadgetry and staff. The evening was something of a nightmare, with technical mistakes at every turn; we played scenes in total darkness when light cues were missed, and one set did not come on when it should, which meant that Eleanor Bron and Greg Hicks had to play a long romantic scene, for which they normally sat, standing lit only from their waists down.

If the stage staff in the Lyttelton were edgy on the first night, so were the actors. Before we opened there was a huge company row. One of the advantages of being with the same people for a long time is that you begin to recognise behaviour patterns and they cease to alarm you, but this was our first production together and we were not yet used to the extraordinary temperaments in the company. At the end of the year together we had learned to ignore the statutory walk-outs by one actor, the lacerating abuse of another, the regular tears of one of the actresses and the superior remarks of another; I learned to expect Ian's total collapse of confidence two days before opening night, and if he did not urge that the show had to be cancelled I wondered if he was all right. My 'professional nervousness', as Teddy called it, made me eligible for membership of certainly the nuttiest company I have ever belonged to. All of which I can now recall with an affectionate smile, but at the beginning it was nerve-racking.

So, what with the rows and the technical cock-ups, we did not do a good first night and the audience was decidedly tepid. As a result the reviews were very good. An enthusiastic audience often antagonises the critics. Thus, ironically, the company was successfully launched.

Malfi continued to be accident-prone throughout its run. Sets stuck, swords broke, heels went down holes in the stage affixing people to the floor, and long trains regularly caught in doors and nails and under people's feet. It even affected other productions. An entry in the *Love for Love* report book, which was Peter Wood's group play performed in the Lyttelton Theatre while we were doing *The Critic* in the Olivier, read:

'A roll of sellotape fell off the lighting desk and hit the motor button for the *Duchess of Malfi* show, which is why we had snow in high summer coming down on a group of bemused musicians. It looked very pretty and perhaps could have been explained away as blossom falling from a very tall linden tree. (If the *Malfi* company object to us using their snow they can use our parrot.)'

Edward sent a memo saying: 'Only if the parrot is painted black.'

Edward is a great one for memos. He fires them off in all directions. He is never averse to telling you what he thinks to your face but really prefers, I think, poking a well-turned note under your dressing-room door. Edward has to have a say about everything – even the state of the National Theatre corridors. This note was sent to our stage director:

> I agreed with your tannoy announcement the other night – people in *Malfi* should certainly lift their trains where possible. Cigarette ends or not, my watered silk is beginning to show signs of wear already.
>
> However, in some areas of the building it is very difficult to manage to negotiate doors and trains at the same time. What I'm really working up to is that when I had nothing better to do the other night, I was standing in that sordid little corridor which I think of as the pool room corridor, upstage prompt side, and counted 36 fag ends on the floor. There were also a number of empty beer glasses on the floor just in the way of any uncarried trains, and counting the empty beer glasses in the stair case corridor, I believe the number came to 35. There is something not only inconvenient, but incredibly depressing, about this pool room goods entrance appearance, and without flying in the face of any time-honoured folkloric tradition, maybe you could make the right noises in whatever department is concerned to improve conditions.
>
> PS I've never seen a single cigarette end in any of the dressing-room corridors, but one shouldn't jump to any self-satisfied conclusions about this. Still, this only points up the fact that this area of the building for some reason gets less respect than any other when it really should have more, after all, it's the gateway to the stage. The most important place in the building.

However, this reverence for the stage and concern for unprofessional behaviour back-stage was not always apparent from his own behaviour on it. Edward would, I think, be the first to admit that he verges on the absent-minded. One of the climactic scenes in *Malfi* is the spectacular strangling on stage of the Duchess. Just a few scenes later I, as his mistress, have to ask him, the Cardinal, what has become of her. One night he replied with absolute confidence, 'The great Duchess of Malfi is poisoned,' which the audience might not have noticed if he had not added after a pause, 'Oh – and strangled.'

My big moment in the play was my death scene. This Webster has contrived to be caused by the Cardinal forcing his mistress to kiss a bible, after which he malevolently tells her that the book is poisoned. Whereupon I writhe and gurgle a lot and die over a stool. Philip urged me not to get a laugh on this, which was not easy at the best of times, but even less so on the two nights that Edward forgot to bring on his bible. On the first occasion he held out his empty, cupped hand and said solemnly, 'Kiss this very little book', and on the second, 'Kiss this cross', at which he thrust my head against his stomach where dangled his crucifix, thereby leaving an imprint of my white make-up on his immaculate black. I then had to stifle my giggles, hanging upside down over a stool while Ian had a long speech, at the end of which he dragged my shaking body into the corner, hissing, 'What *are* you two doing?'

Edward's excuse for these lapses was pressure of work (though it did not stem the flow of well-turned memos). And it was intense. Ian and he were playing two leads in *Malfi* and both were rehearsing leads in the double bill due to open in September. Ian had originally not wanted to play Mr Puff, mainly because he did not want to hog all the good parts, but partly also because of Olivier's legendary performance. Like so many things clouded in time I discovered that Olivier, in fact, had taken a lot of flak for it, but it was now recalled as a triumph. However, the more I studied the play the more I realised that Mr Puff could be played in a totally different way to Olivier's fop. Puff was, in fact, a sort of PR executive of the time, a con-man who followed the market. He finally puts on a play, trying to throw in everything that he saw in current popular successes. I also discovered that Sheridan's language works well when said in his native Irish brogue. And, after I read that a lot of second-rate Irish playwrights flocked into London about the time the play was written, I thought it might be fun to try it. Eventually I wore Ian down and he agreed to have a go at the part. So, with Edward playing a difficult lead in *Hound*, their workload truly was enormous, particularly as they were, as they had promised they would be, constantly supportive of Tom and me.

Having this back-up was a rare experience for me. It made my work as a director far less lonely and helped when coping with tricky situations.

Bill Dudley was still working under huge pressure and at first, I think, was not comfortable with a woman director, or at any rate this one. He did not really approve of my insistence on allowing the actors a say in the design of the costumes, and got very fed up with my aversion to green sets (inherited from Frankie Howerd who will not have the colour on stage). He was affronted when I brought back a palette of colours copied from a cartoon exhibition at the Victoria & Albert that I wanted to incorporate; and his problem in getting a proscenium arch on the Olivier stage was bad enough without Tom's and my constant carping about sight-lines in the extreme corner seats. Acknowledging his superior experience of the space, I don't think I would have had the courage to persist with my demands without the backing of the other three, but we nibbled away and finally found a common language, not to mention a marvellous set for which Bill, rightly, won an award.

My next undertaking was to create some connection with the Olivier stage staff. It was obvious to me that half the trouble in the Lyttelton with *Malfi* had been a lack of involvement in the play of the crew. We didn't meet them until the technicals, they were doing different shows all the time, and many were casuals who only came in on odd nights. They had little or no contact with the actors, so I decided to try and change this in the Olivier. I knew our evening was going to be hugely complicated technically and it seemed foolhardly not to involve the technicians from the start. I asked if I could talk to them, or at least meet them, but this caused panic in the management offices. I was warned they were a bolshie lot and I should leave it to their various heads of department to deal with them. They had, in fact, already refused to wear eighteenth-century costumes for the scene changes. But I insisted on seeing them, so it was that a few days later I rather nervously talked first to the prop-men and then went on stage to confront a large group of the other staff, sprawled on the seats of the stalls, eyeing me suspiciously. I explained that I wanted them to be involved in the show, to come to rehearsals if they liked, to help Tom and me organise the changes and suggest any alterations to the set that they thought necessary. They were slow to react because, as they later explained, nobody except for Richard Eyre with *Guys and Dolls* had bothered to consult them like this before. From that day onwards the men, and the two women on the staff, were wonderfully helpful to both of us. They took to calling me the Boss and seemed to forget their initial unease at dealing with their first woman director.

It was actually less easy to unify the acting company. Some of them

A tentative approach by a young John Thaw in *So What About Love?*, 1969

Six years later he's sleeping in a tent with two new daughters – Ellie-Jane and Joanna

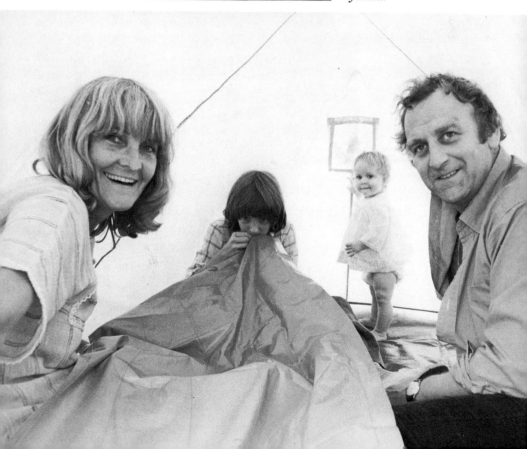

Hugh Quarshie, Peter Chelsom, Colin Tarrant and Roger Allam are almost as embarrassed by my Mrs Goth as I was: with the RSC in *Titus Andronicus* in 1982

With Denis Quilley in *Sweeney Todd*, 1980. More bodies in pies, this time set to music

Above: Just to show I can be sweetness and light, here I am as Mrs Darling in *Peter Pan* with Joss Ackland and The Lost Boys at The Barbican, 1982, on an evening when the set arrived

Below left: Peter and the Children

Below right: Am I being vulgar again? Angela Lansbury, Dame Peggy Ashcroft and Patience Collier take it in their stride in *All Over* at The Aldwych, 1972

Above left: Geoff Burnett of Nat West Bank finds himself launching the RSC tour, ninety thousand pounds worse off after meeting me at the zoo

Above right: Ms Hancock, Artistic Director of the RSC Touring Company, doing a bit of directing

Below: Our mini-epidaurus

were a delight to work with; it was helpful to have such experienced
comedy performers as Roy Kinnear and Hugh Lloyd, but I was slow in
learning how to cope with the difficult ones and the relaxed atmosphere
necessary to create comedy took a long time to achieve. It is a very tricky
play to get right, being extremely witty yet full of broad gags – in fact,
two different plays rolled into one – and it is difficult to strike the right
note that does not sacrifice one for the other. Working out humorous
business is always depressing, and without an audience it can feel very
foolish. Something that seems brilliantly funny when you do it for the
first time, often on inspiration, seems ludicrous when you work it out in
detail and repeat it over and over again to get the timing right. 'Trip,
look at floor, look up, double-take on floor, walk back, step over imaginary
obstacle', and on and on, again and again. Greg Hicks protested violently
during a rehearsal that a joke with a prop was unfunny but, later in the
run, I had to ask him to stop milking the huge laugh he got with it as it
was putting minutes on to the running time. Then, with a stage as vast
as the Olivier which has to be peopled, it needs meticulous care to
synchronise all the actors so that no move at the back detracts from the
central action, particularly if it is a subtle piece of business or a quiet
throw-away line which has to be seen or heard by the entire auditorium.
All these strategies for making an audience laugh take patience and
serious thought. There were some unique talents in the company and
when, after six weeks' rehearsal of the two plays, we moved from the
rehearsal room to the theatre we were more of a team.

Tom and I were pretty daunted when we were shown our seats at the
desks set up in the stalls for the directors to sit at while running the
technical rehearsal. First of all, there was the lighting plot to be set with
David Hersey, the lighting designer, and then all the changes and cues
to be gone through before the actors joined for a dress rehearsal. The
Olivier being so huge, the directors have to use a microphone in order
to make themselves heard over the chaos. Tom took to it like a duck to
water, saying he felt like the captain of a huge ship. But when my time
came my voice waivered on my first command. I could not afford to be
self-conscious for long, however, as we discovered technical faults in the
collapse which demanded last-minute revisions by me. The whole thing
was very dangerous and I felt more like the director of a circus.

Somehow we got to the first preview, and Tom and I cowered behind
the glass of the directors' box at the back of the auditorium. All my good
resolutions were thrown to the wind as I chain-smoked Tom's cigarettes.
By this time we were convinced that both plays were the unfunniest

things in the history of the theatre, so we stared in increasing amazement and delight as the laughs started to come and went on throughout the entire evening. The pageant and the collapse of the set at the end of *The Critic* had the audience cheering and the curtain-calls, which I had not had time to set, went on and on. One of the audience grabbed Tom and me as we left the box and said: 'Oh, thank you, what a laugh. I usually come to the National Theatre to be punished.'

The press night for the double bill was less successful, the critics putting the usual dampener on cast and audience alike. Nevertheless, some of the reviews were all right, although several accused me, as usual, of vulgarity, one even saying I had 'perverted' Tom. If they had only heard some of the awful gags he only half-jokingly suggested they would have praised my relative reticence. I have grown used to their condescension towards me, but Ian was distressed by the tone of some of them. I tried to explain that the critics take some people, like him, more seriously than the likes of me, and pointed out how difficult it must be for Michael Billington the *Guardian* critic to treat with any respect someone with whom he had stood in the greengrocer's queue in Chiswick. Possibly his accusations of my 'lack of taste' and 'coarseness' were influenced by my choice of vegetables. Anyway, I too had not much respect for his intellectual snobbery in bewailing the fact that one of Sheridan's most obscure jokes with the tag 'nem con egad', which I had forced poor Roy Kinnear, against his will, to keep in, did not get the huge laugh Billington thought it deserved, whereas some business put in by Hugh Lloyd did. He did not bother to commend the fact that it came in one of the scenes I had unearthed which was rarely performed at all. What is more, nobody in the audience understood what 'nem con egad' meant but him, and me because I had looked it up in the dictionary. We cut it later. Roy was right. Billington was wrong. Anyway, all the presumably 'tasteless', 'coarse' punters loved the show and the management were greatly pleased that now Edward and Ian's company began to do capacity business in the Olivier as well as the Lyttelton.

We had little time to savour our success for the next day we had understudy rehearsals for *Hound* and *Critic*. I was understudying several parts in my own and Tom's production, and the women I covered watched closely to see if I could practise what I preached. The next day I embarked on yet another test, one of the biggest I had ever faced in my career, in the company's third and last production.

12 : Good Times and Good Timing
London, Paris and Aberdeen

THE RIGHT PLACE AT THE RIGHT TIME — DIFFERING AP-
PROACHES TO ACTING — REHEARSING *THE CHERRY ORCHARD*
— TECHNICALS AND PREVIEWS — HYPNOTHERAPY — *THE
CHERRY ORCHARD*'S FIRST NIGHT — THE FUTURE OF THE
COMPANY — MISHAPS ON STAGE — THE GOOD LIFE IN PARIS —
THE CRITIC AT L'ODÉON — THE BUBBLE OF SUCCESS —
ABERDEEN

Having learned from experts and experience, I think I can justly claim
that on the stage I have good timing. My timing of my career, on the
other hand, has been less successful. Had I begun it a bit later I would
not have these terrible feet, for a start, from slogging round the agents
in winkle picker shoes trying to 'oust the tradition of sweet young things';
if I had finished ousting sooner and 'made it' earlier, perhaps when
David Merrick, the famous American producer, offered to take me to
New York with *Rattle* in 1964, I would not have missed the 'international
career' he promised me because I decided, being thirty-one, to have a
first baby instead before it was too late – 'Godammit woman, *I'm* offering
you *Broadway*!' Then again, if I had got to the RSC sooner when I was
younger I would not have been too late to play the Rosalinds, Violas and
Kates; but on the other hand I would have had to be later to coincide
with the fashion for 'toughened individualists' like Glenda Jackson in
the classics, or earlier to be there when it was acceptable to play those
roles later when you were in your fifties, as had Dame Peggy and Dame
Edith Evans. No, all told, I seemed utterly devoid of the attribute that
we all know is far more important than talent in the theatre, the ability
to be in the right place at the right time. Until, that is, I managed to be
at the National Theatre on 19 July 1985.

The company's choice of a third play, to be directed by Mike Alfreds
and presented in the small Cottesloe Theatre, had proved to be a difficult

one. We wanted it to be different in style from the rest of our repertoire to stimulate our interest as well as the audiences', and it had to provide decent parts for those of us with meagre ones in the other plays. Yet again I haunted the London Library, only this time I had to rifle through the literature shelves as well because of Mike's interest in presenting adaptations of novels on the stage. At meetings we discussed the merits of our different ideas, but we kept coming back to Chekhov's *The Cherry Orchard*.

Mike was very keen to do it with our company because he felt this particular group could move it away from the usual rather heavy treatment into the near farce that Chekhov had originally intended. It was also an exciting prospect to do it in the tiny space of the Cottesloe where the audience would be virtually in the room with us; a changed perspective that transforms even the best known plays, as it has *A Doll's House* in the Pit at the Barbican, *Ghosts* at the Young Vic, *View from the Bridge* at the Cottesloe and *Macbeth* in Trevor Nunn's production with Ian himself. So on 19 July it was decided. *The Cherry Orchard* it was.

One of the attributes actor-managers bring to the job is a more open approach to casting. I doubt if anyone but Olivier would have had the imagination to cast Maggie Smith, with her revue background, as a heart-rending Desdemona, for example. Similarly, Ian and Edward had no outward qualms in suggesting I play Madame Ranyevskaya, nor, fortunately, did Mike Alfreds, with his penchant for adventurous casting, reject their suggestion. The company also generally agreed it was my turn for a big part. Thus, for once I managed not only to be in the right place at the right time, but also with the right people.

The company had now become a real ensemble; tops were occasionally blown, fur periodically flew and each member remained resolutely individual, but the group's growing prestige drew us together in a fierce pride in our work and a determination to make the last show as successful as the other two. Ian and Edward ignored all the misgivings of more orthodox friends at their choice of me for this classic Chekhovian *grande dame*, and were unwaveringly supportive. In Mike Alfreds I encountered the perfect director to coax a performance out of me and to overcome any awe I might have at playing at the National Theatre of Great Britain (as Ian insists on calling it), in a role that has been played by some of our greatest actresses.

As with Ian with Puff, there are few actors who relish following Olivier in a role and the same applies to actresses with Dame Peggy Ashcroft, who was by all accounts a wonderful Ranyevskaya. This reluctance is not always because you know you will inevitably be compared with them rather than being judged without any preconceptions, but sometimes because if you have seen a superlative actor play a role there seems little point in doing it as everything has already been said about the character. I felt that after seeing Uta Hagen in *Who's Afraid of Virginia Woolf?* and Vanessa Redgrave in *The Seagull*, for example. Fortunately, I had never seen anyone in *The Cherry Orchard* and if I had Mike's methods would soon have made me rethink what I had seen.

One could not find two directors more different than Philip Prowse and Mike Alfreds. Working with both Philip and Mike in such quick succession illustrated that there is no definitive method of preparing a performance. With Philip it is wiser to set what you are doing and stick to it, for if one night you should decide suddenly that your emotion called for a new move down-right or a collapse into a chair, the chances are you would get out of your meticulously pinpointed light and do your emoting in a black-out. With Philip's exquisite, flamboyant costumes you would be mad not to use them to advantage by planning effective gestures and poses – something that Jonathan Hyde, who is used to working with Philip at the Citz, did to devastating effect in *Malfi*. This kind of pre-planning necessitates a very structured approach. The feeling of a scene has to be discovered at rehearsal and then analysed and worked out in terms of gestures, moves, inflection, pace and tone of voice which can be repeated nightly to achieve the *effect* of that feeling at each performance. Indeed, it is not even necessary to feel it yourself at rehearsal, you can simply recreate external behaviour that you have cold-bloodedly observed in yourself or others that demonstrates that feeling. For instance, an actress can make the sound of crying, and even put a substance into her eyes to create phoney tears, and I guarantee an audience will be just as affected as if she put herself through an emotional wringer each night. What could have been more moving than Olivier's rolled-up eyes during the negro spiritual in *The Entertainer*, or more stirring than the shout of Crispin's 'Daaaaaaaaaaaay' in *Henry V*?

However, that technique and the close plotting of Philip were thrown to the winds by Mike. With him nothing was to be set. No move, no inflection, no approach to a scene, no climaxes, no gestures, no moods, no relationships.

If anything, to achieve this sort of freedom the approach was even more pedantic than Philip's. We had to know everything possible about the person we were playing as well as the others in the piece, allowing at the same time for the unpredictability of human nature; to be so inside our characters that if someone else on-stage did something different we would respond on the spur of the moment exactly as our character would. We had, in short, to *be* the person.

To bring about this absorption before we even started rehearsal we had to read the script over and over again, writing down in full everything we said about ourselves and everything anyone said about us and comparing any differences between the two. We searched the script for facts and evidence about our characters – she has two children, one died, she drinks a lot of coffee, takes pills, kisses and embraces people a lot – until every detail was noted. We sat round a table for the first week of rehearsal discussing all these observations about our own, as well as the other characters', lives. We also did background reading on Russian society, the revolution and the landscape.

During the rehearsal period we went through all sorts of exercises to get to know the play and the characters better; we played each other's characters in turn in mime or little imaginary scenes while the actor playing the role sat and watched. I was surprised how enlightening it was for me to see Ian moving about as he imagined Madame Ranyevskaya would because, as Lopakhin, he had to idolise me, and it helped me to know what sort of woman he would admire.

To begin with we did not do the actual dialogue of the play but went through it, working out the actions. 'I come in, I tell you I am happy, I ask you if you are, I express pleasure at your reply.' When we eventually got to the dialogue, we had to make choices as to which of several possible alternatives we preferred. Mike's literal translation and his Russian assistant's comments made it clear that so many of our accepted English versions are absolute distortions of Chekhov's original.

One of the main problems for English actors in foreign classics is eliminating our natural reticence and careful thought-processes – our British reserve. A characteristic of Chekhov's people is their mood changes, laughing one minute, crying the next, and we did many things to try to shed our nationality, including starting each day with vigorous Russian dances. We worked scenes over and over again, taking different things as our focus – the weather, each character in turn, money, nostalgia, the future – and I was amazed at the variety of quite valid interpretations of the text we kept discovering. One of the most productive run-throughs was at the end of a long rehearsal day when we were all tired and got the giggles. Most directors would have stopped the rehearsal, probably angrily, but Mike made us continue and we struck a whole new vein of childish laughter, even at tragic moments, which unleashed for us the infantile nature of the characters. Chekhov, after all, set two of his four acts in a nursery.

Mike wanted us eventually to heighten our style of playing so that it became almost surreal. The play is like a kaleidoscope and the colours need to be flashing and bright. This is a difficult concept to describe. It is best illustrated in plays by Joe Orton, or latterly on TV in *The Life and Loves of a She-Devil* by Fay Weldon, when after discovering the essential truth of a scene an actor has to push it a bit beyond naturalism without being mannered.

We were helped by going to a rather sleazy private picture-house in Soho where we were shown films lent by the Russian Embassy. The dominant atmosphere was surprisingly volatile and light, exactly like the Soviet orchestra I had heard in Belfast. Recently I went to an exhibition of Russian costumes from the Hermitage Museum in Moscow and they were full of shimmering, rich colour, so far away from our dour modern perception of Russia with solemn men in sinister hats and dark overcoats. Paul Dart, our designer, was attempting to remove this impression by having no walls or windows in the set, but merely an impressionistic framework of floating white curtains in front of a sky-blue backcloth. The costumes were coded into a palette of colours to match the mood of the scenes – pink, yellow, red and mauve. None of your 'traditional' Chekhovian sepias and blacks.

After two shows and nine months to come together, the company was well able to take advantage of these methods and do the various exercises without being inhibited by the fear of looking foolish. There were one or two dissenters who did not find the approach very productive for them; but I was in my element – it was perfect for me. Despite my thirty-seven years in the business I have no real technique, so Mike's methods are easier for me than Philip's, much as I also enjoy his. I usually rely very much on living the moment and on my response to my fellow actors. Even my good timing is merely being tuned in to an audience, rather than a knowledge of the mechanics of how to get a laugh. Whatever the emotion I have to portray I need to find an equivalent in my own past experience, which I can usually do having lived a fairly — chequered life. Sometimes exactly the same, sometimes just similar: I have not committed murder, but I have felt like it.

I had never felt so akin to a part. When I first read the script I did not like Ranyevskaya at all: feckless, irresponsible, changeable, neglectful of her family (particularly her daughter), unrealistic, selfish and foolishly romantic. I had no problem with any of these qualities. I was much more worried about her class. Mike soon put me at rest about that by pointing out that the family were land-owners, not aristocrats, and anyway that class was largely a state of mind. The upper-class were different from me in as much as they felt poised and confident and responded differently to the way other people treated them, and we did various exercises to achieve these outward accoutrements of a rise in social stature. He also pointed out that Ranyevskaya was not a conventional 'lady': properly translated, Chekhov makes her brother Gayev call her 'depraved', as opposed to the usual watered-down English translation of 'loose woman' or 'easy going' (a fact that gave me some comfort when that defender of old-school Chekhov Michael Meyer criticised my performance on BBC Radio 4's *Kaleidoscope* on the grounds that Ian, as a peasant, was more 'Oxbridge' than me. *Oxbridge* – after all those bloody Russian dances!).

I had few problems with the emotional side of the character, although using my usual method of relating it to my own experience led to some pretty curious substitution of images. When Ranyevskaya looks out of the window and imagines her dead mother in a white dress in the orchard, I saw mine in a flowery dress walking down King's Cross Road. But the anguish I felt was the same – very different backgrounds but the same nostalgia, the same sense of loss at its passing. During rehearsal the company were taken aback at the endless flow of tears I produced as they grovelled on the floor searching for my contact lenses. To quote Chekhov himself, I was 'in mourning for my life', and enjoying every minute of it. I was in tune with the play, the part, the company and Mike's methods. Until, during our last week of rehearsal, we moved from the rehearsal room to the theatre. Then things began to go wrong.

First, there was the set. During the previous seven weeks in the anonymous surroundings of the rehearsal rooms, I had created in my imagination such a vivid idea of my Russian estate and home that a few floating curtains and blue back cloth with sugar-pink clouds were a rude shock. Not to mention the furniture. 'My darling bookcase and my darling table' were rather shaky plywood and cane numbers, about as Russian as Habitat. The rest of the cast was equally shocked and, never reticent at the best of times, we told Mike so, accusing him of forcing (uncharacteristically) a concept on us, particularly with the floating down of the curtains into a crumpled heap on the floor which ended the play. The whole thing just did not feel right. The pink ice-cream cone clouds were slightly toned down to appease us, but the rest stayed. And he was right to keep it. Despite all our work on lightness, not to mention seeing the model of the set at the start of rehearsal and approving it, we were still not genuinely prepared for the revolution away from our English perception of subtle colours and heavy furniture in Russian plays. However, we got used to it over the three days of technical and dress rehearsals before we faced an audience at the first preview.

This was when my personal problems began. I was suddenly aware of how Mike's technique had eliminated all thought of an audience from my mind. Usually when plotting moves you are always thinking of their sight-lines, and when planning the way scenes should be played you have at least one ear cocked to their future reaction. We had done none of that. So, when on that first preview they laughed and coughed, they felt like intruders into my world. As I looked out-front at my cherry orchard I was terribly conscious of it being a sea of eyes, averting its gaze when catching mine, and I worried about the people in the front row being dampened by my tears. During rehearsals I had managed to believe I was ravishing enough for everyone in the play to be in love with me, and I could have kept up the illusion had I been up on a stage with a few soft lights. But, in the confined areas of the Cottesloe with people peering up my nostrils and counting my wrinkles, not to mention flinching at the sight of the grotesque cold sore that had chosen to encrust my upper lip, my self-confidence crumbled. All the old insecurities came winging back over the first few previews; I could not for the life of me remain inside the woman's skin and with no structure to fall back on, not even a plotted sit or gesture, I floundered about the stage feeling utterly lost. When we had been tuned in to one another we had miraculously moved into groupings every bit as elegant as anything Philip could have devised; suddenly I was bumping into people, fighting for the same chair and stepping on other people's lines and laughs. In Mike's method everyone has to contribute to every moment or the ball falls out of the air. He was as appalled as I: I had quite simply lost my nerve. He sat and chatted to me in my dressing room and tried to remind me of what it had felt like in rehearsal. Very gently during the previews he guided me back on to the rails, but although I got a bit better we both had to admit that I had lost a lot of the openness that had made my performance so free in rehearsal.

It was a familiar pattern. A press night looming, the thought of being sneered at from a great height yet again by some of the critics and over something I cared so much about, was pushing me into the very sort of performance that would deserve their disparagement. My husband, coming from a similar background to me, is propelled by the attitude of:

'I'll show the bastards.' Mine, despite my father's competitive spirit, is: 'I probably won't.' 'Lose your inferiority complex – you don't need it,' urged Trevor Nunn in a letter to me. More easily said than done. Or, so I thought. And here follows a passage that could well be worth the price of this book to you.

Before I started the job at the National I went to a health farm for a few days (something I have frequently done if I want a quick rejuvenation), and while I was there attended a lecture by a hypnotherapist. I was extremely sceptical at the claims of his speech at the time, but I now felt I had nothing to lose but my panic so I went to see him privately in London on the morning of the press night. After a long chat (during which he explained how the mind can get set into negative patterns that can be replaced by new positive ones), he simply asked me to close my eyes and counted backwards from ten to one. He then suggested to me that when the five minutes was called that night, instead of thinking I wanted to be sick I should think how much I was looking forward to portraying this character in this beautiful play, and while on-stage I should quite simply *be* her. I would ignore all outside distractions and live, move and speak as I already knew this woman would. After a few more encouraging words urging me to be true to myself rather than other people's view of me, he counted from one to ten and told me to open my eyes. I was convinced that I had not been in any kind of hypnotic trance but had been wide awake all the time and nothing would be changed. How wrong I was.

During the rest of that day of the first official performance I certainly had no recurrence of the Richmond Park *Sweeney Todd* nightmares and I was not, as usual, utterly convinced that I would fail, but I was none too confident either. Then, exactly as my hypnotherapist had predicted, as the stage manager's voice said over the tannoy, 'Five minutes please', I felt a novel rush of excitement. I could even bear to listen to the murmur of the audience as they waited for us, something that normally struck terror into me. When I walked down to the stage with Edward he *was* my brother Gayev, and when I ran on to the stage it *was* 'my darling nursery'. There was one wavering moment when I looked out at the orchard and caught sight of the impassive face of one of the critics but, whereas normally my mind would have been distracted, somehow it jumped back into the play. It was a miracle. All those groundless, destructive fears of previous first nights seemed to have dissolved. I actually enjoyed myself. After the show I was relaxed and happy, and received the praise of my family with great satisfaction instead of believing

I could have done better. I went to the company party in the bar and enjoyed myself thoroughly.

I was told next day about Michael Meyer's dig about my lack of Oxbridgeness and genuinely found it funny rather than upsetting. I did not rush out and buy all the papers when the reviews came out but *The Times* and the *Guardian* were delivered anyway. I first read Irving Wardle in *The Times* and he did not even mention my name. Quite an achievement, I suppose, to be ignored in a leading role of a major classic. Calmly, there and then, I decided to join the ranks of the many actors who do not read their notices. I even threw away the *Guardian* without looking at it. I was no longer masochistically inclined to discover whether or not I had vulgarised a great play ('Yes, Sheila Hancock is very good, but I find her rather common,' said Dilys Powell in 1967, when the rest of the critics on a radio discussion programme praised my performance in *The Soldier's Fortune* at the Royal Court.) For once, I knew I had done my best and if the critics did not like it, hard luck.

Again, my timing was at fault. Later that day an excited Ian, followed by Tom, phoned to congratulate me on my rave reviews, then my Auntie Ruby rang me and the postman told me the *Daily Mail* said I was wonderful. But I had made up my mind and it seemed hypocritical to change it just to read nice things. Thus I have never read what are probably the best reviews I have ever received, judging by the extracts in the hand-out advertising and the congratulations I received. However, my decision only to read, in future, reviews of shows I direct so that I can discuss them with my actors will probably prevent a lot of heartache. Old notices in faded copies of *Punch* and *Country Life* are always leaping up and biting one in dentist's waiting rooms anyway, so you usually get round to them in the end, but by then you are doing something else so you are past caring – the timing is all.

Anyway I did not need to read the reviews to find out if *The Cherry Orchard* was a success. Queues formed at 6.00 am for returns, as the show was sold out for the entire run. Offers came in to take the play to all parts of the globe, including Russia, and there were immediate requests for a West End transfer. In this Thelma Holt, who had left the Round House and joined the National as its touring manager, was to be thwarted by the company's reluctance to commit itself to further plans. Some of us were worried about the production transferring from a small intimate space to a larger conventional theatre – particularly Ian who had had a bad experience with a similar transfer of *Macbeth*. Others were playing much smaller parts than their prestige in the theatre warranted, which was all right in the repertoire but could be harmful to their careers if viewed out of this context. Some of us also felt a West End transfer was not an appropriate accolade for the company. We had proved ourselves as an ensemble of great versatility and were surprised and hurt that no suggestion was made for any of us to continue at the National when our contracts finished in four months' time. I was not privy to inside discussions so it could be that it was mooted – I cannot believe it was not.

In retrospect I feel it was sad that *The Cherry Orchard* was seen by so few people, although at the time I was one of those against it having a further life. Bad timing again, or bad judgement. It had its off-nights, but on the whole it was a remarkable production and because it did not continue longer it is now virtually forgotten, unlike, say, *Les Liaisons Dangereuses* which went from the Other Place to London to New York, albeit with a slightly changed cast from the original in Stratford. I am sure that if we had tried harder and thought more carefully, despite the obstacles the company could have continued. It was entirely our fault – or those of us who vetoed it – as the National very much wanted us to transfer to the West End. Our wish to continue on the South Bank instead was plainly difficult to accommodate, planning being finalised far ahead in such a complex operation. Anyway, Ian was contemplating a production of *Wild Honey* in New York and Edward a series on television playing Lord Peter Wimsey. With the salaries to be earned elsewhere being so much higher than at the two national theatres, it is difficult to keep artists who are in demand for very long. A deputation of some of the company came to my dressing room one night to ask if I would take over the leadership of the company if Ian and Edward left so that maybe the company could stay on or come back later, but I had to point out that I thought that would be impossible, and I considered I had to be asked rather than suggest myself.

Anyway, I doubted my ability to match Edward's tenacity and Ian's tornado-like energy. I had my work cut out with Ian on stage. Nobody I have worked with is more unselfish as an actor than he, but he has such charisma that it is easy to shrivel up in his presence. Playing scenes with him in *The Cherry Orchard* was like a marvellous duel. In the scene where he announces that he has bought the cherry orchard I never knew what he would do, and every night it was a fresh earthquake. Sometimes he would crush me in a bear-hug and kiss away my tears, sometimes he would hurl hatred at me. Underlying all our actions were gauntlets thrown down to see if the other could pick them up. There are some actors who have this force which makes them the 'centre' of any stage. They simply cannot efface themselves. Nothing could have been more eloquent than Olivier's back on-stage when he tried to give the focus of the scene to somebody else. Similarly with Ian, but in this company he was surrounded by actors, used to playing leads, doing the small parts and pretty forceful personalities themselves, so the stimulation of this, plus his passion to make the ensemble a success, pushed him to great heights as Lopakhin. All told we were something of a sensation but, except for a few 'well dones' from the other actors in the Green Room, life on the South Bank churned on in much the same way.

Thelma Holt had planned a rather diverse tour for us to wind up our year as a company. In February we were scheduled to take the *Hound* and *Critic* to L'Odéon Theatre in Paris for a week as part of a European Theatre Festival. After a short spell back at the National performing all three shows again, we would set off in March for a week in Aberdeen with *The Cherry Orchard*. We would then do our last performance of all three shows on the South Bank, before embarking on a final trip to Chicago where we would present them for a month in a World Theatre Festival. As all the theatres were different shapes to those at the National, much adaptation of the sets and blocking (as the setting of moves is called) had to be done; the blocking of *The Cherry Orchard* remained unplanned but we had to think about projecting it in a large theatre. We still had the usual understudy and word rehearsals, necessary as a refresher each time one of the plays returned to the repertoire after a period of doing the others. With all this work, the company was pretty tired. This pressure resulted in some illness amongst the actors. Understudying in *The Critic* was a nightmare with everyone having to cover several parts, as well as play several of their own, and be able to make the costume changes between each. In January 1986 the disaster that I feared happened when Hugh Lloyd was off in *The Critic*. So complex was the knock-on effect that Edward that night seemed to be playing everything. It got to a point where the audience applauded immediately he appeared in yet another crooked costume, to offer yet another accent and funny walk in a desperate attempt to be a dozen different people. He was never off-stage. In the end, Ian and the rest of the company were openly laughing as he shot on yet again from the wrong place, frequently in the wrong scene. 'Wait a minute – who am I now?' was his comment having bounced on stage wearing the costume for one part with the hat of another.

In the best Joan Littlewood tradition, Edward was never averse to chatting to the audience. Neither was Roy Kinnear, with whom I had learnt this technique in *Make Me an Offer* at Theatre Workshop in 1959. A particular obsession of Edward's was the sight-lines – especially in the Olivier. He and Roy, as the critics in *The Real Inspector Hound*, had to sit in the same position for almost the entire play. There was a curtain stage-right that was supposed to be fixed back by one of the stagehands at the beginning of the show to prevent them being masked from several rows on the edge of the auditorium. I was sitting in my dressing room one night, being a dutiful understudy, when I was transfixed by a dialogue over the tannoy. Edward later gave me the following transcript of the ad libs as he remembered them to demonstrate to me how long he had been deserted by the back-stage staff, ignoring the fact that it would have been a brave stagehand to come on in the circumstances:

MOON: Birdboot.
(EDWARD)
BIRDBOOT: *(Attempting to go on with dialogue, thinking 'I am going mad')* Do you
(ROY)   believe in love at first sight?
MOON: I am going to do something unprecedented.
BIRDBOOT: Are you?
MOON: I am going to stop the show. You see, due to a technical hitch, there
              are up to fifty people on that side who can't see us.
BIRDBOOT: Do they care?
MOON: Well, we must give them the benefit of the doubt.
BIRDBOOT: Well, yes.
MOON: Now that we have stopped, somebody will come on and see to that
              curtain.
                               (Pause)
              I hope they *(the audience)* don't mind me stopping. I mean this is a
              sort of interval in the play, isn't it?
BIRDBOOT: Well, it is now! *(Big laugh)*
                               (Pause)
MOON: I suppose there *is* somebody back there.
                               (Pause)
              Perhaps they have all gone home. It is Christmas after all.
BIRDBOOT: Have a chocolate.
MOON: No thanks.
                               (Pause)
              I think I am going to do it myself. *(Nips across footlights, approaches*
              the proscenium arch and deftly tucks the curtain behind the clamp. Big
              round of applause. Returns to seat)
MOON: Shall we go on?
BIRDBOOT: All right.
MOON: Camps it round the Old Vic in his opera cloak and passes me the
              tat. *(Usual silence – this line never gets a laugh)*

BIRDBOOT: That went well. *(Big laugh)*
MOON: I can't understand why that never gets a laugh. Shall I try it again?
BIRDBOOT: Go on then.
MOON: Camps it round the Old Vic in his opera cloak and passes me the tat.
BIRDBOOT: *(Makes well known characteristic upward gesture and 'woof' noise, simulating big laugh reaction from audience)*
    (Dialogue continues as scripted to end of play.)

I fear I could not bring myself to reprimand even the last unnecessary departure from the play.

Being the leaders of the company Ian and he were always keeping a weather eye out for mistakes. In *Malfi*, in the middle of one of his most moving speeches, or more often one of mine, Ian's Wolfit-like eyes were apt to flicker around as he checked the lights. This general vigilance stood us in good stead one night during *The Critic*. In the set collapse, he and Jonathan Hyde had to hit very accurate marks just before two flats with holes in the middle crashed to the ground Buster Keaton-like over them. One night Ian's beady eye realised Jonathan's mark had been put down inaccurately and he hissed a warning at him just in time for Jonathan to avoid a very nasty accident.

There was another near tragedy during the firework display in the finale of *The Critic*. (Oh yes! We had fireworks too *and* a battle between miniature ships, several of which sank under gunfire.) One performance Julie Legrand, playing Queen Elizabeth I, was taken aback when Simon Dutton suddenly lunged at her and started beating her about the back. Fortunately, her costume was very thick which was why she was totally unaware that she was on fire. It got a very good laugh from the audience, but increased the alarm of the cast at the hazards they faced. Stephen Macdonald was heard to remark lugubriously on this occasion: 'I thought acting was meant to be pretend.'

It was at times like this that I cursed the fact I had devised such an accident-prone show, and that I was lumbered with being in the theatre on double bill nights because of my understudy duties and therefore was on hand to cope with things when they went wrong. I saw the point of disappearing after the first night, like some directors. My presence was hard on the actors too and they, like my RSC company, learnt to quail at my advancing notebook. Or bridle. The company could still not be said to be all sweetness and light, but by this time I was used to the odd outburst and had occasion to be grateful for their trusting one another on-stage when we arrived in Paris, on the first leg of our period of touring.

I had exactly two and a half days to mount *Hound* as well as *The Critic* (Tom Stoppard being unavailable until just before opening night), and with only a skeleton English crew, grappling with their schoolboy French, and a lot of chauvinist *porcs* who were at first not too keen at all on a female *metteuse en scène*, life was pretty *difficile*. As we wrestled to get the sets up and lit and endeavoured to communicate in franglais the complicated, life-endangering technical operations, I realised the company would have no chance of getting on the stage for a dress rehearsal on this modified set, in a completely different type of theatre to the Olivier. It did, however, mean that they could see a bit of Paris instead, and again I cursed my luck at being an on-the-spot director trapped in the theatre with the glories of Paris outside.

It was in Paris at fourteen that I first learned about 'the good life'. My school organised a visit during my summer holidays to work as an au pair for two months. My employer was an elegant wealthy Parisienne, with oiled jet black hair who divided her time between a flat in Paris and a beautiful house in Fouras near La Rochelle, where she received many artistic friends and, when her husband was absent, to my utter amazement, lovers. She was intrigued by my naivety and fiercely protected me from the marauding French youths who seemed to find my Englishness attractive, yet at the same time she would dress me up and caress me herself in front of her lovers, muttering things about my 'jeunesse' to the nodding, wistfully smiling men. I was fascinated by this sophisticated, faintly decadent woman moving in a haze of expensive perfume and sex. It was a strange new world for a young Bexleyheathen and no mistake. When the latest lover departed she would sit up half the night talking to me about *l'amour*. She introduced me to the delights of good wine (which I had never even seen in my life, let alone tasted), garlic, frogs' legs, snails, Pernod, salad dressing and Gauloises. At home we had a joint on Sunday, cold on Monday, shepherd's pie Tuesday, stew Wednesday and considerably less than that during the war. Good, wholesome economical food. I had no idea until I went to Paris what a joy a civilised meal savoured with friends could be. Or that it could last so long. The great advantage of 'abroad' is that people seem to know how to pass the time of day better than us; to linger in a cafe watching the world go by is not considered idle. You can take your children with you and keep them up late without cluckings of disapproval from other customers, and grandma goes along too, highly respected and fussed over by the rest of the family (although this would have been a mixed blessing with mine).

As well as the strange encounters with her lovers, I was allowed to take part in the *soirées* at Madame T's. Indeed, she usually called upon me to perform my *St Joan* speech, which I might have done less confidently had I heard of one of the men I later discovered named in my diary as Jean-Paul Sartre. I have since wondered if the unusual woman with him was Simone de Beauvoir, and curse my ignorant childhood that to me they were just a 'nice lady and gentleman'.

Four years later I worked in Paris for a while scrubbing floors and serving in a restaurant while in the process of hitch-hiking round Europe. That was when I saw my first real live paintings. I had seen the odd print in books, but they did not prepare me for the layers and slashes and thicknesses of the Van Gogh's in the Jeu de Paume, or the colours of the Monets and Gaugins. This gallery utterly bewitched me, but the Mona Lisa gallery in the Louvre was the one I visited most often. The main attraction here was the proper lavatory that was situated in one of the corners, a rare luxury in the rough world I inhabited, the chief discomfort being the nasty little holes in the ground with foot rests either side that served at *toilettes* in the dives I then lived in. Even on this less luxurious visit, Paris seemed wonderfully stylish to me. I somehow managed to wangle an invitation to a Jacques Fath fashion show and had my first glimpse of *haute couture*, although my own *couture* did not appear very *haute* when someone stood on the loose end of my rope-soled sandal and it slowly unravelled as I crossed the perfumed room to reach my chair.

I always feel a bit guilty about enjoying myself in England, but never in Paris. If I walk in London late at night, I always get the same sinful flutterings I experienced as a child when running down the empty streets late for school. In Paris it feels quite normal. Day or night – anything goes. I simply love being a foreigner, too – to feel no responsibility for the politics or injustices of the country. A blissful lightheartedness takes me over when I am in Paris. And not just in the springtime.

Before this visit in February 1986 I had never seen Paris in the snowtime. The frozen fountains and white expanses of the Jardin du Luxembourg area round the theatre were an eerie sight, and in the unusual trafficless calm it was hard to believe that this student area had once been the site of such turbulence. In 1968, during the riots, Jean Louis Barrault had handed over L'Odéon Theatre to the students to use as their headquarters. They had repaid him by wrecking the place and ransacking his theatre wardrobe.

However, when we arrived, apart from a rather nasty painting on the ceiling which we were told was done during the student occupation, it was again a beautiful theatre, and the company loved it after working in the Olivier. It is not easy to play comedy in the latter when you have to deliver a throw-away tag or show a raised eyebrow reaction to a widely spread half-circle of 1,160 seats; the Greeks were not into that sort of subtlety when they designed the theatre at Epidaurus on which the Olivier is based. I am not sure whether it was being in an old-fashioned, proscenium-arched theatre, or whether the French listened better than the English audiences because of their difficulty with the language, but the double bill went even better in Paris than it did in England. I had been worried that our plays would be a little lightweight at the end of a European Festival that had included productions of Corneille by the brilliant resident director, Georgio Strehler, and Ibsen by Ingmar Bergman. On the contrary, our timing was perfect as the audiences were ready for a laugh. We were a riotous success.

The French stagehands started to treat me with great respect when they heard the audiences' nightly cheering, and I was delighted when I was told that all the French critics, as well as the audiences, appreciated our send-up of the xenophobia and the farce business and the witty lines alike. The British Ambassador told us at a party he gave for us during the week that we had done our country a great deal of good. We did not get a telegram from Mrs Thatcher, but then we were not a cricket team.

We did not get a lot of thanks from the National Theatre either. After this triumphant week in Paris, on the day we returned to the South Bank we all found buff envelopes awaiting us containing our notices. It was a necessary formality as our year's contracts were due to end in three months, but it could have been better timed. I tried to soothe everyone's ruffled feathers and to shame the management by sending out a congratulatory memo to all the staff and actors. Thelma Holt, who was also trying to humanise the organisation, gave us a cake, but the well-meant inscription on top 'Roll on May 25th', was interpreted by over-sensitive actors as her wanting to get rid of us too. In fact, she had thought we all meant it when we put on the usual bravado about how we could not wait to leave anyway. We were still packing them in for all three shows but I suspect our depression at the thought of being on the way out, surrounded by actors in the other groups in the middle of putting on new things, must have affected us. Certainly, Mike was not very pleased with one performance he saw of *The Cherry Orchard* when he wrote notes to us all saying: 'You have made your contribution to Deadly Theatre. Would you please return to Lively Theatre. Please all think and prepare before all performances. You can't just go on . . .'

We had by this time finally forced the National to cancel the plans for a West End transfer of *The Cherry Orchard*, so we had got what we asked for and could not complain. But we did, of course. The latest row was about the size of the per diems on our next trip a fortnight later up to Aberdeen. It was, I think, the old problem of all big organisations. Although Edward and Ian did their best to liaise, everyone felt neglected. Not appreciated enough. Used. Why were we working so much harder than the other groups? Why were we being pushed off on tour more than the others? Why was everybody not kissing our feet and telling us we were wonderful all the time?

The sad fact is that success is often like that. Once the first-night flowers have faded, you just have to go on every night and do the play like any other worker does their job. What is more, nobody else is really all that interested in your phenomenal success. Success in the theatre is transitory, too. You can be flavour of the month one minute and box-office poison the next, so it is essential to get your priorities right. I once asked Edward why, unlike most men I know, he put his family first and he replied that when he was on his death bed, he would rather be surrounded by a loving family than his old notices. Nevertheless, it is still silly to throw away success when it is so elusive, which is what we did with *The Cherry Orchard*. One of our reasons for doing so was proved ill-founded when we did the play for the week in Aberdeen during March.

At the time of our visit the town was feeling rather like us. After the boom time of the North Sea oil discoveries it was now facing an imminent decline into unemployment as oil prices plummeted. House prices were dropping and businesses closing, but on the surface the town still felt prosperous. It was certainly not gay like Paree, though, in any sense of the word. Little craggy Scotsmen were outnumbered by hordes of larger men from all parts of the country who worked on the oil rigs. I have never seen so many drunks in my life, and me a publican's daughter. The rigs are teetotal and, after a fortnight on duty, the men are gasping for a drink when they arrive back in Aberdeen for their fortnight's leave. Most of them seemed to quench their thirst in our hotel. They made a change from commercial travellers, mind you. As did the devastatingly good-looking Swedish football team who were playing the Scots and caused a few of our hearts to flutter – both male and female. No, we were not short of good company in Aberdeen.

The harsh appearance of the granite city belied our very warm welcome. When I arrived at the theatre there was a parcel awaiting me from the guard on my train, who had brought round my scarf which I had left behind. Eleanor Bron and I then received a lovely cherry tree on behalf of the company, presented by the Lord Provost before the opening performance to commemorate our visit, which I believe now languishes on the windy Lilian Bayliss terrace on the South Bank. It was refreshing to see that some of the wealth of the city had been poured into its arts facilities. The theatre we played at, His Majesty's, was designed by the great Frank Matcham in 1906 and had been recently magnificently restored by the council. They were shrewd enough to realise that a prosperous theatre can regenerate a whole area. In the same street is a remarkable art gallery and there are numerous museums and churches to visit. I was in my element. I dragged Ian round the town, weighed down with guide books, and bored him rigid with my crash course in Scottish history. He retaliated by making Tristram Wymark and me accompany him at the crack of dawn to the fish market on the docks, where a new-found Scottish friend plied us with champagne as we clambered over the boxes of newly landed fish. I was told the last woman to visit had been the Queen Mother and, apart from one woman gutting fish in an evil-smelling shed – a job that has taken over from Peter Jones' glue factories in my awfulness index – and another on the tea stall, there was a marked lack of the gentle sex. This probably accounted for my welcome being even warmer than Ian's. Classical actors are less familiar to fishermen and dockers than TV personalities, as was proved by our introduction as 'Sheila Hancock and Peter McTellern'.

They are a bit vague about names in Aberdeen. Apparently one of the papers attributed Mike Alfred's translation of *The Cherry Orchard* to Alfred Marks. Hugh Lloyd, however, provided the best example. The BBC were re-running the classic *Hancock's Half Hour* in which Hugh had appeared, and another TV series he made with Terry Scott was also on during the week. An Aberdonian stopped him in the street and said joyously: 'You're Terry Lloyd aren't you? I saw Shirley Hancock in the fish market.' When Hugh looked a little blank, he continued: 'You know – you were in her show on Sunday.' You certainly get a measure of your true value in Aberdeen. But the play got the usual honest response of people who are not reacting as the critics have ordained. And that was how I realised that my fear of the detrimental effect of putting the production in a conventional theatre was unfounded. It actually went better. Too late – the die was cast. But if our visit to Aberdeen had been timed before the decision about a transfer had to be finalised, my vote would certainly have been different.

Especially after an encounter I had with a woman who, like Hugh's man, had no idea of my name. Fortunately, in my quest to master the Aberdeen accent I secretly recorded what she said, so I can replay it in moments of disenchantment:

'Oh, you are the lass I saw last night. Beautiful. I woke up in the night thinking of you and I was quite happy to lie there, loving you all.'

It's not such a bad job, after all.

13 : With a Bang, Not A Whimper
Chicago

The company's exit from the South Bank coincided with that of the
Greater London Council — only they made theirs with a bang that
shamed our whimpering departure. My children and I had enjoyed
many events organised by the GLC, which the Government deemed so
dangerous that it had to be abolished, but the final knees-up was the
best of all. During the shows at the National on the night of 31 March
1986, we could hear the fireworks exploding over the river outside and
in every wait between entrances we rushed to the windows to watch the
fabulous displays. After the show, a few of us pushed our way through
the vast crowds enjoying the concerts to watch pearly kings and queens
dancing to reggae bands. From the terrace of London's County Hall
(now destined to be sold off to the highest bidder by the new non-elected
London Residuary Body), Elgar was boomed out over the river, rockets
banged and lasers beamed as Tony Banks and Ken Livingstone lowered
the GLC flag for the last time. For some reason, possibly passive
resistance, it stuck half-way and refused to budge. As they eased it back
up the pole and tugged and pulled, the huge crowd went wild. They
were powerless against the decision from on high but at least they could
laugh at it.

I had a bit of a smirk too at the farewell tea-party given for the company
by Sir Peter Hall. This was held during the three-week period in April
when we gave, with varying degress of regret, our last performances on
the South Bank of all three shows. With so many people and so many
plays at the National, actors usually slink away quietly and, unless Diane

takes it into her head to tannoy fond farewells, plays disappear from the repertoire unnoticed by anyone save those taking part. So for Sir Peter to give us a tea-party was a nice thought, but so used was he to giving his set-piece speech about how bad the funding is for the National Theatre that he went into automatic pilot and gave it to a group of actors who were about to lessen his burden by joining the dole queues. In the circumstances, it was a little hard for us to express much sympathy. Anyway, we had done our bit to keep the National Theatre flag flying. Indeed, we were to carry it back abroad during the last month of our contracts to Chicago to perform all three of our shows in a World Theatre Festival: *Malfi* and *The Cherry Orchard* for one week each and *Hound* and *Critic* for two weeks.

I had never been to Chicago, although I have always had a good time in New York. It is not the sort of good time I have in Paris, sitting back and relishing things. It is more brash and energetic than that. I feel alive in the States, but totally alien – and a bit of a joke. The Americans make me feel quaint. I did as a child when I made the GIs laugh at my cockney accent to earn my chewing gum and sweets, and again in 1965 when I went to New York with Joe Orton's *Entertaining Mr Sloane* and, accompanied by my mother, I sauntered up Broadway with Melanie in her pushchair. People seemed to stop and stare at us. Blonde, blue-eyed children were unusual in central New York, as were people sauntering, particularly grey-haired ladies wearing hats and gloves ordering people not to push so rudely. The double-takes quadrupled when we were joined on our strolls by Joe himself, black eyes sparkling under his leather peaked cap and muscles rippling under his tight white T-shirt and sprayed-on jeans. My memories of him enjoying my mother's roast beef and Yorkshire pudding on a sweltering, humid New York Sunday contrast strangely with his violent death and the uncosy life-style revealed in his diaries. My mother thought he was 'a nice boy who needs feeding up', and his regard for her was revealed in his uncharacteristic reticence when she questioned him on the use of the strange objects in the windows of the sex-shops we passed – a service industry which had not yet reached England. These, along with the hamburgers, police sirens, incomprehensible disc-jockeys and other American phenomena, which have since become the norm in England, make New York now seem a less startling contrast than it did in the 1960s.

I can still only take America in small doses, but the odd homeopathic exposure is very therapeutic. For someone so floppy, the American positive-thinking approach – the 'get up and go' – is tremendously stimulating. As is the belief that anyone can make it. Their naive enthusiasm is a wonderful antidote to my British cynicism and laziness. The late Alan Schneider, the New York director of *Entertaining Mr Sloane*, was nonplussed by us English actors' apparent lackadaisical approach to rehearsals. He would have worked day and night if we had allowed him. 'A cup of tea wouldn't go amiss,' was our constant whimper. He would shake his head in disbelief, just as he did when I objected to his proposed sacking of an American actor in the company. There is a pernicious clause in their contracts which allows this, so that the actors are on trial and anxious for the first few days of rehearsal when they should be feeling their way gently into a role. The actor in question was not very good, but I felt sorry for him and I urged that he should be kept on. Alan very reluctantly agreed, to placate me, but was mystified by such a sentimental attitude: for him, the success of the show was more important than one bad actor's hurt feelings.

I had encountered this same uncompromising professionalism when working with Bette Davis on the film of *The Anniversary* in 1967 at Shepperton Studios. She knew exactly what the public wanted to see her do, and when our director, Alvin Rakoff, tried to change it she demanded his removal. She knew her job and herself inside out. She supervised her own lighting, which is why she looks so much better and younger than any of us in the film; she usually perfected her scenes, however complex, in one take; she always said any lines off-camera for other people herself even at the end of a tiring day; and she knew everything there was to know about cameras and film technique. Like Alan, she believed there was no room for sentiment, but I discovered she too was vulnerable. I was very in awe of her but on one occasion, after she had done a brilliant take, I plucked up my courage and told her so. She clutched my hand and said, 'Oh, thank you honey. The highest compliment I've had on this film so far is "Print it,"' (the order a director gives when a scene is good enough to use). I was very sad when I heard on the grapevine that she felt we were unkind to her. She is a legendary actress, and my admiration was only increased when I saw her fighting to guard the uniqueness which I knew from her autobiography, *A Lonely Life*, she had paid so highly to establish. Even if I did not always approve of her tactics. But then, I often do not approve of American tactics.

On 15 April 1986 they chose to repay terrorist attacks allegedly organised with the help of Gadhaffi (although there is subsequently some question over the evidence for this) by a bombing raid on Libya, for which some of the planes took off from USAF bases in England. This action was supported by Thatcher and a man on LBC Radio, who said: 'Well, yes, I fink it's time we showed old – er – whatsisname – a lesson.' The *Sun* doubtless dreamed up a few gotcha-like slogans, as in the Falklands War, but on the whole the British people were pretty shocked; especially those living near the bases who had managed to convince themselves that they would never actually be used. Shortly after this, one bomb was intercepted in a TWA plane and one actually went off, as did another in the British Airways office in Oxford Street. All told, not incidents likely to improve my chronic aerophobia, happening as they did just before our TWA flight to Chicago on 25 April. There was nothing for it but to resort to my hypnotist.

Having promised my family that I would remember I was a guest in the USA and keep my mouth shut, I clamped on my Sony Walkman earphones and listened to my hypnotist's voice reminding me to relax as we took off for the New World. We practically had the plane to ourselves. All the Americans, fearing reprisals, had left London quickly after the raid and no more were venturing to come over. On top of that, the TWA stewards were on strike and the plane was serviced by retired or novice blacklegged replacements, which meant the service was not of the usual standard. But I was perfectly happy. After take-off I removed my earphones and beamed at Ian, commenting how smooth it had been. White and shaking, he pointed out that, first of all, we had been delayed while a plane landed from Tripoli and diplomats and journalists had alighted just beside us, guarded by armed soldiers. After which, our plane had taken off rather jerkily through a violent storm. I had been blissfully unaware of all this.

Even in my trance, however, I was disconcerted by a conversation we had with a middle-aged hostess, who Ian was convinced was the pilot's wife's best friend who had agreed to come along for the trip. It did occur to me that she and the other fumbling amateurs would not be much of a match for a determined hijacker, and when we saw her myopically checking the hand luggage I asked her what she would do if she actually found a bomb. She thought hard for a moment and then informed us that she would go and tell the pilot. If he could not think of anything better, she would take it to the back of the plane and pile cushions and curtains against it in an effort to make the blast go outwards. Then followed a graphic description of how easily things could get pulled out of a plane. Warming to her theme, she told horror stories of little cracks in windows that had burst open, sucking out rows of passengers. Ian eventually managed to stop her and she tottered off to get us some very cold tea, which was understandable as for some sinister reason all the water on the plane had frozen up. Were it not for my hypnotist, I have no doubt that I would have had to be strait-jacketed to prevent me running amok. Indeed, I doubt if I would ever have got on the plane in the first place. Which would have been a pity as I would have missed seeing a wonderful place.

As with Milton Keynes, I found it enlivening to visit a city that revels in being modern. Chicago first consisted of a few wooden shacks in 1830. The name is Red Indian for skunk, wild onion or powerful – nobody seems quite sure which. It is a model of free enterprise, starting with the likes of a dentist called Sears who plied his trade round the early settlements. When people asked him to bring them goods, he compiled a catalogue and from that humble start built a business empire, now based in the vast Sears Roebuck skyscraper. In search of similar fortunes, people have poured in from all over the world, settling into village-like communities which still preserve the traditions and lifestyles of the various ethnic groups – Polish, Irish, Hispanic, Italian, whatever. Businesses of all sorts sprang up with the advent of the railway, including the gigantic slaughterhouses in the famous Stockyards. Chicagoans must have learnt not to be squeamish at the sight of blood, particularly during the fourteen years of prohibition that turned the city into a stronghold of gangsters who wiped out about seven hundred people, often in broad daylight, sometimes with machine-guns. Yes, they know all about terrorism in Chicago. It is a dramatic place. The early town was destroyed twice by fire, the second time, in 1871, razing the place to the ground and making way for the revolutionary buildings of modern Chicago.

All that is left of the old town is the ugly Water Tower, around it soaring the skyscrapers which Chicago pioneered. (It was in Chicago that nuclear power was first developed too, but I will pass over that.) They have a proud tradition of great architects, including Frank Lloyd Wright, and the houses he built, standing in their well-kept lawns (that seem to be waiting for Mickey Rooney to cycle across, throwing papers, or Judy Garland to lean back on the front doors, singing), show the same brilliant use of materials and colour as the buildings of later generations. Viewed from a boat on the lake on which Chicago is built, they glitter and glisten – blacks, browns, pinks, greens, golds, reds. Nobody in Chicago writes letters to the paper when a new experiment in architecture is tried. There was a vast exhibition of modern art on the pier while we were there that would have us English winging, 'But what does it *mean*?', but Chicagoans were 'Woweeing' and 'Yeahing' loudly with enthusiasm. None of your polite whispers.

They are enthusiastic even in their worship. When we arrived, bedraggled and jet-lagged, our hotel on Michigan Avenue rang with 'Hallelujahs' from the various revivalist meetings being held there. Born-again Christians, Daughters of the Revolution, Moral Rearmers were at it like knives. I sat in on one or two of the fundamentalist meetings during my stay and marvelled at their childlike trust. Watching the television chat-shows too, it was wondrous to behold the shining eyes at the banal utterings of their hosts and, mindful of the slight disapproval I had sensed back home when I married a man nine years my junior, I was intrigued during one of these programmes at the spontaneous way the Americans clapped and whooped when a woman with capped teeth and drawn-up face shyly said she was sixty-two and in love with a boy of twenty.

I also got caught up in the quest for the body perfect. Along the block from our hotel was a brand new health club called Charlie's. One of the old skyscrapers had been converted into acres of pools, steam-baths, running tracks, studios, halls filled with machines dedicated to 'total fitness'. Every day, I donned my black leotard and tights and steadfastly wrestled with weights and computerised torture apparati, even when I occasionally caught sight of myself in one of the mirrors looking like a geriatric earwig. Gradually, as they saw the new spring in my step, other members of the company joined the club which, being open twenty-four hours a day, was the perfect place to sweat out any over-indulgence after the show.

My coach was a second-generation American of Ukranian descent called Don. I was beneath all but his most cursory notice until he read a newspaper article about me, whereupon I discovered the power of publicity in the States. Charlie himself sent a message of thanks for the mention I had made of his club and I was offered a free 'healthy' lunch. Don treated me to another one himself in the outspoken hope that in future articles I would mention him by name.

Career was overridingly important to Don. When I asked why, he told me he wanted: 'To be rich, happy, and retire early.' He was eighteen at the time. He was doing a Business and Self-Improvement course in the evenings, and his conversation was so full of the jargon he had learned that I had to keep asking for translations. He was saving money to set up as a funeral director because he had calculated that there was seventy-five per cent profit in it, particularly if he established himself in his own Ukranian neighbourhood and provided a unique service to fit its taste in funerals, of which he had useful knowledge, albeit little regard.

I was curious about his family history but he simply would not discuss it. I asked him if he was upset about Chernobyl, which was close to his town of origin, but he said that although he believed his mother and grandmother had been anxious for relatives still there, he was not, as he had no feeling for the country. 'It is not a lifestyle that interests me,' was his curt comment – except presumably as a business gimmick. Despite still living in a traditionally Ukranian atmosphere, he had no knowledge of the country of his ancestors, except that the Soviet Union was the enemy. He did not even know that they had once been allies and that twenty million Russians had died in the last war; but he knew all about the Communist threat that would cause the next, if we were not constantly on our guard. I tried to share my fascination with Russia, engendered by *The Cherry Orchard*, but he made me feel like a dangerous subversive. This brain-washed all-American boy had no time for international understanding – no time for anything but improving himself.

And this in a city that is thumping with fun. Everywhere you go you can hear jazz: in hotel foyers, in the numerous clubs, on street corners, someone somewhere seems always to be blowing a horn or tickling the ivories. It was a welcome change from the muzak that infiltrates every-where in London. And then there is the food. In New York the food is a disappointment, luscious-looking multi-layered sandwiches that taste of nothing; in Chicago we found several fabulous restaurants. As befits a centre of meat distribution, steaks abound, and nowhere in the world are there so many varieties of bangers served in so many different ways. But no delicacy surpassed egg, bacon and coffee at three o'clock in the morning in the marble splendour of the Hilton Hotel. Except perhaps the huge bags of toasting hot pop-corn to be purchased in a little shop on the Magnificent Mile. Not just the gooey white stuff that I crunched in the one-and-nines as a child, but dozens of different nutty, chewy varieties.

It seemed a shame that Don's health regime would never allow him to touch any of this, or alcohol either. The fun the Americans have with their drinks makes our gin and its and whisky and water seem awfully dull. To sit with friends in the cocktail lounge, 1,127 feet above ground in the Hancock Building, toasting my namesake with Whisky Sour or a Pina Colada, looking out at the views of the city is a bit of all right. Good old Hancock. The lift here is the fastest in the world – except when I am in it. I am not too happy in lifts at the best of times and usually prefer to walk up the stairs, but not when there are a hundred flights – even with my amazingly developed gluteus maximus. On my first ascent, the lift juddered to an unscheduled halt between floors twenty-four and twenty-five and stayed there in suspense for several minutes. However, once up at the top, I managed to dismiss thoughts of imagined illustrious ancestors passing judgement on my relative unworthiness and enjoyed myself thoroughly.

I had to dismiss a lot of disturbing thoughts in order to enjoy Chicago so much. When I travelled round Britain I felt I had to rub my nose in my own country's dirt, but America, like France, is not my responsibility. I did not go and look at the slums on the Southside which are said to be some of the worst in the world. I tore up the hate-ridden leaflets that were saturating the town, calling for the sacking of those on TV who 'think it is OK for homosexuals to teach in schools'. I jammed wax ear-plugs into my ears to shut out the frightening obscenities that came through the paper-thin walls of the adjoining hotel room to mine. The accents varied from Tennessee Williams to Phil Silvers, but wherever they hailed from, without fail – as the drink flowed – they broke into impersonations of Frank Sinatra singing 'Chicago' and their vocabulary gradually narrowed into a virtual non-stop use of the word 'mother fucker'. Well, I suppose it made a change from 'Have a nice day now.'

I did not want to hear or read in the papers about the graft in high places that lingers from the reign of Mayor Daly. Or the corruption that has never been quite wiped out since Al Capone ran the city. I did not want to delve into all that any more than they did – it was in the past. After all, there were only fifty-eight gang murders in Chicago in 1985, according to a news report of the latest one.

When a few youngsters calling themselves 'anarchists' made a bit of a scene on Michigan Avenue, I tried not to regret their aimlessness compared with the sincerity of the thousands in 1968 who marched in the name of love and peace along the same avenue during the Democratic Party Convention. 'Yippies' they called themselves then. I wondered idly whether it was the savage beating they received from the Chicago police, or the disillusionment of Vietnam later, that had reduced the challenge of American youth to this silly 'anarchic' charade which was much frowned on by Don. Our idealistic marches are not so well-attended these days either, but wherever I go in London I still see young people being outlandish and looking marvellously shocking – I did not see any outraging of adults going on in the parts of Chicago that I frequented. They get a bit drunk after the prom balls, the boys in their white suits, the girls in their pink and blue puff-sleeved, old-fashioned evening gowns, but the grown-ups smile indulgently at this traditional part of American life. This behaviour they can understand. Young and old linked 'Hands Across America' together on a sunny day in May, egged on by President Reagan, and, like Don, they felt proud of their country and wiped a tear when the President called them 'Fellow Americans'. Living in a country that size, composed of so many ethnic groups, it must be a comfort to be a fellow anything. Considering their lamentable record of crooked or second-rate presidents, it is touching to see the faith they still put in the present incumbent, through thick and thin – well, thick mainly.

But I suppose that is what I find so refreshing about Americans. They are eternally optimistic. With comparatively little history to burden them they are open to change. They want to believe everything will be wonderful and it was this quality that stopped me sounding off when, on hearing my English accent, they plied me with free drinks in return for helping America in the Libyan raids. My jaw ached from clamping back comments that would shake their conviction that the whole world was grateful for their heroic act. Only on one occasion did I lapse and I was deeply sorry for it afterwards.

A rather flamboyant shoe-salesman was distracted from trying to find plimsolls to fit my large English feet when their uniqueness amongst the smaller American clients, together with my voice, gave away my nationality. His exclamations of delight drew all the customers and staff round my bare toes, applauding and thanking me emotionally for being a good ally. (It was hard to visualise a similar event taking place in Harrods.) One woman asked sympathetically if it was frightening in London at the moment, the impression in the media being that England was virtually under seige. Before I could check myself, I quipped that it had been a lot better before their President Rambo started throwing bombs around. The stunned silence and hurt disbelief that followed my remark made me feel as though I had said something obscene at a children's party.

Just as I have to ration my anxiety to little England, I usually have no worry left over from human beings to concern myself overmuch with animals, but in Chicago a furry intruder was a major problem. I was watching another chat-show in which a pack of American matrons were in full cry against a man who had left his wife for a younger woman. Appalled at the naked hatred and hurt my sisters were exposing to the viewing millions, this militant feminist was suddenly confronted by a (probably male) mouse. I was so startled by this invasion of my swish room that I flew out down the corridor to enlist Ian's help. By the time we crept timorously back, the mouse had disappeared but there was clear evidence of his presence and Ian boldly telephoned reception, demanding action. Having been promised an 'exterminator', Ian retired and I awaited the arrival of this saviour, sitting on my chair with my feet up on the television set containing my fellow members of the ferocious sex. A huge man arrived who turned out to be the hotel jack-of-all-trades, his least favourite of which was exterminating. His behaviour as he looked at the mouse droppings and chewed carpet was reminiscent of Humphrey Bogart when he discovered leeches on his body in *The African Queen*. 'Oh, nasty little bastards – oh, I hate them – oh God, how awful.' His solution was to bung up the holes we discovered between my room and the next with newspaper as he was only in charge of half the corridor and next door was someone else's responsibility. (Would that President Reagan and Co were as reluctant to fight battles outside their own territory.) True, it did not seem a heroic solution, but if the hotel had mice or the White House had the odd rat, that was not my problem, so long as they did not come near me.

Apart from my four-legged visitor, I allowed myself only one other small fret – about the advance bookings for our shows. This being the first attempt at a World Theatre Season in the city, it was a bit slow taking off. The local arts scene is very healthy. Apart from the superb orchestra and opera, Chicago boasts several fine theatre companies, including Steppenwolf and Body Politic. They were all splendid and progressive, but with memories of the lethal but healthy attacks on the American way of life of Mike Nichols, Elaine May and Lennie Bruce, who had appeared there, it was a sad let-down to find that the satire group, Second City, had declined into gently prodding safe targets. But they were packed out while we were half empty. And not just us. The fact that there were top companies from Israel, South Africa, Spain, Italy, Japan and Britain playing in theatres all over Chicago left the citizens even colder than the wind, judging by the size of the audiences. After the success of *Nicholas Nickleby* the RSC is well-known, especially in New York, but I am afraid the National meant nothing to Chicago. In a frenzy of PR, Ian set about changing this, and I saw how very important the theatre was to him as he drove himself to exhaustion promoting the shows. 'I hate not being wanted,' he said with hurt disbelief, and it became clear that this feeling most actors know well was unfamiliar to him. Edward and he rushed around addressing meetings, leading workshops, being cutely British on radio and television chat-shows, until gradually business improved. Our first week with *Malfi* was not at all good, our second with *The Cherry Orchard* improved, and by our third and fourth with the double bill the theatre was packed. It was an extraordinary achievement because our repertoire was not easy for the Americans.

I was deeply concerned about the Sheridan before it opened. The technical rehearsals were not made easier by the fact that our skeleton English crew were forbidden by American union rules even to touch the scenery or props or give orders to the staff direct. All instructions had to be given through the stage director. A dead ringer for James Cagney, he curtly put me in my place when I tried to direct him by snarling: 'I *date* actresses.' I was also anxious that an audience with little classical tradition would be confused by a play in which the humour relied heavily on sending it up. I need not have worried on either score. Jimmy ran the show superbly with an iron-fisted control of his men, and the audience took a wider view of *The Critic* than a mere theatrical joke. As one reviewer put it, 'It gives us colonials a fine view of the English making fun of the English.' After a rave review in *Time* magazine a few days after we opened, we were home and dry for the rest of the run.

With the production launched, my only professional reason for staying in Chicago was my understudy duties. Back in li'l ole Chiswick, my husband was single-handedly caring for a houseful of extended family, gathered to welcome relations visiting from Australia. Assessing that thanks to Charlie the company were in peak condition, I felt safe in persuading Julie to take over my understudy covers for the last few days so that I could go home early. I bade a fond farewell to my fellow diddle-ohs and, whimpering a bit, set off for the airport where I was greeted by the violent storm that seemed to accompany me on flights to and from Chicago. Two mornings after my return I woke to find a message on my ansaphone from Ian, saying Claire had injured her ankle and the understudy masterplan had resulted in Julie having to go on in *The Real Inspector Hound*. For ten months I had sat in the dressing room like all good understudies waiting for my big break, and as usual I had managed to be in the wrong place at the wrong time. Or perhaps not. Julie was apparently wonderful. And so was home. The 'little May flowers', the soft sunshine, the smallness.

*

A month after my arrival back in England, a story broke in some of the press that brought home an aspect of our less attractive small-mindedness. Trevor Nunn and Peter Hall were accused of making too much money out of their work with the RSC and the National. I laughed at the thought that, even were this true, they would be counted heroes for it by Don, Charlie and most of America. Or even by some people in England, were they footballers, city gamblers, Sir Ian MacGregor or TV game winners. The fact that they have, with brilliance and dedication, led two companies that match in excellence and output anything achieved by British industry, seems to have escaped some people's notice. Better theatre politicians than I have expounded the watertight case for the benefit of the huge revenue and prestige which the Arts bring to this country. (Mrs Thatcher herself, on her recent visit to Moscow, suddenly remembered that people had told her that our Arts were highly rated, and offered them magnanimously to Mr Gorbachev as a sop to the Russians.) That two of the theatre's leading workers should have left their posts in the wake of scurrilous slurs, after years of grinding work, is a mark of the attitude of some of the media towards Britain's artists. And therefore, it follows, of many of the people who read the stories. Both men have faults but corruption is not one of them. It probably was time for them to move over and make room for others, but not like that. Still, this is life in the theatre, I suppose. Or anywhere really. 'Up one minute and down the next;' 'Pride cometh before a fall;' 'It never rains but it pours' – my father would have found a phrase to make sense of anything, however perverse – anything in this whole rambling saga.

I said at the beginning of this book that I wanted to take a good look at what lay ahead of me in the light of a searching re-assessment of my past. So, what have I *beheld*?

Well, experience has not improved me. Suffering has not enriched me. I know there are certain things I can survive that I would not have thought I would. There are still others, that I dare not name, that I doubt if I could. But others have. Two people survived their child drowning in a sewer. Eleven million people in this country survive on or below the poverty line.

Things in my past look smaller. Not policemen – they were bigger – but theatres, the shops, the pub at King's Cross, the communities, the bombs, the threats, the prospects, they were all nowhere near as big as today. It is because things have got bigger and bangier that I have begun to whimper. That is what people always do when they get older. Enough of this. I have looked back in anguish over thirteen chapters. So, *ME.f.OF,or,L.f.Gk theatron f.theaomai*-BEHOLD – the future.

14 : The Future

I cannot think of anything to say about that. I just thought it might be unlucky to finish on Chapter Thirteen.

Index

Wisbech 110–11
Wisdom, Norman 150
Wolfit, Sir Donald 18
Women's Movement 7, 161–8
  directors and 163–4
  groups 161–2
  and history 164–5
  and Margaret Thatcher 165–8
  and men's clubs 165
  and tokenism 163
Wood, Charles 161
Wood, Peter 183, 194
Wood, Victoria 162

Woodbridge 114–18
Woodward, Nannie (maternal
  grandmother) 120–1
Wordsworth, William 107
Workington 96–103
World Theatre Festival 209, 219, 227
Wright, Frank Lloyd 222
Wymark, Tristram 216

Yarborough 53, 57, 58, 63
Year of the King, The 20
Yes, Minister 26
Yonadab 189–90